THE *Belle*
OF BELFAST

To Barbara,

I hope you love the
Stores.

♡

X.

Anne Marie.

THE *Belle* OF BELFAST

A love story of great courage,
heroism and bravery

ANNE-MARIE FOSTER

NEW
HOLLAND

First published in 2015 by New Holland Publishers Pty Ltd
London • Sydney • Auckland

The Chandlery Unit 9 50 Westminster Bridge Road London SE1 7QY United Kingdom
1/66 Gibbes Street Chatswood NSW 2067 Australia
218 Lake Road Northcote Auckland New Zealand

www.newhollandpublishers.com

A record of this book is held at the British Library and the National Library of Australia.

ISBN 9781742576190

Managing Director: Fiona Schultz
Publisher: Diane Ward
Project Editor: Susie Stevens
Cover Design: Andrew Quinlan
Internal Design: Peter Guo
Proofreader: Angela Sutherland
Production Director: Olga Dementiev
Printer: Toppan Leefung Printing Ltd (China)

10 9 8 7 6 5 4 3 2 1

Keep up with New Holland Publishers on Facebook
www.facebook.com/NewHollandPublishers

DEDICATION

Based on a true story, this is dedicated to my mammy who has survived a life that would have sent many a one to an asylum. It's a tribute to her courage, bravery, tenacity and the love of her family.

To every human being that has ever felt marginalised by what they believe, the colour of their skin, their gender or their intellect, 'In my Father's house are many mansions ...' (John 14:2). There is a place for everybody. We are all meant to be here. It is also a tribute to my Irish heritage.

The names of people, places and some events have been changed to protect the innocent. Historical events listed are true.

CONTENTS

INTRODUCTION
Berny

As long as I can remember, the name 'Jack Kennedy' has been part of my life. When I was a little girl I imagined a lot that he might be my daddy; the man whose Irish dancing medals I found in the secret drawer so long ago. The tall, sandy-haired stranger I'd been introduced to at the Oireachtas in Dublin when I was eleven. The only man my mammy ever loved. I dreamed, too, of the place where he lived called Canada, where I fancied we could have a happy life and a lovely house with lace curtains like Protestants did.

A place where my mammy would be happy. Where Jimmy-Paddy could walk and talk, where Gerry would be understood. A place where there would be enough to eat every day. Where school teachers didn't hit the childer, and I'd be smart instead of stupid. A place where it didn't matter if you were a Catholic or a Protestant and everyone could have a street party on the glorious twelfth of July. A place where nobody called you a 'fenian bastard' or shouted 'no surrender.' A place where I wouldn't be afraid and where I could dance and dance and dance …

PROLOGUE
Berny

I stared again at the hands on my kitchen clock, checking for the umpteenth time what time it would be in England. Eleven hours! Yes, I had it right. It would be just before 7 o'clock in the morning. Ma would have been up and dressed about an hour ago. I wanted to make sure I didn't disturb her morning prayers or meditation from The Big Book.

I was nervous. I had a small chance to tell her before she'd be busy with Jimmy-Paddy, getting him off to 'school'. I knew what I was about to tell her would be one of the biggest shocks of her life, and I needed to make sure she'd be sitting down and not distracted. Maybe I shouldn't ring her; maybe I'll send her a letter. Maybe if she reads it first it won't be such a shock.

But a letter could take weeks by Aussie post. Wouldn't she want to know as soon as she could after all these years? What if the news is too much for her? What if she has an angina attack? No, she has to know. She'll never forgive me if I don't tell her. I'll break the news gently; make sure she's sitting down. I'll tell her to make a cuppa first.

God, I better ring before the day goes on, or I'll have to wait until tomorrow. I'll not sleep a wink carrying this with me to bed. My hands started to tremble, my breath rising higher in my chest. My thoughts were racing faster than a hare on a hot griddle, my veins pulsing in my neck.

Shit ... why had I just put milk in my tea? I don't even take milk! God, I just have to do this. Pick up the phone dammit! Breathe ... breathe ... no ... wait.

Write it down. Yes, yes, that's an idea. I scramble for a notepad in the wooden tray beside the phone.

'Just do it for God's sake,' I berated myself. 'Don't put it off any longer.'

The hands of the kitchen clock were still moving forward tick ... tick ... tick ... Were they speeding up? Don't think. Just go with your gut instinct. She'll want to know. Slowly, my shaking hands lifted the phone and as I punched in the international code my heart began to thump in my chest.

Ring ... ring ... don't you dare chicken out. Ring ... ring ... maybe she's already out at the market? Ring ... ring ... again I glance at the clock, biting the skin off the side of my thumb. Shit, now it's bleeding. Where's a tissue? Why is it that when I'm nervous I could almost bite the skin off my bones? Ring ... ring ... Pandora's box ... Oh my God ... just breathe ... ring ... ring ...

Then I hear her voice.

'Good morning and who's ringing me at this time of the day?'

'Ma, it's me, Berny,' I say trying not to let my nerves choke me.

'Ach, Berny, hello love and top o' the morning to you. What time is it in Aussie land? Are ye not away to your bed?'

I laughed anxiously.

'No, Ma, it's just turned eight o'clock at night here. It'll be another few hours before we head off to bed. Funny isn't it, you just starting your day as we finish ours?'

'Ach, how's everybody doing? What about me darling grandchilder?'

'Ah, Ma, they're well, eaten' me out of house and home and growing like weeds!' I laughed nervously. 'We're all well.'

'And what about your weather this week, is it any cooler? Dear God, I was so worried about youse in that heat. That place is as hot as Hades sometimes.'

Oh how was I going to do this?

'We've had so much rain, Ma, it's flattened all the daffodils I planted, but that's Australia for you—when it rains it comes in torrents. It surely is the land of droughts and flooding rains.'

'What about yourself, Berny? How are ye doing?'

This was my chance; it was now or never. Breathe ...

'Ma, I have something to tell you, but I need you to sit down.'

'Jesus, Mary and Joseph, what's wrong? Is it the childer?'

'No, Ma, it's good news but please ... sit down and I'll tell you.'

'What is it, Berny? Alright I'll sit down.'

'Ma, it's about Jack Kennedy. I've found him. He's alive and living in America.'

The phone went silent. I didn't know what was happening at the other end of the line. Oh Jesus, what if I've just killed her?

'Ma ... Ma? Are ye there?' After an age, came her whispered reply.

'Y-e-s ... I'm here.'

'Ma, I've told him the truth about what happened all those years ago ... that it wasn't your fault. He knows everything. He wants to see you. He's coming to England.'

Then I heard it, low at first, and deep—the soft, agonising sobs as fifty years of emotion spilled over the wall of my mammy's broken heart.

PART 1

BELFAST 1931

ON MAGGIE
Isabelle

I guess there's only one place to start with a story like this and that's right back at the beginning.

It was 1931 and Belfast was vibrant and alive. My daddy Alistair McKitterick thrived delivering fresh vegies in his trusty, aul Bedford van to businesses all over town, from the Smithfield Market in the heart of Belfast to local fruit merchants. We didn't have a lot of money and our family was growing rapidly. Maggie McKitterick, my mammy, was expecting baby number eight, which was me, and I was due any day. But she was struggling in her pregnancy. Her back ached and she worried whether there would be enough food for everyone. There really was no room for another baby and my Aunt Josie had never even had one child. Mammy loved her sister dearly. Sweet Josie, wanted only one thing in life—babies.

I could just picture Mammy straightening up in her chair, heavily pregnant, stretching out her back and pushing a cushion behind it, letting out a deep sigh. She must have been wishing to God and his Holy Mother that the baby would hurry up and be born because many a time, with the babies born after me, I heard Mammy say that if Daddy came near her again she would 'cut the bloody skull off him as well as the bits that dangled between his legs.' Poor Mammy, the more she would have thought about the baby she was carrying, the guiltier she must have felt about my poor Aunt Josie wanting a wee child of her own so badly.

You see my Mammy and Aunt Josie were not just sisters; they were the best of friends. They shared everything including the very knickers they wore. While growing up, they would have talked I'm sure about meeting their handsome heroes, how many childer they'd have and how wonderful their lives would be.

Josie especially wanted a hoard of childer.

She loved the wee ones and whenever she got the chance she was minding anyone's child she could get her hands on. Often, when I was wee, I heard her call them 'God's little angels on Earth.' She could soothe a fretting child quicker than a bottle of milk laced with whiskey. She just had the gift.

Mammy told me Josie would make a great mother; she knitted more matinee coats and bootees for her bottom drawer than anyone else round the doors. She had even put a pram away in Doggart's Emporium on Lombard Street and was paying it off at a shilling a month ready for when Don and her got the good news.

Now everyone thought my Aunt Josie was tempting fate. It was bad luck to buy a pram before you even had a baby in your arms. A pram wouldn't be needed for the first month anyway due to the 'churching' that the Catholic Church insisted on to cleanse the mother of the carnal sin of giving birth. This compulsory ritual made sure a mother and child stayed close to home for at least six weeks after the birth of a baby. Mammy could say nothing to Aunt Josie, though, because it would have been a cruel and soul-destroying thing to dampen the joy in anyone's eyes who wanted a baby so badly.

Now when Josie met Don she was head over heels. It was said to be a match made in Heaven. When Don looked at Josie, the light in his eyes shone like a new penny. Don too wanted a brood of childer, being one of nineteen himself. His family made no apologies for expanding the numbers of the Catholic Church in God's holy name!

But as each year went by and no babies came along, my Aunt Josie's joy started to fade and Don took more and more to the Guinness, staying out later on a Friday night. The more Don stayed out on a Friday night with the Guinness, the more Josie blamed herself for not giving him any babies.

She said she felt useless as a woman ... as a wife.

'Why can't I give Don the wee childer we both want?' she would say. 'A "barren woman", what use was that? Wasn't that what God intended for a woman? To have childer?' If I can't even make babies, what use am I altogether?'

Father Flanagan never said anything to Josie's face, but after mass she knew he was looking down his nose at her and Don for not producing a baby. Josie wanted to scream at everyone, 'it's not like we haven't been trying.' It just wasn't fair; there was Mammy, breeding like a rabbit and no sign of stopping. My Aunt Josie would have given her right arm, if only she could have had just one wee child of her own.

Each year Josie watched on as Mammy had one baby after another. Her resentment forming a lump in heart that just got bigger with each new baby she brought into the world. Mammy could read her sister like a book; she sensed every emotion her sister was going through. She decided to talk to Daddy. She'd wait until he got back from the market. She'd tell him how desperate Josie and Don were for a wee child. She'd let him know how well looked after the baby would be, and how it would just be living up the street!

They'd be able to see it grow up, it's not like they would be giving the baby away to some buck stranger, it would want for nothing, be brought up like royalty, who wouldn't want that for their own? It would be a gift to give Josie the new baby. They'd be good to it and it would ease the pressure, make more room for everyone. Daddy lit his pipe as he finished his dinner. But when Mammy had told him her plans to give their baby to Josie his face went pale. He said nothing; he just let her talk on.

He knew well money was getting harder to stretch. There hadn't been any extra work at the markets for months. Even extra vegetables

9

were becoming scarce. He could sense the logic of Mammy's words, but something deep in him couldn't come to terms with it. This was, after all, his wee child too.

Daddy's thoughts wandered back to when he was a wee boy himself and his own da had told him what it was like to be left orphaned. His granda had abandoned his granny, going off to Oklahoma in America in search of gold, only to end up a penniless pauper. His poor Granny had gone to an early grave leaving her five childer alone in Dublin; the oldest two boys having to steal what they could lay their hands on from the Moore Street Market just so they'd all survive another day. If it hadn't been for the kindness of an aunt in Belfast the whole lot of them would surely have perished.

What galled Daddy more than anything was, had history been different he should've been a wealthy man. He wouldn't have had to struggle to make ends meet. For while his granda Seamus had been chasing after gold in America, granda's sister Mary, who never married, had headed Down Under to the goldfields of Ballarat in Australia and struck it rich! Millions, they say, she left when she died and not a soul to leave it to.

When Daddy's Uncle Willy seen the advert in *The Irish Times* for relatives to come forward and claim Mary's fortune, Willy told no one, not even his poor brother Seamus or his wee sisters. He kept the lot for himself, living like a lord squandering the money away for the rest of his life.

'What use had all that money been to Willy anyway?' Daddy had said. 'He'd never had a day's happiness for it and bad luck and tragedy seemed to follow him.'

It surely was a true saying that 'if ye put a poor man on a horse he'll ride to blazes'.

It was funny, though, that no one could ever tell where exactly Mary McKitterick had made her fortune in Ballarat. The location of her goldmine remains a mystery to this day. There was no certificate of mining, no maps or anything else—all of which led tongues to wag.

Before you knew it, Mary McKitterick's reputation was as large as her fortune. How else would a spinster woman make good in such a den of inequity in the arsehole of nowhere in those days? It was said by some that apart from Mary McKitterick's 'face being her fortune', she was no fool and wasn't a woman to be crossed. She'd done it tough alright and learnt the hard way how to stick up for herself in a land that was full of convicts, thieves and skulduggery. Oh aye, ye had to have your wits about you in those days.

You couldn't trust banks to look after your hard-earned coin, because they too were apt to crash, taking your money with them. So Mary kept her own money safe, tied in a piece of oilcloth, fastened to the end of the bucket where she drew her water from at the end of her backyard.

Each night, she'd take her earnings for the day and when it was dark, slip out as if she was fetching water, and lower the bucket into the well carefully adding another day's takings to her rapidly-growing bundle. The rest she tucked into the right side of her calico dress in what she called her 'titty beg' strapped to her ample chest.

As Mammy let out a deep sigh, Daddy's thoughts were brought abruptly back to the present. He looked at her, the hurt in his eyes clear as day. He wasn't mad, just sad. Sad that she felt he wasn't able to provide for them. He was sad too for the wee baby that wasn't even born yet.

'Ach Maggie, we'll manage somehow, work will pick up. I swear I'll be first to the market tomorrow and make sure I'll get extra grub. Don and Josie will have their own babies soon. Now don't talk so, or the wee one inside you will know what you're saying.'

Mammy was raging and wanted to scream at him. *Why was it when it came to the childer it was like talking to the wall?* She thought. She sighed again and turned from him, looking down at the other childer playing at her feet and her heart cried for Josie. *In the name of God what was she going to do?*

It was a long labour—there was no midwife, just Josie who attended to each and every one of Mammy's births. Josie was starting to get worried; this was the longest labour Mammy had ever endured. She'd already changed the bedclothes twice and for all Mammy's pains there was still no sign of getting ready to push. Josie sent one of the older girls down the stairs to boil another pan of water and put the tarls by the fire to warm them. She then wrung another cloth out in the basin and gently wiped Mammy's forehead.

The next contraction hit hard and all she could think of was damn Alistair McKitterick for getting her in this state again. *If this was what GOD wanted of her then damn God too! Dear Jesus how was she ever going to tell Josie what he'd said about the baby about to come into the world?* Not only was her body weary, but her heart was broke.

'Oh Jesus, Mary and holy St Joseph, ahhhhhh, was this really what God meant women to go through every year of their lives?' Gasp, gasp ... 'Ahhhhhh,' she cried as another strong pain shot through her whole body. She clasped her sister's hand digging her fingers in till her knuckles turned as pale as alabaster.

'J-o-s-i-e, I don't think I can do this any longer, ahhhhhh.'

Josie started to tremble; she'd never seen Mammy like this before. Mammy had turned ashen white; the colour of the sheets she was lying on. But just as she was about to shout for Daddy to get Doctor Quinn, Mammy started to push with what little breath she had left in her body.

When Daddy heard the cries of the wee baby, he took the bare wooden stairs two at a time to see Mammy and the child. She was exhausted and spent. Daddy, unable to speak, lifted the tarl.

'It's a wee girl,' Josie said drying her hands. As he peered into the warm, rumpled bundle his heart leapt.

'Ach, Maggie ... another wee girl and my God, she's the nicest one yet.' As he gently lifted the baby into his arms he said, 'We'll call her Isabelle after my mother.'

From that moment on Mammy knew Daddy would never part with her. Mammy let out a long sigh, glanced sideways at Josie and eased herself back onto the sweat-sodden pillows. Both of them knew well there'd be no baby for Josie that night.

GROWING UP
Isabelle

Well … it looks like my daddy had been right; I was indeed a lovely wee child. I was no trouble to Mammy and I thrived. For some strange reason, though, as I grew up, I felt different from our ones. I looked different too—the only one of eight childer with my daddy's piercing blue eyes.

'Aye, you're mine alright,' Daddy used to say every time he looked at me with my flaxen hair, white as the driven snow, thick as a bull's lug, that fell in ringlets and waves right down my back. I felt different too. I'd no fear of anyone—not even nasty Isa Mullen who lived down the street could scare me. It was our boys who got a thick ear from her.

Many a time I was called out of our house to fight our boys' battles in the back alleyway. I usually got the better of the offender. Daddy made me put on a pair of boxing gloves and spar with our ones to toughen them up. Imagine that—me, only a wee slip of a girl. 'Ach, fir God's sake, Alistair McKitterick, is that all ye can do with your time?' said Mammy waving her hands in the air in exasperation.

'Haven't you got enough wee lads, now ye have to try making her into one?' But Daddy never took Mammy's words to heart. He loved it when he saw me getting the better of the boys.

'C'mon, boys, now ye wouldn't want a wee girl to get the upper hand, eh? Bejesus, I'll make men of you all yet. You wouldn't wanna be sissies now would you?'

'No, Daddy.' came the chorus, as another punch flew my way.

'Are ye sure, boys?' Daddy would carouse slapping the boys round the legs with a tarl.

'No, Daddy.' Came the reply even louder than before and I knew it was time to duck. I boxed and sparred that much with our boys, I was deaf in my left ear by the time I was ten. After the boxing matches, Daddy always slipped me a penny.

'Ach, Maggie,' he said as he laughed tapping his pipe, 'sure Isabelle's the only one of them with any guts or gall.'

I wasn't afraid of anyone in the street. I was terrified of only one thing—anyone seeing the tiny creatures that encrusted my scalp. I knew I was lousey. My worst childhood memory wasn't of the blitz when Hitler bombed the bejesus out of Belfast. No, I was only afraid that Maisy Stewart, who sat behind me in the classroom at school, would spot what was crawling down my back.

Then, in an instant, one day my worst fears were realised when I heard the voice behind me say, 'Please, Miss, there's something crawling on Isabelle McKitterick's jumper.'

Oh my God, the humiliation. My face burned with shame as I was called out in front of the class and sent home not to return until I was clean.

The job of getting rid of the walkers and lice was never ending. How could I stop the crawlers walking all over my head and down the back of my jumper when we slept with four in a bed and all they had to do was crawl from one head to another in the middle of the night? The very thought made me feel sick.

Determined to rid myself of the walkers, I spent hours with a fine-tooth comb and a piece of rag working tirelessly through a blanket of waist-length blonde locks to clean myself. As I got each of the crawlers out of my hair, I'd beat them with the comb till they didn't move. But the nits—the thousands of nits—I had to place between my thumbnails and squash until I heard the 'crack' then I knew they were stone dead.

The sting of summer sun had begun to fade and the days took on a misty, lazy hue. The winds changed and it was cooler at night. People in our street were worried about what was happening in the world. Everyone who had a wireless listened nightly for word about what was going on. The childer weren't allowed to utter a word when the BBC News was being broadcast.

Everyone crowded into our living room round the wireless. There was talk of war and of countries being invaded by a man called Hitler. There were tales of extraordinary cruelty, of people being slaughtered just because they were Jewish or handicapped or just because they were old and of no use to Hitler anymore. Some were saying that Hitler was trying to make a race of his own kind of people, with blonde hair and blue eyes. This scared the shit out of me because I figured I'd be the first one Hitler would get because I had blonde hair and blue eyes.

Mammy and Daddy were very worried because they knew if Hitler were to invade France as well as Poland, he'd be across the English Channel as quick as a fiddler's fart—over the Irish Sea and into Belfast. They knew too that the Harland and Wolff shipyards just a few miles away from our house would be sitting ducks for Hitler's bombs—we could all be in real danger.

Then it happened. It was 3 September 1939 and I was just eight years old. Everyone was crowded into our living room to hear the broadcast on the wireless. You could have heard a pin drop. Don and Josie were there as well as Jerry and Kathleen McClure and their tribe. The McClures always had the snotters tripping them no matter what time of the year it was. Their Ma Kathleen tried to tell the street it was because they were allergic to the milk, but Mammy reckoned that was balderdash, that Kathleen was through other and it was more to do with dirt and neglect. No there was just no excuse for being a dirty mare. The twins were even quiet on the floor, rolling their marbles back and forth, as all the other childer sat on the stairs, three to a step.

'Shush,' snapped Daddy, as the wireless crackled into life and the familiar, posh English accent of Prime Minister Chamberlain filled the room. I sat stock still as he told the people of Britain that they were now at war with Germany.

An audible gasp broke the deathly silence as the devastating news sank in. Kathleen McClure exclaimed, 'Jesus, Mary and Joseph, may God have mercy on us all.' Others made the sign of the cross on themselves, kissing the holy medals hung round their necks for protection. Josie dropped to her knees and began to say the *Rosary*, right in front of everyone, which I couldn't believe because the *Rosary* was only said in private, not in front of everyone else. Even childer knew that—we all sensed the panic. The twins started to cry, everyone started talking at once, some saying we'd be blown to smithereens with the shipyard so close by.

I didn't know whether to cry or run. It was Daddy who stood up to quell the panic, declaring in front of everybody to 'get a grip on their drawers.' There'd be nobody put him out of his house no matter what his fecking name was. He was staying put, war or no war. He'd fought in the Irish War of Independence and was no stranger to defending himself. If he could get that Hitler fella up a dark alleyway, he'd knock seven colours of shite out of him, the big cowardly bastard, picking on the weak, the poor and the aul. Many a night when the war really started, when the sirens wailed heralding the warning that the German planes were coming, Daddy marched all of us two by two, holding hands, up the nearby hills to the graveyard.

'Lie down everyone, get the wee ones and cover their ears,' he barked.

'Not on the graves, Daddy, there's dead people under there.'

'Ach it's not the dead you need to be frightened of, child, but the fecking living.' But our Daddy knew no lights meant safety and there'd be nothing but damp grass, silence and darkness lying atop the graves.

We all lay down, doing as we were bid. Nobody dared move until

Daddy gave the all clear and we made our way back down the hill and country laneways till we were back home. Then it was straight to bed without even having a wash. I wondered why all the families in the streets weren't lying up at the graveyard when the blitz was on.

Our Nell told me that our Daddy was very smart, because he'd fought in the great War of Independence, so he knew what to do when bullets and bombs were flying. Our daddy was a real soldier and a hero with medals and everything, who'd fought with the real IRA. The other daddies in the street hadn't and they didn't have 'gumption' like our daddy. Nell's belief in our daddy's bravery and abilities reassured us all that our daddy knew what he was doing and that 'gumption' was the thing that would win the war and keep us all safe.

The screeching and blasts of the exploding bombs pounding the Harland and Wolff shipyards could be seen and heard as clear as day. The sky lit up like daybreak as the flames leapt up hundreds of feet into the night sky.

Daddy told us we'd be safe there in the graveyard, but it was no thanks to the bastards over the border in the Free State who lit the Northern Irish border up with a thousand fires, showing Hitler's planes exactly where to drop the bombs and incendiary devices in the heart of Belfast. Daddy was furious not only with Hitler for starting the fecking war in the first place, but also with the people who were supposed to be his own countrymen. Men he'd fought alongside, shoulder to shoulder, covering for each other, comrades in arms, united under the republican tricolour of green, white and gold. He never thought in a million years that those very same men would turn on the men they fought beside—all because the Free State wasn't at war with Germany. Did they have no conscience, or worse still, did they have no fecking gumption? A blind man on a galloping horse could see that Hitler fella was one bad baste.

Now there was talk everywhere of sending childer from cities and towns away to the country so they'd be safe from Hitler's bombs. Half the childer in England had been sent to homes in the countryside till the war was over. But Daddy was determined that we were going nowhere. He said you wouldn't know who might be looking after us, or where we'd end up; it might even be an 'Orange man's' house we could be sent to and God only knows what might befall us at their hands. No, Daddy wasn't taking any chances with us or our eternal souls; we'd be safe with him and Mammy.

Daddy firmly believed that the family that prayed together stayed together. He was staying put; neither Hitler nor any other dirty louser was putting him out of his home. We'd manage, sure, each and every child got a rations book and not even half of them would use their coupons up, so there'd be enough food alright. There were so many childer's ration books in our house that, when other families' cupboards were bare, Mammy could get brown paper, twist it making a poke, and fill it halfway up the sides adding some cocoa and bit of sugar so we got a treat that no one else got round the doors.

When I thought nobody was watching, I'd sneak into the cupboard, stand on top of the potato box, pull down the big tin that held the cocoa and make an extra poke for wee Francis Foley down the street. Francis had a hump on her back and couldn't walk straight, due to being dropped by her aul aunty when she was a baby.

Daddy had a laste that he used for mending our shoes. He kept scraps of leather and before ye knew it your shoes would be as good as new, not a bit of rain or snow getting in. Not like some poor childer in my class at school who didn't have any shoes at all. Some childer just walked about in their bare feet, even in the winter. Mammy said the poor craters would've been better off in the poor house. At least they'd have had a pair of boots on their feet. But the poor house was the last resort and a shameful disgrace, so childer walked about barefoot because having no shoes at all was still one step up from the poor house. At least you were still free.

When Daddy wasn't mending shoes on the big, cast iron laste, it was turned upside down and placed on the scullery table while he made toffee. He slapped the warm, golden liquid onto the cold metal of the laste, stretching it out and rolling it up, while everyone's mouths watered begging for a bit. Daddy would laugh at us all gathering round calling, 'Daddy, is the toffee ready?'

'Ach now wait till it cools now, or it'll scald the bake off ye.'

Our house was always a buzz with the noisy clatter of babies and childer. The front door of the house was propped open permanently with the shoe laste in summer, because there was always somebody calling in to see Mammy for a 'wee reading' of the leaves, or trying to make sense of a fitful nightmare they'd had, knowing full well that Mammy was the only one for many a mile who could tell you what dreams meant with any accuracy.

The older ones often had a younger child on their hip because Mammy couldn't possibly see to everybody. Each one of us had jobs to do. Mammy's back was near broke carrying all the babies inside her. She felt as if she'd been pregnant her whole life. Nell made sure Mammy's orders got carried out, or as Daddy put it, Mammy made the bullets and Nell fired them. She picked up where Mammy left off. I thought our Nell had a beautiful face and even though the others seemed to be shit-scared of her, I wasn't. Though she was very strict, I knew she was fair.

When Mammy was busy feeding the next new baby, or even doing her readings, Nell kept order in the house better than a queen bee in a hive. Daddy said our Nell could run the country and did a better job than half the feckers in power. Everybody in the house knew their real Mammy was Maggie, but we all knew Nell was our second Mammy—you questioned our Nell on peril of your life.

I loved my mammy; she was always kind, especially if you weren't well. She sang to us all the time and there was nowhere else you'd want to be, but snuggled up in Mammy's shawlie beside the fire. Sometimes I wished I could be sick, even if I weren't, just so I could get a snuggle in the shawlie. But the shawlie always seemed to be full, of either a new baby or someone who was really sick.

Year after year the babies kept coming for Mammy. Fear of mortal sin and preventing the 'planting of the seed' on top of eternal damnation was much worse a worry than where the next meal was to come from and how many mouths had to be fed. Somehow Daddy managed to get hold of extra grub at the market when no one else could and so, even during the war years, there was enough for every mouth.

FAMILY ENTERTAINMENT
Isabelle

It would be fair to say that most families during the Second World War made their own entertainment. You were considered well off if you had a wireless. There was nothing better than sitting round the living room on Saturday nights listening to the plays that were broadcast on the wireless— as well as the BBC News. Most homes didn't have a telephone. If needed, the phone box at the end of the street was used, or someone simply got on their bike and peddled to the doctors. My family was no different and so Daddy especially encouraged us childer to sing, dance and play the piano. Even the washboard and spoons were used along with the tin whistle.

All of us got music lessons from Mrs McDermott who lived down the street because it was very important to Daddy that we were taught music. But, by God, Mrs McDermont was not one to be messed with. Daddy paid her in free rations, which was as good as money. In return she expected her pupils to pay attention or out would come the ruler. Music books were passed down from one child to another, the pages carefully turned to keep them in good order. The same song would often be heard again and again, like *Over the Waves*. Daddy played the concertina and Mammy the mouth organ. Jimmy played the violin—but only when he was tanked—and I played the piano. There was also a button-eyed accordion, a banjo and a clarinet, which were all shared among the other childer. We had the making of a grand Irish band.It took me only a minute to pick up the beat, strike a chord and off everyone would go. I was a natural at the piano. I was so young when I started playing that my feet didn't even reach the floor and two of the older childer would push the pedals of the piano when instructed. I loved these times in our house. Everyone seemed to be happy, especially my Mammy and Daddy. Mammy seemed to forget her aches and pains and would sit and let one of the childer take out the pins that held her French bun in place, unfolding her waist-length, nut-brown hair, stretching out the loose curls that were held in place.

The childer got to count the hundred strokes of the brush. You had to do one hundred strokes to strengthen it, make it glossy and smooth. The counting had to be done under your breath so as not to disturb Mammy's stories. When it was my turn to brush Mammy's hair, sometimes I was so scared I completely forgot what number I was up to and had to start again, causing a right ruction because somebody else was waiting for a turn. I wished our house was filled with music and stories every night because on those nights, nobody was gulldering or fighting.

The storytelling started with Daddy regaling us of his time when he fought in the great War of Independence against the Black 'n' Tans.

'Oh, they were wicked bastards,' he'd announce and then tell of how he and his comrades 'got one over on them', how eventually they were disbanded due to their evil nature, and how there'd been a hue and cry about their very existence.

Everyone crowded round to listen, especially me because apart from story times like this, my Daddy was a man of few words.

I was fascinated by Daddy's explanations of Ireland's politics and history and how one country became divided in two never to be reunited again.

'Tell me again how Ireland lost its teddy bear's head?' I'd ask.

I never tired of hearing about his battles. When Daddy had told his story and lit his pipe, Mammy would begin her tales and in the dim light, with just the oil lamp glowing and the flicker of the coal fire in the grate, and the north wind howling like a banshee outside, Mammy began. They always started with an eerie 'shusssh', then she closed her eyes and threw her head back as if she'd just become possessed by some unseen spirit.

Hush descended in the room. I was scared stiff when Mammy started her ghost stories. So real were the tales of strange knocking sounds that heralded the coming of troubles and the black magical properties of the hawthorn bush that I wouldn't even go to the toilet across the backyard at night because the hair on the back of my neck would stand up with fear.

What shook me more than anything else was that I knew exactly what my mammy was talking about. It wasn't the first time I'd heard strange footsteps and seen the shadowy outlines of a woman walking across our bedroom floorboards at night. She walked with a limp and a walking stick, tap ... tap ... tap.

One night the steps stopped right at the side of my bed and I froze with fright wetting myself. I felt the presence so strongly, I thought I'd die right there. I was too afraid even to stick my head out from under the thick overcoats and have a look. The strange thing was that the others in the bed seemed fast asleep and nobody heard the footsteps except me.

When I told our ones, they said I was full of imagination and to say another prayer for the 'repose of souls'. When I told my Mammy about the happenings, she looked straight through me telling me to be a good girl and to tell Father Ryan at confession on Saturday night.

'But why do I have to tell Father Ryan, it's not another sin, is it?'

'Well ... he knows about these things. They get trained in the seminary to deal with it. We don't want any evil coming into the house especially now you're a bit older. That's when they come you know ... poltergeists ... the spirits of naughty childer ... moving pictures and smashing glasses ... oh Jesus, Mary and holy saint Joseph, no, I wouldn't want that, I've enough on me plate to deal with. Now go on with you and get to your bed.'

This news about poltergeists made my blood run cold, even worse than the thought of headless, dead nuns. Many a time, too, especially if I were sick, I could feel myself leaving my own body, you know, rising out of it, looking right down at myself as if I was up on the ceiling looking down as clear as day. Floating right out of the bedroom, down the stairs, watching everyone in the living room sitting, talking, except nobody could see me.

One night I floated right out the front door, down to the bottom of the street to the Rock Pub, except I felt scared and floated back up the street to the house, in through the front door (even though it was closed tight), up the stairs and right back into my body again. Our ones said that if I kept telling people, they'd think I was a buck eejit and 'not all there' and I'd be put away in the nut house. So I never told anybody else about leaving my own body and floating anywhere, or about the ghosts I saw in our bedroom at 26 Stonemore Road.

As Mammy rocked in her chair, while one of us took turns to comb her long locks, the more soothed she became and the more dramatic her stories were, completely captivating everyone in the house. At such times, Daddy sat well back in his rocking chair re-lighting and sucking on his pipe, bringing it back into life, drawing deeply on its sweet baccy, listening away to her. Bye she told a good tale and he thought too how lovely she looked with her beautiful waist-length locks cascading over her shoulders as she spoke. Aye the girl he wed was still there.

Daddy said that if he didn't know any better he'd think that the tales she told were real, too. Everyone believed every word that came out of Mammy's story-telling mouth. Often, like some sort of a star encouraging an encore, she'd cut the story short, only to have a chorus of terrified childer beg her to carry on until it was well past bedtime. Daddy never interrupted Mammy's stories—he knew better.

It wasn't only ghost stories that Mammy told; she could tell you what every dream you ever had meant. She had a book of dreams that she kept in the corner of the living room cupboard and when she got a minute she was always reading about their meaning. Dreams fascinated her and, along with *The Little Messenger* that came from the piety stall at church, there was nothing else much that Mammy ever read.

When us childer had bad dreams Mammy told us it was 'just the wash tub of your mind getting rid of the rubbish.' A dream about somebody dying meant new life. One of Mammy's favourite things was reading the tea leaves. Everybody who wanted their fortune told in the streets of The Falls road went to Mammy to get their leaves read. She could predict a plethora of events and odd happenings. Her ability to see into the future was beyond question. She told Nan Jamieson down the street that she was having another baby and Nan didn't even know herself till a month later that she was expecting. The shock of the news gave Nan Bell's palsy—Nan's whole face drooping on one side for months on end. There was no doubt about it: Mammy had 'the gift'.

She told her friend, Vera Quinn, that she could see a death in her house and hadn't Vera's whole litter of puppies been born dead? Well ... it was still death. She told Mary Malloy that there was money coming to her and that very same week her husband John's premium bonds hit the jackpot. They all moved out of Malone Road and started living like lords. She predicted, too, that they'd never have another day's luck, because they never passed so much as a brown penny her way in the way of thanks and her doing the very prediction. Mammy could also sense stuff about people. She knew just by looking at somebody if they'd 'make aul bones', and before you knew it, the poor craters were dead and buried, God rest their souls.

There was one time Mammy and Daddy had gone up the street to the wake of Jock O'Rourke—everyone in the street paying their respects. Jock was an arsehole; he'd always been bad to his wife and had a disposition that was as sour as rhubarb. Very mangy with his money, too, he was. But at a wake, nobody dared speak ill of the dead. So if the dead person had lived a really good life everyone said, 'he was one of the best' while drinking till they couldn't stand and toasting their life. That was until somebody started the fight. A wake wasn't a bona-fide wake unless somebody had been laid out cold besides the corpse. But, on the other hand, if someone was an aul get like Jock O'Rourke, people would say 'he wasn't a bad aul soul' because nobody wanted to be haunted by some aul bastard's ghost.

At Jock's wake this all went wrong, because as the candles round the bed were all blew out and the last person was leaving the room, Jock's body suddenly sat bolt-fecking upright in the bed as a low groan slipped out of his mouth and the last breath left his body. There was a stampede out of the darkened bedroom, everyone squealing like banshees making the sign of the cross, somebody shouting 'send for father Ryan!' As Mammy got to the door, her shawl got caught on the door knob and she thought it was Jock after her, and before she could help it, she yelled, 'Let go of me shawl ye humpy aul bastard!'

Well when all the commotion died down they all had a good laugh and a few more porters and Mammy said two novenas to Our Blessed Lady for speaking ill of the dead and the repose of Jock O'Rourke's soul … just in case. Because the thought of being haunted by Jock O'Rourke's sour countenance for eternity was something Mammy wasn't taking any chances with.

None of us wanted to move when the stories ended. Upstairs was so spooky, shadows darted everywhere, and there was no inside toilet. Every stair creaked and groaned, just like the noises Mammy described in her tales of ghostly happenings. I never went up there alone; I'd have died first! But nobody wanted to look like a scaredy-cat either. So they'd pick up a youngster on their hip, tramping up to bed by making lots of noise on the bare, wooden stairs as if somehow the clatter would ward off the ghosts Mammy spoke of.

Half the time I didn't even take my clothes off. I dived under the covers, closing my eyes tight in case I saw something horrific, or found myself paralysed and unable to shout out. Then it would hit me! The same thought, 'I need to go to the toilet,' but no matter how much I tried to take my mind off it, the feeling got worse and worse.

The problem was what lay under the bed. The poo, or pooly, pot was shoved under the bed so in the middle of the night you didn't have to go out to the backyard. I was shit-scared that if I got out of bed and dropped my drawers to do a big pooly, a big hand would grab me! It was worse if you needed a pooly later in the night because the pooly pot was full with all the others using it and you had to take time being careful not to splash anywhere, and that meant more time for the 'big hand' to grab you.

It was a strange thing that on the nights when Mammy told her stories, not even saying the *Rosary* (which was the most powerful prayer of all) could quell the fear that rose inside me. I was especially scared of stories about headless nuns. Somehow the spectacle in my mind of floating, headless dead nuns in their big swishing, starched habits made my blood run cold.

Although I was pretty much afraid of nothing and nobody, there were still a couple of things that filled me with dread. School was one of them and, like I said, I dreaded Maisy Stewart sitting behind me in class, knowing she might spot the 'crawlers' that infested my hair and then everyone would know I was lousey. The teachers must have had diplomas in cruelty because they needed no excuse to thwack you quick as look at you with the big, long, brown leather strap that hung on a brass hook by their desk.

Order, obedience, cleanliness and Godliness were the order of the day. No one 'stepped out of line'. I tried to keep my head down and stay out of trouble. I didn't ever want to feel that strap across my hands. But somehow I always managed to stand out from the rest of the class. God damn my flaxen, white hair. Suddenly Miss Connor's eyes lit on me. I put my head down and tried to slip a bit further under the desk.

'Miss McKitterick, stand up!'

I felt a familiar heave in my stomach. *Oh, this was it, what was I going to get wrong today?*

'Have you been to mass this week?'

'Yes, Miss,' I replied my face flushing scarlet for no other reason other than I hoped to God I knew the answer to what she was about to ask. I didn't want to look like an eejit in front of the whole class.

'Have you read your catechism?'

Just as I was about to reply she boomed, 'All of it? You know, not only will you *not* be able to make your confirmation and become a soldier of Christ, or receive the Holy Ghost, but you'll be lucky to see the gates of Heaven at all! A soldier of Christ would be able to name the gifts of the Holy Ghost, Miss McKitterick. Name me the gifts of the Holy Ghost.'

'W-i-s-d-o-m, Miss.'

'Wisdom and what?'

'Wisdom and k-n-o-w-l-e-d-g-e, Miss.'

'Any others?'

'Yes, Miss,' I said, my voice faltering, 'wisdom, knowledge and c-o-u-r-a-g-e, Miss.'

'Oh for Heaven's sake, it's like a dead man trying to draw breath.' With a dismissive shrug she asked the class, 'Can anyone else name the seven gifts of the Holy Ghost before Christmas?' A flurry of hands shot up including Maisy Stewart's.

'Please, Miss, please, Miss.'

Miss Connor pointed and said with a loud sigh, 'Maisy, stand up and recite for the class the seven gifts of the Holy Ghost like a good girl.'

Maisy didn't hesitate. 'Wisdom, understanding, knowledge, courage, counsel, fortitude and piety, Miss Connor.'

As Maisy turned to sit down she stuck her tongue out at me and I vowed that if I got the chance I'd pull that stupid tongue right out of Maisy Stewart's rotten head.

'That's better thank you, Maisy, now back to you, Miss McKitterick, surely you should have no problem naming the Stations of the Cross?'

My ears began to buzz; I was panic-struck. *Which one of the Stations of the Cross came first?* Miss Connor calmly swanked back to her desk, as my eyes followed her. She lifted the big, leather strap from its hook, flopping it across her hands. My face flushed redder. I couldn't think of anything but what it would feel like. I clenched my hands in dread.

'Well?' she boomed, 'cat got your tongue?'

At that she brought the big, thick leather strap down hard on the wooden desk—thwack! I nearly jumped out of my skin, my eyes as big as saucers. I knew I was next to get it.

It must have been all the praying I did, I don't even remember starting the lines. But one by one I named every one of the Stations of the Cross, much to her disappointment. I was told to go back to my seat without so much as a thank you.

She hissed in my ear as I slid back into my seat.

'You'll get into Heaven by the skin of your teeth, Isabelle McKitterick.'

At lunchtime, the schoolyard boomed with the high-pitched voices of childer calling for each other, and playing hopscotch and chasey. They sang all the songs of the day.

'I'll tell me ma when I get home, the boys won't leave the girls alone; they pulled me hair and they steal my comb, but that's all right till I go home. She is handsome, she is pretty, she is the Belle of Belfast city; she is courtin'—one, two, three. Please will you tell me who is she?'

This was my song. I was the only child in the school with such 'white as snow' hair, as mentioned in another part of the song. Others sang, 'My Aunt Jane she called me in, she gave me sweeties out of her wee tin, half a bap with sugar on the top and three wee sweeties out of her wee shop.'

I tried to keep away from any teacher in the yard. Some of the older childer disappeared round the back of the school sheds, out of sight to light the butts of woodbines they'd stole from their ma's and da's coat pockets. They found them anywhere, in bags or even out of a bin on the way to school.

As lunchtime ended, the second dread began to fill me more and more: going home. 'Please God don't let my mammy and daddy fight again tonight.' Over and over I'd recite the prayer, until the teacher caught me muttering.

29

'Stop that at once, Isabelle McKitterick, muttering is for craters who are backward or mad. Are you backward or mad?' Miss Conner never let up on me.

'No, Miss.'

'Well stop that nonsense, before I take the strap and knock some sense into you.'

'Yes, Miss.'

'Yes, Miss what?'

'Yes, Miss Connor.' The walk home got slower and slower. I looked at anything to take my mind off going home: 276, 277, 278 ... railings on the church fence; three doors that were painted red; twenty manhole covers in the road; fifteen babies in prams. Even hunger couldn't make me walk any quicker and as soon as I got in the back door, it started.

'Where in under Jesus have you been, wee girl, half the street's been home an hour ago.'

'She's been dillydallying, Ma, I saw her, and she's afraid she'll have to brush the yard,' Brian chimed in. God I hated Brian. Why was he always trying to get me into trouble?

Now Daddy was usually a quiet man and much of the time he knew when to let Mammy's mithering go in one ear and out the other. It wasn't that he didn't care about what she was saying, far from it, but often he felt there was nothing he could do about it. He had as much choice about having babies as she did. He brought home every penny he earned. He mended the childer's shoes. He fixed up every broken bit of furniture there was. He'd even made the attic into another bedroom to make extra room for them all. 'What more did she want from him?' he'd say.

But Mammy had given him thirteen childer so far and her back was broke with the onslaught of constant work from morning till night. Her bones ached and her spine was starting to twist, which made it hard to stand for long. There was always somebody sick in the house and always somebody lousey with the walkers. The work was just never ending and she was done out. It was either shite or sick she was cleaning.

30

On this night she promised herself that Daddy would listen to her. It wasn't unusual for the 'nagging' to turn into a full-blown row. It wasn't the first time that Daddy could 'stand Mammy's moaning no longer' and stood bolt upright at the heavy, wooden dinner table, upending it and sending everyone's dinner crashing to the floor—every morsel of food unfit for anyone to eat.

Tonight I could feel it. My stomach was in knots again; a sure sign of the night to come. I was pleased there was no room for me or the younger ones round the table. Instead we climbed the stairs each with our own step, pretending we were in a posh restaurant in Belfast. From the top stair I had a bird's-eye view of the living room below. The fire was hissing from another scuttle full of damp coal that had just been put on. Mammy was telling Daddy it was no good the coal being damp as it wouldn't give out as much heat as a matchstick. I knew if anything started I could scurry backwards up the stairs and cover my ears.

Now you know Daddy mended all the family shoes and when a hole poked its way through the soles and the cardboard had worn out, he would heave the heavy iron laste up onto the table, carefully placing a patch of leather where it was needed and glue it in place. The laste was made in the shape of an upside-down foot and so heavy only he could lift it. When it wasn't mending shoes or used for cooling toffee, it was used as a doorstop, letting the breeze blow through on a fine day freshening the place up. That night, we were all just about finished our dinner and I was sitting on my step. Mammy began her lament at Daddy. He lit his pipe trying to ignore her blathering, but she was determined he'd listen tonight.

The more he tried to ignore her, the louder she got. I lifted my dinner, moving myself back up a stair, motioning to the next child to do the same. I could feel the hairs on the back of my neck stand up, which wasn't a good sign. You could cut the atmosphere below with a knife. Straining my neck now to see what was happening, suddenly I heard Daddy roar like a bear.

'WOMAN ... BE ... DAMNED!' and with that, a thump. Mammy screamed out in agony as the heavy iron laste crashed straight into her shin breaking her left leg clean in two.

Everything went deathly quiet as Mammy passed out in the chair. I was terrified. I thought my daddy had just killed my mammy. Frantically I ran down the stairs, pushing the other childer out of the way. The older ones were standing like ghosts, their backs pressed against the wall. I ran over to Mammy, and then looked over at Daddy who was still panting, wiping the spit from his mouth with his shirtsleeve, his eyes glazed like a mad dog. I scanned the room trying to take it all in. Was there not one of them going to do anything? And then something inside me snapped. I glared back at Daddy. How could he do this to Mammy? I wasn't afraid of him; I was more scared of having no Mammy.

'You leave my mammy alone,' I yelled out loud.

A gasp could be heard round the room. The fear was palpable for I suppose they all thought I'd be next to get it.

Daddy stood swaying, his breathing still rapid, fists clenched, taking in what had just happened. But he didn't move, he just stared right back into the eyes that were a mirror of his own and without saying a word, he ripped his coat from the hook where it hung behind the door under the stairs and stormed out of the house, towards the entry to the Rock Pub. Mammy walked with a limp for the rest of her life, which meant she had another woe to add to the list she fired at Daddy.

THE GAELTACHT AND ARDSCOIL
Isabelle

Despite my fear of the teachers at school and constant worry about being lousey, I liked learning; to me there seemed to be something exciting about learning something new. I loved reading books on history and geography too. And in spite of the ongoing cruelty of the teachers and my attempts to keep myself clean and keep a low profile, my last teacher in primary school was an aul cowyard who seemed to have it in for me. Her name was Miss McGrath.

One day, the principal came in to class and announced the school was putting up a scholarship for three pupils to attend the Irish speaking and very prestigious Gaeltacht in Donegal—a place of esteemed academic excellence in language and culture. Pupils would have to sit an exam and those with the highest marks would be allowed to represent the school, their families and parish—what an honour. A wave of gasps and excited chatter spread through the class.

'Children, quiet please, pay attention,' exclaimed the teacher.

I was all a jitter. A scholarship? I loved the Irish language. Everything about Ireland's culture and heritage fascinated me. My daddy's stories were the most amazing things I'd ever heard. I could already say the *Hail Mary* in Irish. Oh I just had to go; somehow I just had to win that scholarship.

I could already picture myself there, imagining what the wild, rugged coastline of Donegal looked like, with the smell of the peat fires burning— even the road signs would be In Irish.

Speaking English was forbidden for the whole three weeks and I couldn't wait to sit that exam. I lined up with the other childer in the class who were putting their names down for the exam. Maisy Stewart was in front of me in the line. Thank God, she wouldn't be looking too closely at my hair for walkers. Just with the thought my head began to itch.

Oh God, don't scratch or they'll think you're lousey, I silently chided myself. That'll be the end of Donegal. *Please God, don't let me scratch. Please St Jude, Our Blessed Lady? Don't let me even look like I'll scratch.* With that Maisy stepped aside, leaving me face to face with Miss McGrath. Instinctively I kept my eyes low, trying not to give the teacher any cause to start on me. But as the teacher pushed the pen forward for me to sign my name, she let out a scathing 'Huh ... so ... YOU ... think YOU will have a cat in hell's chance of passing this exam, Isabelle McKitterick?'

I flushed scarlet against my flaxen hair. I wanted to tell the aul cowyard to go to Hell. But I knew well if I said one word, my chance of going to Donegal would vanish like a puff of smoke going up a chimney.

My fingers twisted tightly in my hands, I shifted from foot to foot and nervously. 'Yes, Miss,' I said.

'Well it will cost a guinea. Only respectable people have that kind of money to spend on education ... for a girl.' My legs suddenly felt like jelly. What if Mammy and Daddy didn't have the money to let me sit for the exam?

'Bring the money to school by the end of the week.'

I couldn't wait to get home that day and tell Mammy and Daddy about the exam and what it was like at the Gaeltacht. Mammy was quiet when I told her, not a muscle on her face moving. But I knew what she was thinking.

What use would it be HER going off for three weeks, when she could be at home lending a helping hand? Now the boys, that was a different story.

34

They'd all have a trade; they'd be husbands and have to support a family of their own one day. Aye, there was sense to educating my boys. That's where any extra money should go.

There was Seamus, already started his glazing apprenticeship and there hadn't even been the money to buy his tools. What in under God was Alistair McKitterick thinking of, filling her head full of nonsense? It was true, the 'road to Hell was paved with good intentions', bejesus I could certainly do with more help round the place if the truth be told. If it wasn't for Nell I don't know what I would have done. Gallivanting off to Donegal my arse ...

Edu ...feckin ... cation! It wouldn't be long till she'd be getting a job at the Belfast Swiss. Oh aye, that would make life a bit easier. What use was it, filling her head full of fairytales and books? That wouldn't stop babies coming. Soon she'd be raising childer of her own, bare foot and pregnant likely, as far as I could see.

When my Daddy had cleaned himself up after his day's work and finished his dinner, I told him about the scholarship and how much I wanted to sit the exam for the Gaeltacht. He didn't say anything initially, just lit his pipe, sucking the baccy to life and then 'put putting' it out of his mouth sideways in small puffs.

I could feel Mammy's eyes burning a hole in the back of my head and I wasn't surprised when I heard, 'Isabelle McKitterick, get into that scullery and clear that table, wee girl, and get those fancy notions outa your head.'

I'd finished clearing the plates off the table in the scullery and come into the living room to sit by the fire grate. It was always the warmest spot. Daddy had been up the stairs for ages and had just come back down. He took his seat and motioned for me to come over to him. He took my hand and without a word pressed a shiny new guinea right into it, then winked at me. I started to shake. I looked from my Daddy to the shiny coin in my hand. I couldn't believe it.

'For me? For the exam? Oh, Daddy, thank you.' Mammy looked over and began to shake her head.

'A whole guinea, Alistair McKitterick, just for an exam? It's for Purdysburn Asylum you'll be. Where in the name of God did money like that come from? There's nothing like that in my purse. Have you been hiding it?'

Daddy waved his hand at Mammy motioning her to sit down, saying that it was an honour to represent your family and none of the other childer had shown an interest. And at that Daddy shooed me off upstairs to put the precious guinea in a safe place ready for school the next day.

As I rounded the top of the stairs our Brian was waiting for me. He caught hold of my cardigan, yanking me sideways, pushing me up against the wall.

'Sizza, the grey-haired rat,' he hissed, low enough so nobody could hear. 'So ye think ye can get away with that? All that money for a fecking school test?'

'Let go of me ye big pig or I'll tell me da.'

'Let go of me or I'll tell me da,' he mouthed back in a mocking tone. 'I wouldn't thank you for your stinking guinea,' he hissed showing all his yellow teeth.

I tugged hard to free my cardigan. His eyes followed me till I disappeared into the bedroom. His mouth tight, his lips a thin line.

'Sisss, I'll get you back one day, thinking you are better than me or any of the rest of us. Why the hell did Da act like a bit of melted butter round you and yet be as hard as nails round me? Bah, it makes me sick,' I heard him mumbling to himself.

The day of the exam results dawned and I thought my legs wouldn't carry me to school. What if I didn't pass the exam and the shiny, new guinea would be lost forever? What would Mammy say about such a waste of money? Oh God, just the thought of the trouble it would cause made me feel sick.

Miss McGrath was waiting in the classroom. The childer sat bolt upright at their desks, wide eyed with anticipation. Who would be going to Donegal? The first name was called, 'Maeve Mc Graunchy, step forward, congratulations you have passed the exam.' My stomach was now in my chest. As we all clapped for Maeve, she stepped forward to stand at the top of the class, beaming from ear to ear, her tight ringlets bouncing up and down as she walked.

'Patrick Kelly. Where is Patrick? Ahhh … there you are now, it's no surprise that you passed the exam. 'Tis the brightest boy in St Patricia's that you are. You'll be headed to Clonard Seminary if you keep your studies and prayers up the way you do. Your family must be so proud of such a pious and smart son.'

Patrick Kelly stood with his back ramrod straight and marched, swinging his arms like a soldier of God, up to stand beside Maeve.

'Take a look, children, fine examples from fine families,' said the teacher with a grin.

I could barely breathe by this time, one more place to be announced. All I could do now was wait. Then something caught my eye. What was covering Maisy Stewart's face? Holy shit, she'd caught the canker sores overnight. If that wasn't bad enough, her ma painted her face purple with gentian violet, the cure for all skin ailments that made you look like a leper from Africa.

Now that was a thousand times worse than having walkers because at least if ye didn't scratch your head, there was a good chance nobody would know you were lousey. So there was Maisy, the shite, who'd caused me to be sent home from school, looking like a leper. It was all I could do to stop the rising chuckle in my belly.

I was brought back to Earth by the sound of the teacher's voice.

'Isabelle McKitterick! May we have your attention?'

I almost jumped out of my skin as I was brought back from my wandering thoughts about Maisy Stewart's ugly purple-coloured face.

'Yes, Miss.' I had prayed so hard to St Jude, the patron saint of the hopeless, for over a month, but I still couldn't believe the teacher had just called my name.

'Well, Miss McKitterick … are you going to keep us waiting all morning? Up to the front of the class and be quick about it before I change the name on this sheet.'

I still wondered if there'd been a mistake. It wasn't until the teacher asked the whole class to clap for the successful candidates that I realised I was going to Donegal. Daddy was delighted, but Mammy never said a word. There was no point; it wouldn't matter what she said or thought for that matter because Daddy would do exactly as he pleased, especially for 'her' as she'd put it. I knew how Mammy felt about such an outrageous waste of money. But Daddy made it clear: it was an honour having one of your childer doing so well off to study the language and culture of their homeland. It's next in line only to the honour of giving one of your own to the priesthood or convent.

Donegal was the wildest, windswept, amazing place I'd ever seen in my life. Nothing but the Irish tongue spoken from morning till night. I thought it sounded like angels singing. This was surely the closest thing to Heaven on Earth. This was the first time in my life that I had called upon St Jude, the patron saint of the hopeless, to intercede for me and, without so much as a thunderbolt or angel to be seen, he had granted my prayers. I wasn't sure if this divine intervention was because I was truly holy as I always prayed to be, or just plain hopeless. All I knew was that St Jude must have gone straight to God himself, for a miracle of this magnitude to occur and any doubts I secretly harboured about the mystery of faith vanished into thin air. Three weeks of Heaven, three weeks of freedom … freedom from Miss McGrath who despised me. Three weeks away from the guldering and fighting at home. Three weeks of having a whole bed all to myself. I could hardly sleep a wink because I didn't want to miss one minute of anything. What did seem strange at first was how quiet everything was; hardly a bus or car would go by, and people still used horses and carts to get about. It was like travelling back to a different time.

It wasn't like Belfast. There were hardly any shops and those that were there closed by lunchtime on Saturday. The only thing open on

Sundays was the pub. But none of that bothered me. The sky seemed endless here and people didn't look wealthy or posh, but nearly all of them smiled passing the time of day.

'*Maidin mhaith, Sibéal, conas atá tú inniu?*' (Good morning, Isabelle, how are you?)

And I'd reply, '*I'm fineáil buíochas le Dia*'. (I'm fine thank God.)

They fed us like fighting cocks; you should have seen the spread morning till night. I wondered where so much food had come from, but then I realised the part of Donegal I was in was over the border in the free state and there'd been no war here, no bombs going off, no childer lying on grave tops, no ration books, no fear.

The day always started with morning prayers, '*In ainm an Athar, agus an Macagus an Taibhse Naofa, o'n*'. (In the name of the Father, and of the Son and of the Holy Ghost, Amen.) The teacher told us that throughout our stay there would be mass said in Irish not Latin. I couldn't wait. Nobody shouted at me for the whole time I was there; in fact, it was the opposite, everyone spoke very politely and slowly pronouncing every word so I could get the sound. I sometimes didn't quite get it straight away, but that made no difference, they were still so nice to me and somehow I got the gist of what was being said to me, like it was inside my soul or something.

The teachers took us outside for some of our lessons. We walked for miles to find magnificent stone Celtic crosses that had been carved hundreds of years before. They told us stories of giants, Pagans, druid priests, great kings, *The Book of Kells* and all about St Patrick, our patron saint, who chased all the snakes out of Ireland.

Each night I went to bed afraid of missing anything, so I kept one eye open as long as I could. It was the wonderful smell of baking bread that woke me each morning. To this day I still remember what it felt like—the sweet delicious aroma of fresh, baking bread, crisp, white sheets in a bed of my own, a window that framed the countryside beyond with only emerald fields as far as the eye could see.

I wanted to stay forever; I felt like I belonged there and was accepted there. And, to my utter astonishment, on my last night as I went into my room I spotted something sitting on my pillow. I picked it up. It was a white, linen hankie with a small, green shamrock embroidered in one corner.

Who would have done this? I clasped it to my chest, and I could feel myself blushing. Someone here must ... like me. I vowed to keep the hankie a secret, in case somebody said I stole it. The note said, '*mian sé,aisling é, é a dhéanamh*' and it was signed '*admirer rúnda*'. (Wish it, dream it, do it, ... a secret admirer.) I didn't care who'd done it, I was going to cherish the wee hankie, keep it with me always. It would be my good luck charm and nobody would know because it was only a hankie. This was the happiest day of my life.

My time at the Gaeltacht fuelled my mind to learn much more about my native tongue and culture and, apart from the day and hour my wee childer were born, it was one of the happiest times in my life. Then you won't believe what happened: when my friends were leaving school heading for the factory, I won another scholarship to the Ardscoil in Belfast, a school for the arts, which let its pupils experience not only the Irish language but the ancient and traditional crafts of pottery and sculpture. I couldn't believe it. I was sure the wee hankie was bringing me luck because I carried it everywhere. Daddy made sure that I had the tools for my sculpting classes, and again there was more than one person in the house who felt my schooling in the arts was nothing but a fancy waste of time and precious money when I should've been out getting a job supporting the family that raised me.

'And what use was there educating girls when they'd be carrying babies for the rest of their lives? No amount of fancy schooling would prepare you for that,' Mammy would say.

I'd been back from Donegal a few months and loved going along to the Ardscoil every day. All the other girls my age in the street were by now out working. It left few people to knock about with. Only the younger ones were about, the others thinking they were all grown up now they had jobs. You should have seen Lilly Foley, Francis's sister, with lips on her like a painted doll, going about like the girl in the big picture, swapping her ankle socks for her ma's stockings and clopping about in a pair of heels that were so big that she fell on her arse one day; the whole street tittering and laughing. I'd no interest in all that. I just loved to be out in the fresh air—I suppose I was still an innocent, big child.

'Jesus, Mary and holy Saint Joseph,' puffed Mammy loudly for Daddy to hear, 'look at that big lump out there in the street, skipping with them wee ones like a buck eejit and her almost fifteen years of age. That's what all that fancy schooling has done for her, educating girls, my arse. I knew no good would come of it. Wasting time as well as money that could be better spent elsewhere. Out running the streets, bah! It would suit her better to be in here making herself useful before the whole fecking street thinks she's not all there. Go on, Danny, go and get pigerina in here before my eyes buckle in my head. And keep away from that big merchant lighting the street lamp. If he sees ye trying to kick his ladder again, he'll cut the skull off ye with the flint he's using.'

'Why do I have to keep away, Mammy? Our Moggie's there swinging on the ropes with Isa Mullen and Maeve McGaunchy. There's about ten of them, why can't I go over and have a go too?'

'Danny, do I have to tell you again it's a girl's game? You're not a sissy, are ye?'

'Aw,' said Danny as he backed out of the scullery at Mammy's admonishment.

'Girls always seemed to have the best fun. What was there for boys to do except throw stones at windows, or chase the Nun's mad dog with a stick up at Riddle's field? Ach aye, that was good fun till the fecker caught up with ye and bit your arse or tore your trousers,' he mumbled.

Danny enjoyed firing stones up in the trees and scattering the crows, with them going crackers protecting their nests. They would swoop and squeal and the Nun's fecking mad dog would be going mad along with the crows. He hummed the song they all sang as they sent the crows mad.

'Crows, crows, your nests are on fire, crows, crows, your nests are on fire … ISABELLE. You're wan-ted!'

'Aye, in a minute,' I called while continuing to play with my very best friend, Daisy. 'One, two, three, jump.' I pretended I was deaf, which wasn't lying as years of being used as a sparring partner for our boys had left me with an ear that I could only hear squealing out of. And besides, the more skipping I did, the less fighting at home I heard and the sooner I'd be away to bed.

'ISABELLE.' Finally Danny got close enough to pull my cardigan. 'You're wanted, pigerina!' Danny acted like a big fella, using one of Mammy's grown-up words. 'Ma says you're a buck eejit skippin' with the wee ones.'

'Feck off, Danny, or I'll kick your melt in.' I was boiling mad that Danny called me 'pigerina' and 'buck eejit'. I'd heard the words used a lot in our house—never in a good way.

'Nah, Ma says you're wanted.'

'Just one more go and I'll come in.' I tried not to let Mammy's words stick in my craw and with another jump I was skipping again.

'I'll tell me ma when I go home, the boys won't leave the girls alone, they pull my hair and they steal my comb, but that's alright till I go home.'

'Isabelle!' Danny yelled again.

I just wanted to hear the next bit; this was my song.

'She is handsome, she is pretty, she is the Belle of Belfast city; she is courtin'—one, two, three. Please will you tell me who is she?' As Danny wasn't giving up, I took one last leap and then left the rope as the wee ones carried on skipping.

'Danny, did you see Mrs O'Donnell going up the street?' I said giving Danny a playful cuff round the ear.

'Nah.'

'I did. She's got a belly as big as a harvest moon; I think she's having a baby.' As we reached the house Danny ran ahead and Mammy rounded on me.

'In under Jesus, wee girl, isn't it time ye caught yourself on, burling round out there like a buck eejit showing your arse? Tisn't right at your age, get in there and make yourself useful, peel those potatoes, wash the dishes and get the table ready.' I stuck my tongue out at Danny 'cause he was sticking his two fingers up at me behind Mammy's back, the cheeky wee shite.

'Mammy, I've just seen Mrs O'Donnell going up the street and I think she's having a baby because her belly's as big as ...'

Smack! My head flung backwards and spun as I was knocked off balance. My hand going straight up to my face, I reeled from the slap. The whole side of my face was stinging, my lip quivered, my eyes started to water, and I couldn't even speak, I just stared at Mammy.

I wasn't game enough to ask why I'd just had the face taken off me because I knew Mammy was about to tell me anyway. 'You ... dirty mare. The longest day you ever live, don't you ever talk like that in this house or before that Sacred Heart picture, I swear I'll skin you alive.' I just stared; I wasn't even sure what had just happened. I wasn't talking dirty; I'd just been talking about Mrs O'Donnell having a baby. What was dirty about that? I knew from that day on never to talk about babies or anything else to do with your body for that matter.

My time at the Ardscoil was over too soon and there were some in the house who said it was about time I started work. Half the street had been there for over a year and it was about time my heels were cooled. I was still a very innocent child and, to the women in the factory, I must've looked like I'd just come down the Lagan on a log.

It wasn't long after that I thought I was dying. There was blood on my knickers; oh God, I thought, now I'd be in for it—even if I was dying—with my new white knickers all spoilt. I knew better than to ask Mammy about it; I'd just have to die quietly and be buried in Miltown Cemetery with my Granny and Granda.

So I hid the knickers under the big, brass bed and lay down prepared to die. I was shocked that I woke up the next morning and was called out of bed to do my usual shift at the Belfast Swiss Embroidery. What choice did I have? It didn't matter where ye died anyway. No one in the house noticed I was on death's door. When I arrived at the factory, I had to walk past the whole line of girls to my spot and walking isn't easy when you're dying.

I walked cross-legged, to hold the aul rag in place between my legs. I couldn't even look at anyone. To my disbelief I heard a couple of the women laughing, nudging each other and I put my head down even further inching my way to my stool where I could die and then be taken home and buried. How could they all be so cruel? A dying dog would be treated better. It was clear that nobody cared if I were alive or dead. As I reached my stool, I felt a hand on my shoulder. It was big Eileen Malone.

'Isabelle, have you got your period, love?' My face flushed scarlet and I started to cry. Finally someone had noticed I was dying.

'Nooo,' I replied, eyes to the floor, 'I am dying Eileen and at this rate I'll be gone by Saturday.' Big Eileen tried not to smile and motioned to the other girls to stop carrying on.

'Isabelle, it's alright, you're not dying, love. Come with me to the toilet and I'll help you get cleaned up.' Like a lamb, I rose and was helped shuffling to the toilet.

Big Eileen gave me a sanitary tarl, called Dr White's, with a loop at each end and showed me how to place it between my legs. Then she cut a piece of string, measured my waist, threaded it through the two loops and tied it round me so I could walk straight. She told me this would happen every month and it was nothing to worry about, but I must stay away from boys.

I was totally confused. So I wasn't dying, I got that. But what did blood in your knickers have to do with staying away from boys? Well, it didn't really matter because I never forgot Big Eileen's kindness that day and the feeling of relief that not only was I going to live, but also I could walk, run and skip round, free as a bird. I vowed to myself that if I ever had a baby girl of my own, I'd never leave her in this state for the sake of explaining something that happened to everybody.

Now my arrival at the Belfast Swiss hadn't gone unnoticed by the fellas. Tommy Peterson had taken a shine to me—him being seventeen meant that he thought he was the fella in the big picture. He fancied himself as my man and it wasn't long before I was spending lunchtime hearing all the craic Tommy spun.

Tommy was going to be somebody; he was headed for the Royal Air Force where he aimed to be an engineer. He wouldn't be hanging round these parts for long, he'd say, he had dreams all right. He told me that he'd be heading for America to make his fortune with the Yanks, and if I would wait for him, he'd send for me and it wouldn't matter in America that he was a Prod; we could be together.

Now I was very flattered by Tommy's attentions, holding hands and all. He spoke really nice and it made me feel well ... special. I liked the thought of living in a faraway land and being rich. It seemed to me that half the people of Ireland were going to America where life was a lot better than in Belfast. I told my wee brother, whom I shared the attic with, that when I go to America he could come too. Ach it was grand to be young, dreaming.

But any thoughts of Tommy Peterson and I becoming an item vanished into thin air when I told my daddy about him. Before I'd even so much as stolen a kiss, Daddy put to bed any notion I had of bringing an Orange man near the house.

'Jesus, Mary and Joseph, wee girl, have you not got 2ds' worth of sense? He's a what? A Prod?' snorted Daddy as he lit his pipe. 'Now listen to me, Isabelle McKitterick, there'll be no Prod welcome in this house. I don't care if his fecking arse is decked with diamonds, do you hear me? Those Orange bastards have kept us down for hundreds of years and they're all the same, tarred with the same brush.'

'But, Daddy, he's really nice and he's going to join the Royal Air Force and live in America.'

'Away where? A-m-e-r-i-c-a, is it? Ach for God's sake, catch yourself on wee girl. Is your head full of marbles? Does he know you're only sixteen years old, the dirty bastard? I'll give him girlfriend alright if I get me hands on him. If I hear tell of any goings on with him, there'll be no more gallivanting on bikes come the weekend. Do ye hear me? You need to stick to your own kind or there'll be no good come of it. A protestant ... in God's name, what'll be next?'

I didn't know what to do because that day Tommy had given me the most beautiful silver ring with a marcasite stone, which sparkled like a real diamond, for me to keep until he could send for me to come to America. I was distraught; what could I do? Tommy was going to America and I had his ring. If I gave it back to him, he'd think I didn't like him and I wouldn't hurt his feelings for the world. How could I tell him my daddy had forbidden me to see him because he was a Prod?

When I told my Mammy the tale, she agreed with Daddy there'd be no Orange man crossing their doorstep. When Mammy asked me about 'this ring business', she said she'd take care of it and put it out of the way because no good would come of it. I handed the ring to Mammy and prayed that I wouldn't see Tommy before he set off to America. Aye, it was better if I went nowhere near the Belfast Swiss canteen until Friday when Tommy would be gone.

Now I loved the lively chatter of Belfast Swiss Embroidery. The older girls thought they were it and a bit smoking cigarettes and all that. They seemed to know everything about life, no matter what it was. They knew all the gossip about everyone and the craic was grand. Of course all young women want to know what the future holds, but very few, if any, could predict it with any accuracy. So during our tea break Siobhan O'Toole told the girls that I could read the tea leaves and this caused more than an excited crowd to gather round me.

They wanted to know what good fortune lay ahead for them. I was a bit unsure and initially tried to put the girls off, but they wouldn't have it. They wanted to know their fortune. Mammy had warned me not to mess with spirit things I knew little about.

'Ach, it's only a bit of fun, Isabelle. C'mon before the supervisor catches us,' said Tilly Reid who smoked one cigarette after another and had a cough on her that would have killed Samson.

'Oh, okay, get me your cup and drink it down, leave the leaves in the bottom. I'll do it, but only for a laugh.'

They all gathered round to hear my psychic predictions and miraculous forecast. Tilly drank her tea, nervously nibbled at her fingernails, flattened her apron and handed the cup to me.

'C'mon, Isabelle, fir fecks sake before that aul tachara comes back.'

I turned over the cup, turned it round three times on the saucer exactly as I'd seen Mammy do it. With a deep breath I rolled my eyes and turned the cup over. I didn't speak, just kept looking at the cup and back to Tilly who was almost shitting herself by this time.

'C'mon, Isabelle, for Christ's sake hurry up will ye.' Everyone was getting impatient nudging each other and waiting patiently for their turn.

I suddenly looked serious; I wasn't laughing anymore. I turned to Tilly and gave her the cup back saying I couldn't read it because there was nothing there. Siobhan grabbed the cup; all the women were so disappointed they desperately wanted to hear Tilly's fortune too. Tilly would have none of it and snatched the cup back off Siobhan thrusting it back into my hands.

'Ach, c'mon … you must have seen something.' I looked round and tried to shy away, which only made Tilly persist more. 'Pleassse, Isabelle, read it for me.'

I turned slowly, looking up till I was inches from Tilly's face and told her that what I'd seen in the cup was 'death'. Everyone stopped talking.

'Death of someone really close, Tilly,' I said, 'soon, very soon.'

At that I stood up and pushed my way through the throng of women who'd crowded round, went into the toilet and vomited. Why did I tell Tilly such shite? It was only fecking tea leaves. What gave me those thoughts? I was sorry I picked the bloody cup up and I hoped to God none of them would tell Mammy, or she'd take the 'head staggers' and start ranting on about poltergeists again.

All the girls on the machine line looked at me as I came back white as a sheet, nudging each other, whispering behind their hands and muttering under their breath. The line supervisor came bustling down between the rows of machines wanting to know what all the commotion was about and for us all to get back to the machines saying, 'Where do these people think they all are? On their fathers' yachts?'

I'd heard it all before, what the supervisor thought of us: *Honestly, these people, bye you had to keep your eye on them. Mr Fenton was right; line work was all they were fit for, especially the fenians. They were lazy bastards, skivers and good for nothing. Could bring a good Protestant workforce to its knees if you didn't keep them in their place. What was the world coming to? Now they also had fecking trade unions trying to cause trouble. Paid holidays indeed and more money for working a night shift, they should be grateful they had a bloody job at all. Bah! It would never get off the ground, the 'lodge' would see to that.*

But we all kept our heads low and no one let on what had just happened.

Tilly Reid didn't come to work the next day and when Siobhan and I entered the factory, everyone stopped talking—just stared at us both. 'What's going on?' Siobhan demanded to know and Vera Duggan shouted up the line that Tilly's da had dropped down dead yesterday afternoon. I fainted on the spot and Siobhan tried to wake me up by slapping my face and told Vera Duggan to get some water. When I pulled round, I couldn't think straight. I knew I shouldn't have been meddling in spirit business. In the name of God and his holy mother, how was I ever going to explain this? A man lying stone dead and it was all down to me. I wished I'd never taken the girls underneath my notice yesterday, all that goading and egging on, and now look what's happened.

'Ach, Siobhan, it's all my fault, talking shite with those tea leaves. Jesus, I'll be for Hell, me ma and da'll kill me if they find out I did this.'

'Don't be daft, it was just a bit of fun and Tilly's da had a weak heart anyway.' Siobhan would have none of it.

But the creepy feeling that came over me never left me all day and as soon as I could, I went to confession and told Father Murray that I'd caused Tilly Reid's da's death by dabbling in the tea leaves. He advised me never to read the leaves again because you never know if ye had the gift until something like this happened, and from that day to this, I never lifted another cup to read the leaves—I left fortune telling to the gypsies.

One night when I was about seventeen I'd been to a dance and I'd missed the last bus home. I was petrified I'd be in deep trouble. Once Daddy and Mammy were in bed, ye disturbed them on peril of your life. Oh Jesus, I'd be in for it alright. I raced up the street and into our entryway, my heart pounding, my flaxen, white hair flying away down my back, and my cheeks flushed pink with the sting of the fresh, autumn wind.

To my horror, the door was locked. Breathless, I rattled the handle, praying the door would open. Oh God, I was in for it now. I'd been told not to be late. I walked back up the path and peered up at the front bedroom window.

'Psst' I said, cupping my hands round my mouth. 'Psst,' I tried again, hoping someone would hear me.

There wasn't a soul or a light to be seen, not a sound to be heard—no one was awake. As I turned to walk back to the entryway, I saw the curtains at the window move and my heart leapt. Oh great, somebody's up and will let me slip in. They'll be none the wiser.

Then I saw our Brian's face staring down at me with a leering smile.

'Brian, open the door please?' I softly shouted, motioning to the front door, but he just stared at me, his eyes burning a hole in my head. And as quick as ye like, he dropped the lace curtain and sloped off to his warm, cosy bed leaving me standing in the cold night air with nowhere to sleep. I could just imagine the sleeket grin that would have slowly spread across his face. He knew that one day he'd get me back and it happened so nicely.

He would've thought about all the times 'sizza, the grey-haired rat' had stolen the show, all the jobs she got away with not doing, all the fecking spoiling his da had done of her, while he went about the place like a nobody. 'That one', he would say of me, had got under his skin since the day and hour she was fecking born. It was time she got her comeuppance. He knew all along that all he'd have to do was wait till the time was right and then he'd feel the warm glow of long-awaited satisfaction infuse his whole body. I knew this was his payback.

The tiles in the entryway were freezing. Ah damn, now what'll I do? Hopping from one foot to another, I thrust my hands under my oxters to warm them up. I'd no option but to bunk down in the entrance for the night. Curled up and shivering I crouched down on the icy-cold floor, trying to huddle right into the corner and to keep outa' the draught that slithered under the front door. I tugged at my coat, trying to wrap it round my legs. I was desperate to go to the toilet too. My teeth started to chatter in my head and I began my prayers.

'Now I lay me down to sleep, I pray the lord my soul to keep. Matthew, Mark, Luke and John, God bless the floor I lay on. If I die before I wake, I pray the lord my soul to take. Jesus, Mary and Joseph, I give you my heart and my soul. Jesus, Mary and Joseph, assist me now and in my last agony. Jesus, Mary and Joseph, may I breath forth my soul in peace with you. Amen.'

Maybe someone would be up early. I tried to sleep, the freezing wind whipping round my thinly-clad body. I heard the clock in the hallway chime one, two, three. Oh God, it was three o'clock in the morning. If I said another prayer, maybe it would start to get light and it would be morning.

Daddy was up first because the market came awake at 5 o'clock each morning. He filled the teapot, its arse blackened from the constant touch of the gas flame, and lit the gas stove. Then tipped three good spoonfuls of tea leaves into it. Bye, he liked a good, strong cup of tea first thing—no weak shite. He left the teapot to boil while he attached the starched collar to his shirt by its three buttons, pulled his braces up round each shoulder, smoothed his hands over his shirt and sighed in gratitude. Mammy took good care when she smoothed the clothes. She always said, 'There'd be no man of hers go out of her house looking like a wrinkled prune.' He made his way into the scullery, pushing aside the washing above his head that had been hung the day before, still damp and hanging from the clothes horse, which was hoisted every night. Best place in the house this was for drying clothes, as the heat from the stove rose up. Mammy never minded the smell of cooking infusing her clean washing, as long as it was dry. Dry clothes smelling of stew was better than damp ones laden with pneumonia.

Daddy started to cut a thick slice of the soda bread Mammy had made the day before. Bye, she was some cook; she always set aside the stuff for his fry the night before she went to bed. No good a man starting his day on an empty belly. She put two eggs, a slice of bacon, half a green tomato and the soda bread on a plate and covered it with a muslin cloth.

The hearth was still aglow.

'Ah, that's good,' he said, reaching for the bellows to puff a bit of air under the fire. 'That'll save a few sticks for another day.'

Once he was done with the bellows, he bent down to carefully place another six lumps of coal from the scuttle on the fire in the grate till the rest of them got up. He rubbed his hands together blowing on them to warm them up; the winter chill was setting in early this year. Daddy always rose early because he firmly believed, 'the early bird got the worm' and 'early to bed, early to rise would make a man healthy, wealthy, and wise'. He sipped his tea, pouring some of it into the saucer to cool it down, slurping it carefully so as not to spill it. Then he pulled on his heavy boots and overcoat, lifted his pipe and baccy, shoving them into his left pocket, making his way to the front door.

When Daddy opened the front door that morning, he nearly fainted when my tiny frame, stiff as a board, fell into the house sidewards.

'In the name of God, wee girl! What's all this? Have you been there all night?'

I couldn't speak and he realised I was half frozen to death. He lifted me into the house beside the fire, rubbing my hands and feet.

'Jesus, get a blanket somebody! Maggie! Come down stairs for Christ's sake.'

Mammy was shocked at the sight of my frozen frame and it took an hour before I could speak. 'In under God, what happened?' I explained about missing the bus and the door being locked and how Brian had seen me but wouldn't open the door.

Daddy suddenly roared with rage. 'I'll fecking kill that big merchant.'

The peace of the early morning shattered like a clap of thunder. In one fell swoop Daddy took off his thick, leather belt with its shiny buckle, his trousers slipping off his waist and took the bare wooden stairs, three at a time, going for our Brian.

All hell broke loose as Daddy cussed and thwacked his way round the top of the stairs smacking the bed post and slamming the belt across the wooden floor, calling for 'the big, cowardly bastard to come out and take it like a man'. The other four childer in the bed cringed, wiping the sleep from their eyes, not knowing what the hell was going on.

Brian fled like two men and a wee lad as fast as his legs could carry him, out the attic skylight, skimming down the rooftop and away like hell's gates down the back entry just as dawn was breaking. He knew when Da meant business and he didn't have to think twice. He'd no desire to feel the weight of that belt and buckle. His only option was to scarper like a mangy cat and wait it out till Daddy cooled off.

I was too sick to go to work; I'd got a proper foundering and had to stay in bed for weeks. Mammy was furious as she was short of my pay packet. I contracted cystitis and a terrible kidney infection from the cold, tiled floor—something that would plague me for the rest of my life. The doctor was called, which also cost a fortune never mind the cost of the medicine on top of it all, and if I hadn't got better Daddy would have killed our Brian. Brian never spoke to me again until the night he accused Harry of being a thief and I paid the price of that for the rest of my life. But that's another part of the story.

ISABELLE MEETS JACK
Isabelle

Now our Molly and I could sing like larks. As teenagers we entered local talent quests, winning prizes of beautiful dresses and stockings —things that you couldn't get hold of for love nor money after the war. Before long, we walked the streets of The Falls road to wolf-whistles and admiring glances, our petite figures framed by the latest designer gear.

We looked and felt like *The Belles of Belfast City*. It was just like in my song, 'I'll tell me ma when I get home, the boys won't leave the girls alone.' And we almost had 'rings on our fingers and bells on our toes,' the gear we won was so fancy—dresses with paisley designs, pure woollen coats with silk lining, silk stockings, enough for all of our ones, and satin gloves. The more we sang the more we won, and we brought the dance halls to a standing ovation many a night. We sang in perfect harmony together—me in the alto and Molly in the soprano. Jesus we brought the house down.

We didn't just sing Irish songs, you know, but all the latest hits from America's Deep South like *Tallahassee* and *Waiting For The Robert E. Lee*. But Molly reckoned if it wasn't for me belting out the notes like I did, we wouldn't have won as much as we did. That's our Molly, though, as timid as a wee mouse and never one to blow her own trumpet.

As a teenager, my passion wasn't only for singing and designer gear, I could play the piano for as long as I could remember and could play tunes just by listening to the music by ear. And although I hated the cruelty of my teachers at school, I had been grateful for the historical tales they'd told, especially about my homeland. I also took to a two-wheeler bike like a duck to water.

As soon as I could, I joined the Northern Ireland Youth Hostelling Association and when none of our ones were allowed to roam the roads of the north, Daddy made sure my bike was fit to ride, oiling its wheels and tightening its bolts and brakes. He knew we shared the same yearning for the open space of the countryside. My feelings for the open road were so strong, like some invisible cord pulling at my very soul—wild horses couldn't have stopped me as the weekend came round. I thought of one thing only, the open road, fresh air in my lungs and the exquisite sight of my beloved homeland with its quilted fields of emerald green. There really were forty shades of green in those fields; God I felt so alive it was electric. 'Thanks, Daddy,' I'd shout as I wheeled the cumbersome two-wheeler out of the backyard, stopping astride the bike only to tie my blanket of flaxen blonde hair back in a ponytail, tucking it down the back of my Aaron jumper.

'Go on, girl, and be back by Sunday tea time.'

'I will, Daddy,' and I took off quicker than two men and a wee lad away down the back entry, down to join the twenty-strong cyclists for a weekend of hostelling. And there would be Siobhan—wild, wonderful, funny Siobhan O'Toole—my best friend in the whole world.

I didn't even notice the boys; we were all just friends, although Dan O'Keeffe who lived up Stonemore Road thought differently. He couldn't take his eyes off me. He followed me everywhere on the bike, always first to help me with my rucksack and to wheel my bike for me. Once again I was very flattered and it made me feel nice. But I only ever thought of Dan as a good pal, a bit like one of our boys, nothing more. But if I'd given Dan the go ahead, he would have been in like Flynn so to speak, and he was a Catholic so he would have got over the doorstep, unlike poor Tommy Peterson. We all looked out for each other, joking, laughing and cycling. Life was thrilling and exciting—another weekend away. This particular weekend the group of hostellers was bigger. We'd been cycling since midday, heading out of Antrim Road, each person taking the lead when they were tagged. I had noticed the tanned legs of the big fella with the sandy hair. I'd noticed him alright, every inch of him, glancing at the way his muscles stood out, well-defined; Jesus, he must have cycled a lot. I'd noticed his strong, freckled arms that were rosy-red with the fresh air, healthy and weather-beaten, the freckles almost all joined together. But I hadn't caught his face as he peddled past me with legs going ten to the dozen and him shouting out 'come on ye boys.' Oh and that voice; strong, yet nice and well-reared, not rough.

We'd all finished our dinner that evening at the hostel and were standing round waiting for somebody to get out the tin whistle or the spoons and get a tune going when I poked Siobhan in the ribs.

'Who's that fella over there?' I asked.

Siobhan's head swung round to see who I was talking about.

'Don't look now you nitwit, I don't want him to think we're having a good skeg at him, or his head will be a big as a bloody balloon,' I chided.

'The one with the sandy hair? Oh him, that's Jack Kennedy, thinks he's fecking Ireland's answer to Fred Astaire so he does,' said Siobhan.

'What do you mean?'

'Well he's Ely Mulligan's protégé—apparently dances like a fecking angel.' Ah, the legs, so strong with those muscles, that would explain it.

'A dancer is he?' I was transfixed, unable to take my eyes off Jack Kennedy and almost fainted when he glanced over and smiled, my skin flushing scarlet once again against my flaxen hair. *Oh God*, I thought, *just when I wanted to look cool, calm and collected, my crimson bake was giving me away again. When would I ever stop looking like a total eejit?*

'Jesus, he's coming over, Isabelle. Don't look for God's sake, act calm, pretend ye haven't seen him.'

So we kept chatting away, smoothing down our frocks and patting our hair at the same time. But Jack took his chance and strolled over anyway. And that's how I met Jack Kennedy. The attraction was instant and overwhelming. I couldn't think straight, couldn't get a word out, as if me tongue was tied in my head. I'd never, ever felt like such a dithering mess in my life before. I was so acutely aware of him looking at me, I found it hard to look back at him without going even redder in the face.

'Ladies.' He wasn't only handsome but, by the way he spoke, he was a real gentleman. 'I'm Jack! How are you both?' Even though he was talking to us both, I knew his eyes were fixed on me.

'Hello, I'm Siobhan and this is Isabelle. Haven't seen you here before.'

'Err, umm, yes, I've just joined the association. Jimmy over there,' he said nodding to his best friend, 'roped me in. He thought the extra exercise would help my fitness.'

'Fitness, oh, what are you keeping fit for?'

'Well, I dance, so I need to get in better shape for the All Ireland. Anyway ladies, if you'll excuse me, I really do have to go and keep an eye on Jimmy before those girls over there eat him alive. Look forward to catching up with you later.'

Again, he was speaking to both of us, but looking straight at me. As he slowly sauntered back to his best friend, he glanced over again one more time and I was mortified that he caught me glancing after him too. And do you know what he did? Winked at me! Flirting like a good 'un. And that said it all.

The whole weekend we seemed to accidentally bump into each other at every turn; it was like we were in some kind of magnetic field: two ends attracting each other. I even bumped into him as I came out of the ladies bathroom and me all flustered because I didn't know which bit of me to try and cover up more, ha! I didn't know where to put myself, but I couldn't stop smiling even though I was embarrassed.

He said, 'We'll have to stop meeting like this or there will be rumours, Miss McKitterick!'

I liked the way he said my name so formally. It was like he was treating me as a proper lady whilst still having a joke. He wasn't like any other fella I had ever met. He seemed to know what he was about, you know, confident and I liked that about him too. The next night, we were all gathered after our dinner and when the tin whistle started, he got up on the floor and started a jig. He danced round the floor and then without warning advanced toward me with each step, right up to me and in front of everyone pulled me up onto the floor, burling me right round as he pummelled the floor with the taps on his shoes. Jesus, I couldn't believe it. I didn't know where to look; I was so embarrassed and delighted at the same time. Everyone went mad clapping and wolf-whistling, egging him on, and all the while my face the colour of beetroot. I was no match for him with the dancing, that's for sure.

As he led me back to my seat he whispered in my ear, 'I have your card marked every dance, Miss McKitterick'. Holy smoke, I was smitten. He was cheeky but he was so gentle and charming as well.

'What was that, Isabelle? What did he say?' asked nosey Siobhan. 'Was it something D-I-R-T-Y?'

'Siobhan O'Toole, you'll be for Hell talking like that you dirty baste. No it was not indeed,' I laughed.

Then if that wasn't enough to happen in one weekend, I had been outside hanging all the wet socks on the line and I knew no more when suddenly he sneaked up behind me, covered my eyes with his hands, and said 'Guess who?' Well before I knew it, I spun round with the wet sock in my hand and had boxed him round the ear so fast both of us fell backwards over the basket of washing, him howling and laughing.

'Jesus, I wouldn't like to meet you up a dark alleyway, Isabelle McKitterick.'

We fell about laughing on the ground now wrapped in the sheet that had come off the line.

'You're an eejit, Jack Kennedy, sneaking up behind me like that, I could have knocked you out.'

'Knocked me out? By God, is that right? You're not big enough to knock the skin off a rice pudding!'

'I'll show you not big enough,' I said as I tried to cuff him again.

He grabbed my wrists, holding me at arm's length, laughing away at me, and without warning pulled me towards him till I was right on top of him, then his lips were on mine, so soft and gentle compared with the make-believe battering that I had given him.

Oh my God, the tenderness, the sweet taste of his breath. He brought his hand to the nape of my neck, gently playing with the hair there; I had never felt a kiss like this before. Then we both started laughing and we couldn't stop. We struggled to get up out of the mangled sheet, and do you know what he did then? Slapped my backside as I went back into the scullery, laden with the now dirty sheet covered in grass. I gave him a look that could kill in mock response and of course he just smiled.

The rest of that weekend sped past way too fast. Even though I didn't want to appear too keen, all the rules Siobhan and I ever applied to fellas like no kissing on a first date, well, that all went out the window. Siobhan couldn't believe it when I told her we had our first kiss that weekend. I couldn't get enough of Jack Kennedy and when I was alone with him, time just stood still, like we were in a bubble or something, and the world outside didn't matter.

I met his mammy and his sister; oh they were the salt of the Earth and they took a real shine to me funnily enough, although his mammy was always telling me I was too skinny and tried to feed me up. Jack always walked me home to the end of our street and it was terrible leaving him.

I'd say, 'You go and I'll watch you'.

And he always replied, 'No, Isabelle, I want to make sure you get into the house alright, so go on and I'll see you tomorrow.'

He watched till I got right up our garden path, but I snuck behind the hedge and watched him till his shadow disappeared out of the street. Neither of us wanted to go first.

There didn't seem to be any big announcement. It was so natural and accepted by everyone that I was Jack's girl and he was my man. We just seemed to click, you know, to get each other. It was almost like we were related or had known each other for many years. It wasn't long before we were inseparable; I thought of him when I closed my eyes at night and also when I opened them. I was already only a wee slip of a thing, not a bit of extra meat on my bones, but I went down further because I didn't even think to eat. But the funny thing was, I slept like a log. I was so happy, I was dizzy. I couldn't wait for each day that I would see him to begin, and I didn't want the evenings I was with him to end. It was as simple as that and nobody or nothing else mattered.

We were the vogue couple that turned heads everywhere we went, with our striking good looks setting us apart from the crowd. The chemistry between us was unmistakable. We lived and breathed every minute together that we could, meeting every night at the bottom of Stonemore Road. I had found my kindred spirit. We shared a love of the great outdoors, fresh air, as well as a deep passion for our Irish culture. Jack told me that when he danced the hornpipe, he felt like a Celtic warrior getting ready for battle, like he was connected to his roots by some invisible cord. I'd never met anybody like him; the connection was both instant and electric. We were made for each other.

Daddy tapped his pipe and smiled. He didn't mind the handsome lad; at least he was of the right faith, and that said a lot because you were halfway there where happiness was concerned. Mammy seethed inside. She couldn't put her finger on exactly what it was, but she didn't like him or trust him. She'd seen him downtown a couple of times, standing round yacking away to a whole gaggle of young hussies. Hanging on his every word they were, making a pure spectacle of themselves. A pack of bitches on heat would have had more decorum, and there he was laughing away, lapping it all up like King fecking Farouk.

Mammy made up her mind to keep a very close eye on any goings on where Jack Kennedy and I were concerned. She was the mother, she ruled the roost in her domain, not him, and there was more in his head than a fine-tooth comb would take out.

'Too cock sure of himself that one,' she'd say. 'Strutting about there like a fecking feathered peacock; like he owns the place, thinking he is something.'

But nightly I would slip out of the house to meet Jack at the bottom of the street. He wasn't allowed near the house to call for me and although he knew that he wasn't approved of, which he couldn't understand, wild horses couldn't stop him from seeing me.

I couldn't understand Mammy's reaction. After all, it wasn't like he was a Protestant. I would close the front door to Mammy's retort, Mark my words, Alistair McKitterick, there'll be no good come of it … I have the feeling on me about all this nonsense.' Daddy would retreat to the outhouse toilet, which was the only place he could get a bit of peace to Mammy's blathering.

'It's your fault! Fecking well spoiling her like you have. It's your fault, do you hear me? You'll rue the day, Alistair Mc Kitterick, encouraging all that cavorting round the countryside like some class of fecking gypo. God only knows what half the street's saying about us, likely that we're raising nothing but a pack of wild hallions, the bloody disgrace of it all.'

But nothing could stop the roller-coaster of love that made the stars in the sky sparkle more brightly every night; we were inseparable. Thursday nights were particularly special. I'd meet Jack outside Clonard Monastery at the end of the novena being said there. He never missed either that or Sunday mass. From there, we'd make our way down to Ely Mulligan's School of Irish Dancing for the practice class.

I'd wait round till the thump and tap of the dancers' feet could no longer be heard on the bare boards, and the beat and rhythm of the hornpipe's haunting music had ceased and his class had finished. I loved to watch him, the way he moved, almost glided, how good he looked, so full

60

of life and energy. I loved the way his muscled legs could flick and twist so gracefully and he never ran out of puff like the other dancers did.

He was Ely's champion dancer and you could see the pride in her face when she asked him to show the class how it was done. He had rhythm and perfect timing alright, but he had something much more too, a quality that just didn't come along every day. He could take you with him when he danced to a place that wasn't of this world. She prided herself that despite him being chased by other dancing schools, he'd remained loyal to her. That said something, aye it did.

Now Ely wasn't the only woman who thought the sun shone out of Jack Kennedy's backside. He was the kind of fella that oozed charisma out of every pore in his body without even having to think about it, just like the film stars in America. Young ones, old ones, even ugly ones who wouldn't normally get a sideways glance, as well as ones his own age, just fell for his gracious charm wherever he went. We'd be walking down the street and have to stop a dozen times a minute while he spoke to this one and that one. We couldn't go anywhere without some woman shouting out to him.

'Hello, Jack, and what about you today?' Honestly he was like the Pied Piper himself the way he attracted the girls.

'Oh hello, Jack. How is your mammy today and your wee sisters? Are you going up to Clonard this Thursday night for the novena? I'll keep you a wee seat, son,' said Nora Devlin (who, if she was any holier would have eaten the altar rails).

It was the way he looked at them—really looked. Paying attention as if they were the only women on the planet at that time. It was more than nice, it was kind of, intimate. It was just the way he doffed his cap at them or held on just that bit longer when he shook hands. And the way he remembered all their names, even at mass, and there were more than a few women there who watched Jack's every move when they should have been concentrating on the holy Gospel, God forgive them. Mind you, distraction and mind wandering was easy in those days at mass. I suppose because every word was said in Latin.

So yes, some would have called him a ladies man and if that were the truth, then he was a ladies man with all of them. He could charm the birds out of the trees and have them all eating out of the palm of his hand, none more so than his own mammy who thought the sun rose and shone on her Jack.

Ely quickly noticed me hanging round the dance class waiting for Jack. At first she wasn't sure if I was going to distract him and cause him to lose his concentration, or even worse give up the dancing. After all the years of hard work and practice that would be a disaster. You couldn't seem to get boy dancers for love nor money in those days. Male dancers were as rare as hens' teeth, most of them giving up when they found girls—their heads as well as their bodies away with the mixer for years on end.

'No self-discipline,' Ely would say, 'only interested in the one thing—that which is below the waistband on their trousers.'

Ely didn't mind me, even though I wasn't much interested in the dancing myself. When I hung round the class, Jack seemed to dance better as if he was putting on a show just for me. So in a way we both got what we wanted. As long as I didn't distract Jack from his classes, Ely was happy to have me knocking about.

We'd head down after the class to Falls Park, strolling hand in hand, or to watch a hurly game. We made our plans for the future and talked about getting married. He'd have his own dancing school, and we'd have our babies. We wanted two, a boy and a girl, and that would be it. For I vowed I'd never go through what Mammy had, having a baby nearly every year of her life. Seventeen babies. Jesus, Mary and Joseph, in under God, what poor Mammy had been through would have put your head away. I'd seen the toll it had taken on her; she was exhausted, her poor body wrecked from it all. No, Jack and I would have two babies. That was enough for any human being.

I'd never been more certain of anything in my life. I loved Jack Kennedy, every inch of him, and he consumed my every waking moment. He also haunted my dreams. Dreams that I wasn't even game

62

enough to tell my best friend, Siobhan, in case she thought I was a dirty baste. This was surely what everyone talked about; this was the love that I read about in books, the kind of love where nothing or nobody else mattered. One day I found myself in a flood of tears, just overcome with the beauty of how we felt about each other. I told Siobhan that if anything were to happen to Jack I'd be for jumping into the Lagan because there'd be no use living without him and I knew he felt exactly the same way about me.

You know, though, Mammy never gave Jack the lickings of a dog; she was very quick to tell me she saw him downtown with a whole load of hussies, all gathering round him and him lapping it up. I was more than a bit put out too. What was she suggesting? Did she think she knew Jack better than me? Did she know something about Jack that I didn't? I told Siobhan when I got to work what Mammy had said.

'Ach, Isabelle, you're not taking any notice of your ma are you? You know she can't stand Jack, hasn't got a good word to say about him. C'mon, girl, get a grip. If you're seriously worried about what she said, go and ask Jack about it. They were probably some girls from another dancing school trying to cajole him into joining. C'mon now don't be a buck eejit.'

'Ach I know, Siobhan. I'm sure you're right, but imagine if I ask him and I end up looking like some insecure half-baked twit.'

'Trust me, that's exactly what you'll look like if you keep this up. You know him, everybody knows him, trust your gut and take no bloody notice of your ma's ramblings. Now come on or we'll be late for the dance.'

And away Siobhan flew before anyone knew she was gone, into the factory toilets, pulling the chain twice to make sure the water was clean and then, as quick as a flash, dipping her comb in and running it through her thick, jet black hair, pushing the flopping waves back in place ready for going out. For the minute anyway, the irrational niggling doubts Mammy had planted in my gullible skull about Jack being a womaniser faded as I concentrated on going to the dance with Siobhan that night and then on the weekend away that Jack and I had planned.

The following weekend Jack and I sneaked out of Antrim Road, borrowing a tent from Jimmy McCoy, and away we skidalled down the road like two men and a wee lad. We told no one where we were going because there'd have been blue murder; we'd have been skinned alive. Going away together, unchaperoned wasn't allowed, especially for good Catholic girls, because in those days that too would have been a sin. We couldn't believe we got away with it. Only Jimmy knew because it was his tent. We reached Portrush and began to set up the tent, unravelling the canvas. It was covered in mildew; bye Jimmy hadn't told us that. But we laughed and told each other we would have to put pegs on our noses. Nothing could dampen our spirits when we were together.

The tent poles weren't numbered, so it took us hours to figure out which way the poles went. When we eventually figured it out we collapsed on the grass, laughing and shoving each other playfully. I was sure I looked like Nanna Mokan, my hair and clothes were so dishevelled from all the cycling and roughing it and getting the tent ready. Jack bent over and kissed me on the forehead and told me I was more beautiful than ever, which made me blush to the roots of my scalp.

We got out the picnic of soda bread, two apples and the rashers of bacon Jack had brought. Jack made a camp fire and when the smoke cleared, he shoved the small pan we had into the coals and began to cook the bacon—the aroma near putting our heads away. As night fell we felt like the only two people in the whole world. Nothing mattered, we were together, and we held hands under the stars, talked about what our lives would be like and how soon we could get married. I told Jack I didn't care what anyone said: when we got married I was wearing white. So many girls were getting married in suits after the war. Not me, on the day I married Jack I wanted to look like a princess.

The next day we were up with the larks with walking boots on. There was a special place Jack wanted to take me. A lookout that led down to a secluded beach very few people knew about. Jack told me the view would take my breath away. I thought I was in Heaven and hoped Monday just wouldn't come. I wished I could stay here roaming the Glens of Antrim with my beloved Jack for the rest of my days on Earth. When I was alone with Jack there was never any doubt in my mind that he was the only man I would ever love.

Jack took me to the secluded beach. We walked for miles to get there, the smell of the seaside filling our senses, heightening the feeling of being alive. I took off like a kite racing along the beach towards the water, tucking my skirt into my knickers, kicking the water as I went.

Turning back to Jack I shouted, 'Come on in. It's brilliant, Jack,' as I leapt from foot to foot. The water was freezing, but I didn't care. There was something about the seaside—a freshness, a freedom—that I couldn't put it into words.

Jack slowly followed me down the beach, but he stopped short of the water, just staring at me, taking in every bit of me. My flaxen hair hung down my back. I tried tucking it behind my ears as the wind swept it across my face.

'Come on,' I squealed in delight but Jack didn't move.

He was transfixed. Suddenly he remembered the camera. He bent down and rummaged about in the rucksack, and without even warning me he started snapping away. Click, click, capturing the moment for all time. It seemed to me that the weekend was over in the blink of an eye and as we headed home that Sunday, I couldn't wait to tell Siobhan all about our magical weekend away.

We were lucky; no one suspected us both of sneaking away together, and if we kept shtum we'd be in the clear. Monday morning came and I felt like I was walking on air, practically skipping down the road to the factory and, of course, Siobhan was all ears, waiting on tenterhooks.

'You went where? You did what? Slept in the same tent, oh Jesus, ye didn't did you? What if you end up having a baby? Your da will kill him,' her face a mixture of shock and elation.

'Now hold on there, Siobhan, it wasn't like that,' I said trying to get a word in edgeways. 'Jack's not like that and neither am I. It was just a weekend away. He was a perfect gentleman, if you must know. We walked for miles and he took me to this incredible beach, where he took my picture and collected shells and we talked and talked.'

'Talked? Yeah right, do ye think I came down in the last shower of rain?'

'Well suit yourself; believe it or don't. Jack's different. He's the one.'

When Siobhan saw the serious look on my face she knew I wasn't joking and she turned saying, 'Isabelle Mc Kitterick, you've got it bad.' Laughing till she near pished herself.

'I never thought I'd see the day. You, with half the fellas in Belfast chasing you, completely ready for the loony bin over a man.'

When Jack met me at our usual spot on Monday night, he told me that he'd had the time of his life that weekend. He also told me he'd been doing a lot of thinking about us, about our future.

'Isabelle, let's get away from Belfast, build a better life for us. They say there are jobs in Canada and the streets are paved with gold if you'll work for it. What do you say?'

I didn't hesitate, I didn't even think of what my mammy or daddy might say, I was completely spellbound and head over heels.

'Jack, I'd fly to the moon if you asked me you know that.'

He smiled at me, slipped one arm round my waist, pulling me tight to him. His other hand slid under my hair at the back of my neck, tenderly cupping my head, drawing me close. His breath swept over my neck and ear, giving me shivers right down my spine, and I felt the hardness of his body. I blushed, burying my head in his shoulder. He knew I was embarrassed by the moment of intimacy that had just transpired. He took his dead end, laughing, throwing his head back, then without a word scooped me up with his other arm, lifting me right off the ground, burling me round till I was near dizzy, and me letting out a mock squeal of delight.

Jack's best friend, Jimmy, was having his end away with every Protestant that would drop her drawers, and acting like fecking King Kong and there was Jack, restraining himself for me. But he told Jimmy one thing was for sure; it would be worth the wait because 'he who laughs last laughs longest'. Siobhan had overheard them; Jack saying how gorgeous he thought I was, not like another soul he had ever met.

'She has an innocence about her that excites me even more than I dare think about,' he'd said.

He said the temptation in his body, never mind his head, was tearing him apart and he didn't know how much longer he could restrain himself. He said his whole body ached for me. He wanted to lie down beside me and caress every inch of me. He couldn't wait until our ultimate joining in wedlock. I blushed as she told me this. To repeat his words, I'd cast an infectious spell on him alright, paralysing his every waking moment as he did mine.'

The patrons on their way out of the pub noticed us love birds, and were nudging each other, smiling as they passed, but we barely paid attention because we only had eyes for each other. The decision was made: we were going to Canada. All I could think about was the snow-capped Rocky Mountains, the Royal Canadian Mounties in their scarlet jackets, and the promise of a life where we would live happily ever after. 'But wait, Isabelle, I'll go first. It could be rough, you know. I'll get a job, find us a wee place to rent, and when I get settled in, I'll send for you.' I didn't doubt him for a minute.

'I'll wait for you, Jack,' was all I said.

It was all that was necessary. It would only be a matter of weeks before Jack would head off to Canada and there was so much to do, planning and packing, and our last weekend away hostelling. It was agreed that's when we would get engaged, tell all our friends, and I thought my heart would burst I was so happy.

A couple of weeks later, though, with preparations in full swing for Jack's departure for Canada, I told Jack I wouldn't meet him that Thursday after the novena. My Aunt Josie hadn't been well and I told Mammy I'd take the soup round to her that night, spend a bit of time with her and bring back any washing that needed to be done. It didn't take as long as I thought; that night Aunt Josie was tired and couldn't be bothered with any narration or craic, so on the spur of the moment, I decided to go on down and catch Jack as the dancing class was finishing. There was still so much to talk about before he set off for Canada.

The dancing class and music was still in full swing, and as I approached the door I could hear the laughter inside. I'm not sure why, but I took a wee duke in the window and there was Jack in full flight. I felt the familiar skip in my chest as I gazed at him without him knowing I was there, but as I watched on another dancer joined him in a two-hand reel.

She was gorgeous, flitting about like an angel. That wasn't so bad, but the way I saw him look at her, gaze into her eyes, swing her round like she was a feather, and her … the way she smiled back at him, all coy like, there it was again, that feeling … Jesus what was happening? I quickly pulled my head back from the window; I didn't want them to see me. I couldn't look anymore. I leaned against the wall of the hall outside, trying to pinpoint what it was I'd just witnessed. My hand was at my throat. I was trying to breathe, but I couldn't. I couldn't think straight and my stomach was churning. What was wrong with me? Jack wasn't expecting me. Shit, was Mammy right? Was this what he got up to when I wasn't about?

I stood there for ages humiliated and shaking like a leaf, then I gathered myself together and made my way home. By the time I got to our house, I was as mad as a raging bull. What the hell was he up to? Was this going to be the way of it? Turn my back for one fecking minute and he's making doe eyes at a buck stranger? Dance, yes, he could dance all he liked, but to look at her like that … then it hit me … it was the closeness … he was just a bit too close to her for comfort. Dancing or not, he stared just a bit too long into her eyes, kept his hand on her back just a bit too long … it wasn't right. It was too intimate and he was enjoying it all just too much. He must take me for a right buck eejit.

'Now I know it for sure, Isabelle Mc Kitterick. You are officially crackers. It was a fecking dancing class, that's what they're supposed to be doing.'

'You didn't see the spectacle, Siobhan, I did.' Why didn't Siobhan believe me? 'The look on his face, you should have seen it.'

'Well he's not supposed to be dancing like he has a pole up his arse, Isabelle, now is he?'

'… and her too, she was just as bad as him, gawking like she'd never seen a man in her life before. He was … was … flirting with her. He was, I swear on the Sacred Heart picture I'm telling the God's honest truth. I didn't imagine it.'

'Ach, you're talking shite, Isabelle. That man loves every hair on your head. Even I can see that even though he's not my cup of tea. What about the flowers he buys you nearly every week, eh? There's more in your house than a fecking florist's shop window. And he's always telling you how much he loves you, isn't he? He wouldn't do that if he was interested in anybody else now would he?'

'Ach Siobhan, you're not listening. I love Jack—with all my heart I love him, but actions speak louder than words. Talk is cheap.'

'Aye, well, I personally think you're halfway round the bend and I hope you're not paying any heed to what your ma's saying, for let me tell you something this day, doing that will cause you both nothing but heartbreak, mark my words.'

THE ENGAGEMENT
Isabelle

Our last weekend away came round in the blink of an eye; I could hardly contain my excitement. Siobhan had given me a good 'ballicking' about trust and all that and, to be honest, when we sat and talked it out, I could see what she was saying and decided not to say anything to Jack. It was a good job really because only a few days later he was asking me all sorts of questions about rings. He tried to act all casual asking me what I liked, what colour stones were my favourite, what shape I liked. Thank God I hadn't taken the head staggers and started on him over something that was probably nothing. Siobhan was right: I was full of imagination.

Nobody knew the great news we were going to announce. Not even Siobhan had a clue what was going on. Jack had made me promise not to tell a living a soul. He told me he wanted it that way because he wanted to see the look on all their faces when he broke the news. But secretly he wanted it kept quiet because he was worried about what Ma and Da might say. He knew he wasn't liked, God only knows why, and he didn't want to take the chance of anyone putting their spoke in about us getting engaged before he put that ring on my finger. By the time he did, there'd be nothing anybody could say or do.

We headed for Carrickfergus on the bikes. The plan was we'd tell everyone we were getting married after dinner that night. We covered many a mile that day, each one of us tag-teaming with the other. Always a shout would go up for someone to take the lead and when the leader tired they'd call, 'C'mon ye boys' and the next cyclist would take the lead and take their turn.

There was always someone bringing up the rear; no one was in charge. We all knew our places and how the pack worked. We looked after each member; no one got left behind. What a grand sight indeed, a bubbling movement of human energy, oneness and friendship racing along the laneways of the north of Ireland. Youth at its most glorious with tanned, muscled legs and weather-beaten, toned bodies.

We reached Ryan's Pass, each rider sliding into low gear to make the slow ascent, changing our breathing, conserving our energy, calling out to one another, 'That's a girl, come on now,' heart rates rising, the boys now slightly ahead of the girls.

'Just keep your heads down, look only two feet ahead,' shouted Jimmy McCoy.

Gritting my teeth as hard as I could, I wasn't about to give up, I pushed myself on and on, two feet at a time, willing myself to the top.

'Nearly there. Keep going,' I heard someone say.

I felt my thighs and calves begin to burn as I stood up to cycle the last few yards to the top.

Many of the boys had already made it to the top and were waiting to cheer the next rider along, clapping, yahooing, whistling and waving as each of us made it to the top. There was a chorus of yells and whistles going up as I joined them breathless and exuberant. Yes, I'd made it! God, it didn't get any easier going up that hill, but the ride down the other side would be grand. You could nearly reach the pub in the valley without using a muscle and it was a well-earned rest.

I quickly glanced behind me; Siobhan was tight on my heels. I smiled to myself. I knew she wouldn't give up if I didn't. We kept each other going that's for sure.

I had just had my wheel fixed and foot clamps fitted to my bike, so I didn't need brakes. This helped me keep pace with the pack on long stretches of road. As I passed the throng of boys cheering everyone on, I started to descend the near-vertical hill on the other side of the pass.

Suddenly I heard the clunk of the gears and the bike wobbled almost tipping over. I panicked as my feet were locked tight in the foot clamps. But I managed to keep going. Just as I steadied myself, I realised I was freewheeling with no brakes and the bike was gathering speed. As I took the first bend I knew I was getting faster and further from the pack, careering out of sight of the others. Jimmy McCoy glanced round and in an instant knew I was in serious trouble. I was screaming, my hands glued to the handlebars, my knuckles as white as alabaster. I thought no one could hear me.

'Jesus, Mary and Joseph! Jack! Isabelle's in trouble!' Thank God Jimmy had noticed.

Jack and Jimmy sped off at lightning speed after me. They rounded the first hairpin bend just catching sight of me as I disappeared again. Quicker and quicker they peddled to catch up, calling out, 'We're coming, hold on.' They shouted and yelled after me but I couldn't hear them. The wind whistled past my ears at a million miles an hour. I could see the next bend and I thought: *this is it! I can't turn the bike quick enough. God help me. I don't wanna die today.*

Just as I hit the hairpin bend I felt a huge shudder and tug on the bike and a big hand gripping the back of my jersey as Jimmy and Jack grabbed me, bringing me to a standstill. I was unable to speak at first, the nerves choking me. I looked at the boys who'd just saved my life and collapsed into Jack's arms, shaking like a leaf, while Jimmy unclipped my feet from the bike's foot clamps.

'Thank God you were here. Thank you, oh thank you.'

Jack lifted me onto the grass and pulled me into his arms, and I rested my body against his chest. I could hear his heart beating so fast.

'God, Isabelle, you nearly gave me a heart attack. I can't tell you what was going through my mind as I saw you dissapearing round that bend. My whole life flashed before me. Holy Christ, Isabelle McKitterick, what would I do without you?'

It took me hours to settle my nerves. I kept picturing what kind of a death I would have had if they hadn't caught me. I would have been tossed over the rocky boulders like a rag doll and into the valley below. All this on the night we were supposed to get engaged, telling everyone we were headed for Canada. To think I could have been killed stone dead. I must have been in shock really because all I wanted to do was sit quietly with Jack. I just couldn't get what happened out of my mind. But I suppose everyone else had other ideas. As far as they were concerned I was alright, 'so let's get on and have a good night'.

When dinner was finished, we were standing round going over the day's events and the drama that had nearly taken my life: me almost meeting my maker, what heroes Jack and Jimmy were saving my life, how far we'd ridden that day, and what a lucky escape I'd had. Siobhan and I had just made ourselves a hot cocoa, and I glanced over at Jack who was laughing and chatting with the other fellas.

I was sure he would announce our news when he thought the moment was right. All of a sudden, without warning, the back door to the hostel was flung wide open and two hussies about my age rushed in. Their voices could be heard above everyone—high, clear and excited. The first was raven-haired and skinny, with a coat that flowed to her ankles in bright red. The second one was stout with red curls that were cropped tight as a knitted blanket and wearing the tightest skirt I'd ever seen. The raven-haired one suddenly shrieked out, 'Jack!' and ran towards him with the speed of a hunted hare and leapt up, throwing her arms about his neck with her two big, bare legs wrapping round his waist. Her coat parted showing a flimsy dress that slid up her thigh, revealing her suspender belt and knickers.

I looked on in disbelief. Who was this and what was she doing flinging herself at my man? The dirty mare, showing her knickers, practically eating him and in front of the whole room. I was furious and mortified at the same time. Here we go again, I thought. I could feel myself go bright red with embarrassment. I silently mouthed at Siobhan, 'What the?' and she put her hands up grimacing as if to say, 'I dunno.' But worse than that, much worse was that Jack wasn't putting her down. He was standing there all smiles, swaying with her, laughing, which was only encouraging her more—the bloody cheek. Oh my God, I'd never live this down. In all the time I'd known Jack he'd never told me of any hussy like this. He'd never, ever held me like that, legs wrapped about his waist. And more than that, he'd never, ever seen my suspender belt and knickers. All this on the back of what I'd seen in the dancing hall just a few weeks ago, not to mention what Mammy had said about him with that bunch of hussies in town. It was just like Mammy had said and here I was witnessing the spectacle with my very own eyes.

I was livid. I felt embarrassed and degraded; this was going to be my fiancé, my husband, and I didn't know if I was coming or going. Well, about to get engaged, eh? And he'd kept a secret like this from me? If he had nothing to hide, why hadn't he explained to me who this woman was? He should've put her straight down and told her he was getting engaged. My mind was going ten to the dozen. If I didn't know about this woman, then who else didn't I know about?

From somewhere deep inside me came a feeling that tore me apart. I'd never felt like this before. Was it jealousy? No, I wasn't jealous of a trollop like that. Was it doubt? Did I really know him as well as I thought? Could I really trust him? And a deep insecurity gripped my heart. Siobhan did her best to reassure me again. 'Ach, Isabelle, you're an eejit. He knows hundreds of women with all the dancing. Get a grip for God's sake before it's too late, and don't be so daft.' But no matter what my best friend said I was left with a feeling I couldn't comprehend. I wanted badly to believe her. I didn't want to feel like this.

Later that night I slipped outside to where Jack was smoking. I sidled up to him, making moves like the raven-haired hussy had. Maybe that was what he wanted. I could show him my stockings. Let him see my thighs. He seemed to like it well enough. And slowly I began to move my hands all over his body, caressing his arms and chest until suddenly he grabbed both my wrists. 'Christ, Isabelle, what are you doing?'

I was confused. Wasn't this what he wanted? I was shocked to see the look of disgust in Jack's eyes. I felt as if I'd done something shameful, bad, dirty. He buttoned his shirt, pushed past me and walked back inside. Oh God, now what have I done? So if it's not that, what was it he wanted exactly? This was turning into the worst day of my life and it was supposed to be the happiest.

I felt so rejected when he pulled my hands away from him as if my physical touch was repugnant to him. I knew he wanted it. Everything that had happened so far told me he did. And there he was making me feel dirty. I wasn't the one flirting with other men, egging them on. I wasn't the one who should feel shame or embarrassment. It should be him. I stood in the walled garden of the hostel alone, with my near-death encounter that day and the wrath of Jack's rejection.

I was mortified and full of deep regret and I knew somehow there'd be no engagement announced that night. How was it possible to feel such hate and love for someone at the same time? This only served to deepen the insecurity and doubt that had woven its toxic thread into the delicate tapestry of my already-fragile heart.

The next few weeks went by so fast. There hadn't been much chance to see each other with shift work and all the arrangements that had to be done. There was so much that had been left unsaid, so much that hadn't been resolved, and the arrangements that should have been made together amid laughter and tears didn't happen. I felt like a black mist had clouded my days, but I was prickled with anger at him too. I had expected that he would have at the very least come round to our house and apologised for his behaviour that night. I didn't care that he wasn't wanted near our house; he should have come anyway if he cared enough.

Jack's ticket for the ship to Canada had been bought, his bags packed. He'd said goodbye to Ely Mulligan, who was heartbroken at losing the best champion dancer she'd ever taught. He promised her, though, that he'd be back, in a few years when he started his own dancing school. They would meet up in Dublin at the Oireachtas. By that time he'd have dancers of his own competing.

Within days Jack would be gone, headed out across the Atlantic for a new life in Canada. He carried both of our hopes and dreams with him. Tucked safely in the breast pocket of his jacket, placed in its green, velvet box was the diamond ring he'd bought for me—the one he'd saved every penny for months for, chosen so carefully, remembering every single detail about what I'd said I liked, right down to the delicate emerald green stone that would have reminded me daily of my homeland. The ring I didn't know even existed.

THE LONG WAIT
Isabelle

I hadn't been able to eat or focus at work for weeks. I made mistakes all the time, and I couldn't be bothered with anyone or anything. Things had been left unsaid between Jack and I over the last few weeks and it just didn't feel right. I wanted to sort things out, I really did, but each and every time I tried to bring it up with him, he made out he had more important things to get on with, or he shrugged it off, played it all down, and made out that I was causing a fuss about nothing. He was such a smart alec, though; he knew what I meant. All I would have needed was for him to reassure me and talk it through with me—something for God's sake—and I would have been alright.

But you know what it's like when something isn't right in your heart. You feel it, but the other person doesn't let on they understand how you feel and just makes you out to be half crazy. Jack not only dismissed how I felt, but I sensed he was lying to me by omission. A bit of harmless flirting is nothing; I'd have coped with that. I knew how popular he was with women everywhere we went. But he wouldn't even accept he was doing it. It was this fact that troubled me more than anything else because it wasn't true. That and the intimacy thing, which made my stomach churn every time I thought about it.

The day of Jack's departure arrived so quickly, and things had been building up in my head for weeks. But I wasn't in the mood for talking to anybody. I cursed Jack under my breath, swearing that I'd teach him a lesson. There was no way I was going to that bloody train station to wave him off. No, I wasn't, and he could go to hell. But as my shift ended I thought better of it. Alright then, bloody hell, I'll go to the train station, of course I will. I didn't want the last time we saw each other for months to be like this.

But I didn't want to let myself down so I decided I'd hide up the platform, where he couldn't see me, and watch to see if he'd turn round and look for me. Aye, that would tell me the truth. If I caught him looking round, I'd jump out and surprise him. Aye, that's what I'll do and then I'll give him my good luck hankie from Donegal. It was something he could carry with him all the time, and I'd crushed some rosemary into it so he wouldn't forget me for one minute.

So along to the train station I went after work as fast as my legs could carry me. It was just on dusk, and all the platforms were abuzz with people saying their goodbyes, hugging each other and swinging their suitcases onto the carriages. I tugged my headscarf tight round my head and kept duking up and down the platform. All of a sudden my heart leapt; there he was, his sister and his Mammy either side of him. I watched as his family said their goodbyes and I saw his mammy crying.

My hand went swiftly up to my mouth, covering my sigh of sadness. I loved Mrs Kennedy. She was the gentlest soul I had ever met and she loved me to bits. She made me feel at home from the minute Jack and I met. I couldn't wait till the day I would be part of her family. I never heard Mrs Kennedy say a bad word about anybody. She was always telling me that the way to a man's heart was through his belly, and that she'd teach me everything she knew about pie-making when we were married.

At that minute I wanted to run down the platform and leap into his arms, but for some inexplicable reason my feet were rooted to the spot. What the hell was wrong with me? Why wasn't I running like Hell's gates down to that platform? He boarded the 6.30 am steam train and pulled down the window to wave to his family. All I wanted was one look. I willed him, *Jack, for Christ's sake look up, I'm here, look up here damn it.* But he didn't look up or look round once, just kept his glance straight ahead. All I could do was watch as the train chugged and chuffed its way out of the station, gathering speed, puffing out steam like a giant snorting dragon.

As the whistle blew, the train disappeared round the bend of the track along with the love of my life. And my wee hankie, my good luck charm from Donegal that I so wanted Jack to keep with him, slipped out of my hand, landing in a puddle of mucky water. I thought I'd die of a broken heart as I cried all the way home.

His trip had been for both of us, to give us a good start for our future, and now Jack was heading out to a country he didn't know and our last memory together was that dreadful night. I wished to God he'd told me the full story about the raven-haired hussy who'd run into the hostel the night we were supposed to get engaged. 'Loose legs Linda' I later heard the local fellas call her. She'd slept with that many men I wondered why she hadn't ended up 'up the duff', until someone mentioned, 'well trodden grass doesn't grow.'

Weeks became months, and I didn't want to go anywhere. Nothing was the same without my beloved Jack.

'Come on, wee girl, eat for God's sake or you'll get consumption,' said Daddy.

He'd noticed my decline, reserved quietness and lack of interest. Even his tales of Ireland's politics couldn't coax a smile out of me. It was getting beyond a joke, the state of me. I was fading away before his eyes.

Mammy looked on but said nothing; she carried on with the business of the house, eager to collect my pay check from the factory each week.

'She'll get over it. Young ones always do. The only way is to pay it no bloody heed. There was nothing wrong with being on the skinny side, and it never did you any harm,' she'd tell Daddy when she thought he was 'making a damn big fuss about nothing.'

Yes, life was a bit easier for Mammy as the childer grew up and got jobs. She thought it was our duty to help out after all the scrubbing and cleaning she'd done over the years. As time went on, I never heard a word from Jack—not a letter or even a postcard. I became a ghost that slipped quietly about the place, lost in the noisy clatter of fifteen childer.

Every day was filled with excited anticipation as I rushed home from the factory to ask, 'Mammy, did any post come for me today?'

But each day the elation was replaced by desperate disappointment and a deep longing for Jack. Days passed, then weeks. Weeks turned into months. Still no word from him, no letter as promised. What I felt for Jack couldn't possibly be wrong. I was sure he would write to me and send for me. We'd be together forever, that was for sure.

What had stuck in my craw was that Jimmy McCoy had even got a letter from him just a fortnight after he landed in Canada, and it was fair enough to write to his best friend, but to not even send one letter to me was unforgivable. I mean, we were as good as engaged. I just didn't have a ring yet.

As each day passed with no word from Jack, my heart broke a little bit more. I missed him so much—his smile, his bubbly banter, the way he held me, caressed me, the fun we had. It was as if the sun had stopped shining. I didn't know how it was possible to be so much in love and feel so desolate at the same time. I really understood how you could die of a broken heart. It's true what they say, you know, absence does make the heart grow fonder, and by this rate if I didn't hear from him soon, I'd be in the cemetery before long.

There was Jimmy, yahooing all round the place saying he was going to join Jack in Canada as soon as he had his fare saved. I was on an emotional roller-coaster and didn't know if I was coming or going. I felt so disappointed and embarrassed that I hadn't got a letter from Jack, but I didn't have the courage of a louse to go up and tell Jimmy I hadn't heard from him, especially as we'd fallen out before he went to Canada and I didn't want anyone knowing my personal business or knowing how I felt.

I didn't want to let myself down and look like some half-baked desperate case, so I said nothing and my heart broke in silence as I thought: *how could he do this to me? After all he'd promised me, after all we shared, after all our plans, hopes and dreams?* But as each day passed I was also haunted by the awful memory of the night before Jack's departure for Canada. God I wished we hadn't fought like we had—all over that bloody mare that jumped on him the night we were at the youth hostel. Jesus, I'd been such a fool. Why couldn't I let it drop? But Jack didn't help matters. Every time I asked him how he knew that woman he got so defensive, as if he had something to hide. He'd just shrug his shoulders and say she was nobody, making me more suspicious. Then I'd kick off saying, if I couldn't trust him now, when would I be able to trust him? And that made him so mad he had stormed out saying, 'Isabelle McKitterick, as sure as Jesus, you'd cause a row in an empty house.' Me shouting after him that he could 'Jump in the bloody Lagan and go to the train by himself for all I cared anyway.' This of course couldn't have been further from the truth.

The Belfast Swiss Embroidery Company had work for many young hands eager to earn a quid and spend it just as fast. Post-war Belfast was struggling back to life and the factory was making it happen. But no matter how many jokes Siobhan told me and no matter how many wild antics she got up to, I sank further into myself. Siobhan was worried, 'Isabelle, get a grip on your knickers girl, it's been months. What if you don't hear from him again?'

'How could you say that, Siobhan? You know him.' I know him. He promised he'd come back for me. I felt it in my heart and soul.

'Isabelle, you're an eejit if you think boys in far off countries don't get a bit wild. You know what I mean? Let it go for God's sake. Sure the fecking road to Hell itself is paved with good intentions.'

Siobhan's words sent a shiver through me as I remembered the night we should have got engaged and the raven-haired hussy who had flung herself at Jack putting paid to that, as well as the stupid row we'd had before he went to Canada, and the desolate feeling I'd had as his train left the station without even a second glance. I felt like the loneliest girl in the world.

MEETING HARRY
Isabelle

Now Harry Savage wasn't just handsome and funny, it was said by some that he could count quicker than a Chinaman on an abacus. He could calculate four-digit sums in his head before ye could blink. They said he had a 'silver tongue' with the looks of Errol Flynn. He would stand round at lunchtime, all suave-like, crossing one leg over the other, leaning casually on the back of the chair. As he got out his tin of Golden Virginia baccy, he teased the solid square with his yellow-stained fingers until he could free enough for a 'rollie' and then, while he was still talking, keeping one eye on what was going on, he would lick his middle finger and slip a fine 'red' paper out of its tiny packet to place the baccy into it, rolling it up, sealing the edge by running his tongue along the paper line, ready to light. Harry always made two rollies; the first he propped neatly behind his ear for later, like 'the fella in the big picture', and the other he'd smoke at once.

Then he'd smile, that million-dollar smile, every tooth in his head as straight as a ruler on a teacher's desk, the whites of his nashers near blinding you with their sparkle. Nope, he'd never regret that move. It's what you did at twenty-one years of age with a few quid in your back pocket—have your crooked, stained teeth removed for perfectly straight white teeth, just like the film stars in America. Everybody who was anybody was doing it and he'd never looked back. He never even took a day off work, going straight back to the factory in the afternoon, with every tooth in his head taken clean out. No more dentists for him.

Harry also kept his round palm-sized hairbrush in his back trouser pocket, taking it out to brush his jet-black shiny hair, which stuck straight up with Brylcreem. He'd carefully make sure he went from the front of his head to the back, keeping the hair sticking up on end, smoothing it at the same time with his left hand each and every time he lit up.

He felt like no goat's toe. Harry's shoes gleamed, polished till they shone like glass. His clothes weren't the finest about the place, but were spotlessly clean. The sharp crease of his chino trousers stood out a mile, with their neat turned up hems, which were all the rage. His cotton shirt was as smooth as silk, neatly tucked in, and with only the best braces holding it all neatly on his trim frame.

He checked his shoes throughout the day and if there was a speck of dust, he'd lift his foot, tuck it behind his other leg and polish it on the back of his trouser leg. His mother, Connie, had taught him well; cleanliness was next to Godliness and in Connie's house, you could eat your dinner off the very floor it was that clean.

In Connie's world there was simply no excuse for anyone being through other. It didn't matter how little you had. To her, pride cost nothing and soap and water very little. So being well turned out and looking decent was ingrained in Harry. Even if you were just off to your work, it was very important to make a good impression and to have clean underpants every day in case you had an accident. Just imagine the shame and disgrace if a doctor or nurse saw your big bare arse clad in dirty underpants.

Harry also kept everyone highly entertained in our lunchbreaks at the factory. How he remembered all the jokes he told nobody knew. Once he started, you had a job to shut him up, 'Did you hear the one about the English man, the Irish man and the Scotsman?' There were more jokes in Harry's head than in any edition of the *Beano* ever printed. He had a memory like an elephant and could recite every race winner that ever ran on Belfast turf. He knew what odds they had come in at, who trained the horse and where it was stabled. It's a wonder he didn't also know how many times each horse had been shod. He had everyone in stitches and his jokes were always clean—no dirty jokes. One thing that Harry Savage prided himself on was the fact that he was clean living. There were no back doors in him. He'd no time for smut or any of that stuff, and if any of the other dirt birds at the factory started on about titties or what they got up to with their girls down the back entry, Harry made himself scarce. He'd no time for dirty bastes.

Harry dreamt of greater things, like being a millionaire, living like a lord, and making it big one day, and the horses were the way to do that especially if you had his brains. Slim and tall, he cut an okay figure alright, and when Harry asked me for a date I thought he was joking. I didn't know him from a bar of soap. He wasn't from round these parts of The Falls road. So, I told him to get lost and that I was already going with somebody.

'Oh, who's that and where's he working?' came the response. I nearly died of embarrassment when Siobhan shouted over, 'Ach, the fella fecked off a year ago and not a word since.'

Mortified, I looked in my lap; I was going to kill Siobhan O'Toole after work. There was my best friend in the world blabbing her big mouth about my personal business to a fella I didn't know or want to know. Sometimes Siobhan hadn't 2ds' worth of sense.

Harry chirped up, 'So the coast is clear? Come on, it's just a date, I promise I won't bite your head off.'

That lunchtime Siobhan made it her business to find out all about Harry Savage. She couldn't stand my long countenance a minute longer.

She said, 'I have to do something. Best friend or not, you're as miserable as sin and it's seriously getting on my nerves. I'm at my tether's end with you. Half the fecking fellas in Belfast are after you, whistling and shouting. You could have your pick of any man you wanted and here you are brushing off another fella, and still hankering after the one that's gone.'

'Isabelle,' Helen whispered as she caught hold of my arm pulling me round the corner at lunchtime, 'Harry's quite a catch, you know. John O'Dowd says he knows him from St Matthew's Harriers Club. He runs like a coursing hare. He said he was spotted by an English football scout looking for young Irish talent; nearly went off to play football in England. Dowdy said it wasn't just any old club either, fecking Manchester United, none the less. Except his da was dead … tragic it was … killed stone dead in a bar brawl … and his ma couldn't let him go, him being the oldest boy and all that.'

'His ma needed somebody to start work. He was only twelve when he got his first job too. He's no slacker, except he told the fella delivering spuds that he'd driven a horse and cart before and it was all going well till the fecking horse took the head staggers, taking off down the road, Harry with the reigns, like something outa the wild west, screaming like a banshee, "Jesus! Fuck! Oh fuckin' Jesus! Ahhhh!"'

Siobhan and I couldn't control our squeals of laughter at the thought of Harry trying to control a wild horse and cart. We near pished ourselves.

When I caught my breath, I said, in between drying my eyes on my apron, 'Well what happened next?'

'Well, bejesus, half the street was running after the horse and cart and the fella who owned the horse, shitting himself, was running the fastest.' That started us laughing again; this was the funniest tale I'd ever heard.

'In under Jesus, how did they get it stopped?'

'Well, out came big John Dooley from the pub, just in the nick of time to see the pandemonium and luckily he leapt on the cart as it sped past, climbed along the back of the wagon and got the reins from young Harry, bringing the horse to a stop, or he'd been killed stone dead for sure. But that wasn't the end of it. When the fella who owned it asked Harry what had happened, he couldn't tell him why all of a sudden the big dray horse had taken off … till the owner found the fecking big beg of oats still full to the top. The poor fecking horse hadn't been fed all day. It was starving,' she laughed.

86

That set both of us off again in gales of laughter this time, holding our sides, almost squatting on the floor.

Helen was now on a roll. 'Paddy Reilly said that Harry can't be beat at the card games they play at lunchtime. He's so smart, sure somebody even thought he was "counting the deck". It was either that or he's a fecking genius. You could do worse. And for fecks sake at least he's got a smile on his bake, not like yourself.'

'Well, a runner for St Matthew's? He can fecking well run in the opposite direction. I'm not interested, and I'm waiting for Jack,' I retorted.

Siobhan let out the biggest sigh, 'Not this fecking malarkey again. I give up, Isabelle McKitterick. Suit yourself. It'll be no fella you'll get in the end.' And as I turned away Siobhan started to sing, 'You'll die an aul maid in the garret.' I stuck my two fingers up in mock response.

Months and months passed and something that Siobhan said stuck with me. So Harry had no daddy? Surely a man who gives up the chance to play football in England to look after his mammy and wee sisters can't be bad. And so, to a chorus of girls' whispering and egging me on, 'Go on ye buck eejit, have a bit of fun,' I agreed to Harry's request for a date.

Mammy's face lit up like a boney on the glorious 12 of July.

'Harry? Well that's a nice name.'

And if she'd been any nicer to Harry Savage, she'd have tripped over herself. He brought her some snuff and he made her laugh with his daft jokes.

'Just look at him,' she'd say, 'clean as a whistle, not posh or prickly, very decent-looking, not like that other big merchant who wouldn't give you the time of day.'

Bye he was handsome too with them lovely new white nashers, and always grateful when Mammy offered him a plate of stew. He finished every morsel laid afore him, showing respect and appreciation. Mammy said that was a sure sign he was well-reared. Best of all, in Mammy's eyes, Harry was staying put, with no plans to feck off to another country, taking any help as well as my much-needed pay check out of her house.

Now Daddy was a different kettle of fish.

'Harry Savage', he'd say, 'umm, Savage isn't a Catholic name.'

And before I could utter a word Daddy continued, 'Now you mind what I've told you before, wee girl, about bringing any Orange man near this house; he won't be welcome.'

'But Daddy …' I tried to get a word in edgeways.

'You've got no idea about the battles that have been fought. Have you not listened to anything I've told you? All the heartache that would be in front of ye and any wee childer you might bring into the world. Life's hard enough. You know it's a fact. No good comes of them kind of relationships.'

'Daddy, please …' But he lifted his hand to silence me and I knew it was no use saying another word, for it wasn't often Daddy said much.

'Once a Prod, always a Prod. They'll stab you in the back, steal the eyeballs outa your head and come back for the fecking sockets.'

Daddy's neck was flushing red, a sure sign he was getting as wound up as the clock in the hallway.

'He's a Catholic, Daddy,' I chirped in, trying to smile.

'A what?'

'A Catholic!' I repeated, this time the smile spread across Da's face as he realised he'd gone on like a scalded cat for nothing.

'Aye … well … what's he doing with a name like Savage then?'

'It's from Scotland. His daddy's people might have been Prods, but Harry's been baptised at St Matthew's. He's as much a Catholic as me.'

'Was his da a convert then? They're often more pious than Catholics born into the faith. What's his da's name then? And where does he work?'

'He's dead. His mammy's on her own. Harry's been working since he was a wee boy to help her.'

But Daddy was quick, 'Dead, what happened?'

'Oh, I'm not sure. I just heard that he'd had an accident at the Black Swan Pub. He fell down the stairs and was killed stone dead.'

Daddy looked perplexed. There was something about this tale that didn't add up. He'd make it his business to find out more. For he knew well the Black Swan in the docks area of Belfast was a well-known den of iniquity. You wouldn't be seen there unless you were a hard man or up to no good. It was said there were more dodgy dealings done in the back rooms of the Black Swan than in the rest of the north of Ireland put together.

But for now Daddy seemed settled. Phew! And Mammy chimed in under her breath that if Daddy 'Hadn't been ranting on like somebody out of Purdysburn, he'd have heard the story half an hour ago.'

Daddy lit his pipe and sucked the baccy hard, puffing quickly as he paced the floor. I heard him tell Mammy that he wasn't so sure about this fella—a Catholic with a Proddy name, something wasn't right. He'd heard tales at the market about them sort from the East end—vagabonds and thieves he'd heard—a lot of them were up to no good.

'But one thing is for sure, Isabelle,' he said, 'at least you're smiling again and there's a bit of meat on your bones.'

Mammy made it very clear what her thoughts and feelings on Harry Savage were: 'A bird in the hand was definitely worth two in the bush.'

Summer was turning to autumn and it was time to gather the clan and head for the bungalow Daddy and the boys had built for their retirement. This having come about after Daddy won the fecking pools. Mammy, of course, claiming the glory for this miraculous turn of fortune in their lives, as she had dreamt about it, as sure as night follows day, and was always telling Daddy, 'There's money coming into the house, I can feel it in me bones, me left hand's been itchy all week.'

It hadn't been a king's ransom, but bejesus it gave him the chance to buy a bit of land at Rushyhill about ten miles out of Belfast, and he set to building their dream house in the country. Here Daddy would be able to have the small holding he'd always wanted, grow his own vegies and finally give his childer the space they needed to roam about. Oh aye, it'd be grand and despite Mammy's mithering about being isolated and lonely, the house was built. Between Daddy and our boys, they had nearly every trade to make the dream come true. Out to Rushyhill they moved, lock,

89

stock and barrel, leaving the cramped cobbled streets of The Falls road and Belfast far behind.

There were acres of hay to be bailed—all hands were needed on deck. 'Why don't you bring Harry with you this weekend? Your da could use another pair of hands and he can kip down with your brothers?'

'Okay, Mammy, I'll ask him.'

Harry was delighted. 'A weekend in the country with my girl,' he'd said. 'Hard work never killed anyone.' He was in like Flynn.

They all worked from dawn to dusk. I loved the farm at Rushyhill with the calls of the curlews and cuckoos in summer. I wished I'd been able to live there when I was a little girl, but I was glad at least my wee brothers and sisters were getting the chance I didn't get. Roaming about the place was my idea of Heaven; I hated the thought of being hemmed in. I could see how happy Daddy was; he loved the land like I did—the open spaces and fresh air. I'd felt so free and so did Daddy. But Mammy never looked happy. Somehow there seemed to be more work for her to do and there was much more cleaning as the house at Rushyhill was a lot bigger than their aul house in Stonemore Road.

Mammy wasn't just lonely out there. She longed to have a look at the shop windows downtown, just to get her head showered. Out there, not even her sister Josie or friend Nancy could drop in for a cuppa tea and wee bit of snuff. Out there was nobody to read the leaves for and there was no street craic. Except for her childer and Daddy, Mammy often didn't see another soul from morning till night and that was what drove her mad much of the time.

Out there she didn't know if Mary McNamara had had her twentieth wee child yet. Poor crater, three more babies than she'd had herself and she thought she'd done it bad with seventeen. Jesus, Mary and Joseph, Mammy had been so exhausted after her last wee boy was born, she hadn't even the energy to feed the poor wee soul.

Thank God my older sister had just had her first baby and had enough milk to fill a crate, so both wee childer got fed well. God knows what would have happened to my wee brother if our sister hadn't been able to feed him some of her milk. And look at the bond there was between them now. Mammy suspected this was something that would continue for the rest of their lives. Out there, you couldn't hear the angelus ringing out from St. Pat's. There was no one to pass the time of day with, no corner shop to have a wee duke into, and no entries out the back where you could find out the entire street craic with the hoards of women hanging their washing out.

Mammy longed to see her friend Patsie whose life indeed was much worse than her own. Patsie's husband was a dirty baste who'd slept with his very own sister, the dirty mare. The humiliation near 'put Patsie's head away', almost sending her to Purdysburn. The husband's only redeeming feature was that he tipped his pay packet over to Patsie come rain, hail or shine. And Patsie wasn't going to the poor house over any incest-ridden fecker. Apart from Mammy, there wasn't another living soul who knew Patsie's awful secret.

That's all Mammy needed on top of everything else; she was now cut off from everything she knew. She didn't know why she'd let Daddy talk her into this godforsaken idea in the first place. We could have built a nice house out on Malone Road but, no, he had to have fecking fields none the less. Here there was just work, work, work, from morning till night and her back was broke. Mammy made up her mind. As soon as she could, she'd be back where she belonged in Belfast. There was no way she was spending the rest of her days in the arse hole of nowhere.

Outside I was revelling in the hazy sunshine and fresh air. I, on the other hand, wished I could stay at Rushyhill forever. As I thought this, I began the sea shanty song.

'Oh the work is hard and the day is long, over watchful waters they were sailing, all along the shores boys, the rocky, rocky shores, as we're sailing for the shoals of herring.' Over and over I sang with the others joining in for the chorus while working the big, wooden rakes with their long handles over the hay, gathering it in rhythm to my songs.

Harry worked like a Trojan and a man with no arms, with an energy that was hard to believe—shirt sleeves rolled up above his elbows, sweat rolling down his brow and back. He kept them highly entertained, too, with his constant barrage of jokes and witty chatter. That was until somebody let Tomo, the billy goat, out of its pen and it charged straight for Harry—it's head low, horns pointed and hooves pounding the earth.

'Holy ... s-h-i-t!' cried Harry, as he took to his heels as if aul Nick himself was after him.

Everybody was on the ground laughing. But Harry's training as a runner meant he was faster than Tomo that day.

He scaled the dry stony wall just in the nick of time and even he started to laugh.

'Which one of you buck eejit's let that fecker out? Was it you, Sandy? If it was, I'll kick your melt in!'

'Wasn't me!'

'Was it you, Seamus, ye lanky big shite?'

'Feck off, Harry. If I'd let it out then I wouldn't have given ye a head start,' he laughed.

'Okay, is that the way of it? Trust me, it'll be twice as fast ye'll have to run when I find out who it was,' said Harry who was still out of puff, but surprisingly still in good form.

My brothers got a rope round the billy goat's neck and dragged it back to the pen while it was still bucking and carrying on.

When the raking was done, I would wander over to the donkey shed, open the door and put the leather strap round its neck and lead him out into the sunshine. I loved to walk the little donkey round the fields to stretch his legs. It was a shame he wouldn't let anybody ride him; he'd just buck them off. I felt so sorry for the poor crater. Daddy said he'd rescued him from a farm down the road and when they got him, you could even see his ribs.

Daddy was sure the donkey had been starved and beaten stupid because he took a long time to tame. I even sang a song as I walked the donkey. Harry got on so well with all the family. Well ... with everyone except Brian, but then Brian didn't get on with anybody especially me.

We made our way back to the house for supper. Young Tom, my youngest brother who loved Harry, ran along beside us sticking his hand in Harry's. The other hand trailing a piece of blackthorn stick he'd found in the field.

'Harry, you know the circus is coming,' chatted young Tom with a grin a mile wide. 'They say there'll be elephants and acrobats and all sorts of stuff, even candy floss by the barrel full. Will you and Isabelle take me? Mammy will let me go if you and Isabelle take me. Go on please, Harry.'

Harry glanced over at me smiling and gave me a wink.

'What about it? Fancy we take the wee fella?'

'Ach, Harry, sure there's no bus; it'll be Shanks's pony. We've only another day here,' I said with a half-reluctant smile.

Young Tom jumped up and down with excitement, punching his fist in the air because he knew Harry liked him and if he asked Harry first, I might say yes.

As we neared the back door of the house I turned to Tom, giving him a hug round his neck and whispered, 'Okay, but only if you're good. And for God's sake throw that blackthorn stick away before ye cross the door or Mammy will skelp your arse. You know she doesn't like that or lavender inside the house. It's bad luck and blackthorn will bring spirits into the house and not the alcoholic kind either.'

At that Tom fired the stick to one side and we all made our way in, kicking off our boots as we went.

It was Saturday night and everyone was exhausted and burnt to a cinder from the autumn sun. The stovetop had two big pans full of Mammy's stew—the aroma putting our heads away we were so hungry. There was a big pot of floury, white potatoes steaming hot and the soda bread on the tabletop was still warm.

There wouldn't be a morsel left tonight. Everyone was taking their place round the table, when Brian shouted, 'Da, have you seen my cigarettes? I left them here. Anyone seen them?'

No one really looked up; we were all too hungry.

'Da, my cigarettes, they're gone. A full packet, where are they?' Brian persisted.

'Have your tea, they'll be about.'

'They're not fecking here. Somebody's taken them.'

Brian was starting his usual antics and standover tactics, and I was embarrassed even more than usual as Harry was a guest. I motioned to him to just eat. Maybe he'd shut up. But Brian had no intentions of stopping; he was just getting started. 'There's no one here who'd take them,' said Daddy impatiently.

'Except the outsider,' Brian snorted.

I nearly choked on my dinner as Harry put his fork back down on his plate and looked up at Brian.

'Do you mean me? I haven't got your cigarettes.'

Without warning Daddy let rip, 'Hey, Mac, I'll have no thieves in this house.' What was Daddy saying? My heart raced at a thunderous pace. 'And are you calling our Brian a liar? No one here would take his cigarettes. You're invited in here and treated like King fecking Farouk and this is what happens? If that's the way of it, you can get your stuff and feck off back to Belfast.'

'Daddy, no.' I was on my feet, 'Daddy, please! Harry wouldn't take the cigarettes.' I glanced round the room, my eyes searching for anyone who'd back me up, but nobody dared go up against Daddy. They knew better.

'Pack your bags, Mac, this minute,' Daddy boomed at Harry.

Harry stood up, his chair sliding backwards as he wiped his mouth. I couldn't take it in. What was Brian saying? What was Daddy thinking? Even Mammy, who liked him, never opened her trap. I could see anger spread across Harry's face as I began to cry.

He said to me later, 'Your lot might be high and fecking mighty, with their fancy fecking bungalow, but where I came from, people might

94

be rough and ready, but they were as honest as the day was long—hardworking, decent people. You knew where ye stood with them. There was no room for shite like this. Now I know who set that goat on me.'

And as Harry's glance rounded on Brian he had wondered what he'd done to him to be called a lousy thief. The silence was broken by my sobs. It was over ten miles to Belfast and a fine misty rain had started to fall. Harry had eaten nothing to speak of and the walk would take him hours. He'd worked like a Trojan for them the whole weekend, only to be treated like this. I couldn't believe it. I was stricken with fear and disbelief at what was happening and my sobs turned to rage.

Mammy had to steady herself when I suddenly screamed at Daddy, 'Well if he goes, I go too!'

I was so shocked at myself I trembled. No one breathed, just watched, the dinner going cold on the plates.

'Well you better pack your stuff, too.'

In one fell swoop, Daddy pushed me into the arms of the very man he didn't even like—a move he would regret for the rest of his life. I was devastated. My daddy, the man I idolised, my hero, my rock, had just deserted me. We both gathered our bags in silence and shock and with just our summer clothes on, set off to walk the long road back to Belfast in the rain.

THE PROPOSAL
Isabelle

The road ahead, back to Belfast, lay in complete darkness, as black as the ace of spades. I was terrified for the first couple of miles. I hated the dark and was too humiliated to say anything to Harry. My gut was all knotted up again and all I could think about was how could Daddy believe our Brian's accusations of Harry being a thief? And why did Jack Kennedy break his promise to come back for me? If he had kept his word, none of this would be happening. Men were shites. I'd never trust another one.

It was getting colder as the fine rain soaked into our thin clothes and I shivered. Harry draped his jacket across my shoulders and I started to cry again; his act of kindness brought me to tears. Harry reached for my hand.

'Ach, come on, Isabelle, we'll be alright. Don't worry about them feckers back there.' And then he told another daft joke, which just made me cry even more. He was being so nice about it all.

We reached the halfway mark and could see the Cave Hill lights in the distance. We sat down, huddling together for warmth, our hair matted with the rain.

Harry suddenly turned to me and said, 'Isabelle, will you marry me?'

I was confused. 'What?' I asked in disbelief.

'Will you marry me? I know I don't have a ring for you, but …'

'Harry,' I interrupted him. *Jesus what was he saying?* 'I … I don't love you, though.'

'Ach, that's nothing to worry about, Isabelle. I have enough love for the both of us. And don't they say love grows?'

So in the middle of the night, freezing cold and soaked to the skin, shocked and traumatised by the fighting in the house, and in an attempt to escape the haunting memories of Jack Kennedy, I said 'yes.'

We had the weekend together back in Belfast before the rest of them came back from the farm. We rehearsed what we'd say. If I wasn't allowed to stay there until we got married, then Connie told me I could live with them. I was grateful for the offer, but it would have been a big disgrace not to leave from your own home the day you married.

So I prayed that there wouldn't be too much trouble about it. After all Harry was a Catholic. Much to our surprise, there wasn't as much commotion as we'd thought. Mammy hadn't been pleased one bit about the neuration at the bungalow that weekend. She liked Harry and thought Daddy had been just a bit too quick on the uptake, so to speak. All that cooking and slaving she'd done and the whole dinner had been spoiled going cold. One thing Mammy hated more than anything was a cold dinner when she'd gone to all that back-breaking trouble. Mammy was made up when she heard the news. There was something about a wedding that made the sky seem a bit bluer, taking your mind off your troubles. Oh she'd have to get herself a new hat. And the wee ones would all have to have their hair cut and shoes mended. And if she set to and made a list of the jobs that needed done, the place would look like a new penny. She'd make the wedding cake because there wasn't a woman about the streets of The Falls road that could make a fruit cake like Mammy, and there'd be just enough time to let the fruit soak in the whisky—exactly two months.

Mammy was so excited; she helped me scour Belfast for white material for the wedding dress. I had very definite ideas about what

I wanted. I'd thought about my big day for a long time. I just never thought in my wildest dreams that it would be to anyone other than Jack Kennedy.

The wedding dress had to be ballet length, which was all the rage, and it would be reminiscent of the in thing, which was rock 'n' roll, but very tasteful and very classy. A fitted waist, a stand up collar, and three-quarter sleeves, and I wanted my sister's dress (as the maid of honour) to be made exactly the same, which had never been done before, but in pale pink. I'd even picked out, in my mind's eye, what my peep-toe sandals would be like.

Now, though, Mammy moaned bitterly, 'What ye want white for I'll never know. Just get a nice suit. That's what everyone else is doing. There's hardly a scrap of material worth having since the war. Hitler and his fecking planes made sure of that.'

But I knew she was secretly pleased that one of hers was going down the aisle in white. And besides, I wanted the dream. So from somewhere came the white satin embossed material for my wedding dress.

We married in my local parish church. My sister and brother were maid of honour and groomsman, and Harry's wee sister Sarah-Jayne was the wee flower girl. Connie was delighted; her eldest was getting married, all respectable like, and her wee girl as pretty as a picture. Connie never regretted the fancy double-barrelled name she gave her youngster; it was nothing like her own, thank God. What had ever possessed her own ma to call her 'Consumpta', she'd never know. It was as close to a disease as you could get. She may as well have called her 'cough and fecking splutter'. Mammy and Daddy put the small spread on back at 26 Stonemore Road. There was no honeymoon.

MARRIED LIFE
Isabelle

Our first night of marriage was spent eating as many chocolate Maltesers as we could stuff down. We fell asleep holding hands. Three weeks later, our ones were all abuzz wanting to know how it was. 'How was what?' was the constant refrain.

'You know … the rumpty-tumpty tickle-your-fancy stuff? Come on, Isabelle, spill the beans. What's "it" like? Is he any good … you know … between the sheets?'

I could feel my face flushing scarlet. Why did I feel like an eejit? I made a smart remark about it being none of their bloody business now I was a married woman, but our ones weren't daft and they weren't about to give up either. I didn't know what to say. I felt so stupid. Fancy being married three weeks and not even knowing what to do. My God, I was mortified.

'Do you mean Harry and you haven't done it yet and it's been three weeks? Jesus, Mary and holy Saint Joseph, she's still a fecking virgin,' they shrieked. 'What was Harry Savage up to? Surely they both couldn't be that green?'

Seeing the state I was getting into, my sister said, 'Ach, c'mon love we're just pulling your leg. Sit down and you can tell us what's wrong.' They realised quickly that their playful enquiries into married bliss were no joke.

There and then is when I learnt the truth about the birds and the bees. I was astonished at what they said. Mary said married relations weren't all they were cracked up to be anyway and it was just something you put up with. Her suggestion was to get a tub of petroleum jelly and rub it everywhere to make it easy. But our Aggie gave me a hug and told me, 'take no notice of that one,' then she turned to Mary.

'Ach, for Jesus' sake, Mary McKitterick, you make it sound so cold. You're supposed to enjoy it and have a bit of fun.'

'Fun Agnes? Fun me arse! I swear you and your Tony are a couple of dirty bastes. You'll have to tell Harry tonight, Isabelle, that you don't have a marriage in the eyes of God till the union is consummated. It's a mortal sin to lose the seed.'

Oh my God, not only was I an eejit but a sinful one at that too. I swore I'd tell Harry that night and made our ones swear 'on peril of their lives' not to breathe a word to a living soul, especially to Mammy or anybody from the legion of Mary, or I'd never be able to hold my head up again.

I'd spent my whole life trying to be good and keep away from sin, and here sin was, even when I was married, trying to drag me to Hell. Maybe the teacher was right, that I'd get into Heaven by the skin of my teeth. Not even married in the eyes of God—oh Jesus, Mary and Joseph, if Father Flannigan finds out, there's no telling what might happen. Oh God, I'll be the laughing stock of Belfast. My marriage not even consummated? This was a mess. I wanted to run a mile.

Harry usually got home from work at 5 o'clock on the dot every day. He didn't miss a minute and Friday was payday. Maybe we could go to the pictures, get a bite to eat and I'd talk to him about what our ones had said about married relations. Five o'clock came and went, but he didn't come home. I waited and waited and had to throw his dinner in the bin and then eventually I fell asleep. It was four o'clock in the morning when the noise and stench of stale alcohol woke me up.

'Harry, is that you? Are you drunk?'

He staggered about the bedroom not saying very much and I tried to get him into bed quietly in case he woke our roommate Willy Spence.

'Where have you been till this hour? You're so drunk! Where's your wages?'

'There's no wages, but I'll get them back tomorrow.'

'Why? Where's the money?'

'Shut your mouth, woman. I said I'd get it back. The card school runs all weekend.'

I froze, my stomach in knots. I'd never seen this side of Harry and it terrified me. And what the hell was a 'card school'?

I reached out again to touch him, but he roughly shrugged me off.

'That's nothing to worry about. Worry about T-H-I-S,' he slurred.

And without so much as a sideways glance he staggered over to where his wedding suit hung on the back of the bedroom door, took out a Wilkinson Sword razor blade and sliced his wedding suit to pieces, while I watched in terror. I couldn't believe what had just happened. I thought I was going to die of shame; I'd just made the biggest mistake of my life. But I knew what I had to do. As soon as he was asleep, I'd go home as fast as my legs could carry me. I waited, lying as still as possible, and when his snores were hard and deep, I quickly and quietly gathered a bag. As dawn broke, I walked across Belfast getting the first morning bus from the city centre back to our house, all the while wondering what I had ever done to deserve this. And wondering too why Jack Kennedy never came back to get me, like he promised, because none of this should be happening to me.

When I got to our house everyone was going about their business, getting their breakfast and getting ready for work. The fire was ablaze in the grate and the smell of fresh toast made me suddenly feel like I was home, and I realised too I was ravenous.

'In under God, looks who's walked in! What time of the morning is this to be visiting, wee girl?' asked Mammy.

I started to tell them what had happened the night before. Mammy suddenly turned from the stove where she was finishing off the fry and shrieked, 'What's this?' as she wiped her hands on her apron. 'We'll have none of that talk in this house, wee girl. You've just been down the aisle three weeks ago. Pull yourself together. Harry's a good man. You've just got to grow up ... and do your wifely duties.'

My God, what? Surely our ones hadn't told on me. Surely they hadn't told Mammy that I didn't know what to do as a married woman. Did she know all of it? Did she think this was my fault? When Daddy sauntered into the living room he was quiet, then cleared his throat and grunted from under his pipe, 'Did he lift his hands to you?'

'No, Daddy, I was just so scared. He's done the wages in at a card school and his wedding suit's been sliced to ribbons. He took a razor blade to it. It was awful.'

Daddy was quiet and pensive.

'Are there any babies on the way, wee girl?'

'No, Daddy,' I said feeling my skin go scarlet.

'Well then, Maggie, I say she stays here and feck him. I knew they were a bad lot those East Enders.'

But Mammy dug her heels in and said, 'Alistair McKitterick, as God is my witness and in front of that Sacred Heart picture and his Holy Mother, she'll not break any wedding vows in this house. What God has joined together, let no man put asunder. You've bloody well ruined her all her life, letting her get away with far too much and I warned you time and time again what would happen. Aye, I did, now I will have me say if it's the last thing I do.'

With that Daddy sat down in his chair and never said another word. And with that declaration, of God's will to be done, my fate was sealed. I had made my bed; I could go and lie in it.

I was devastated, my eyes red raw from all the crying. He would be awake now and he'd know I'd taken off. I'd be going back like a dog with its tail between its legs because I had nowhere else to go. Mammy didn't want me and Daddy had no say in it. I'd never felt this desolate in my life except for the night I'd gone to the train station to see Jack off and he never looked round once. I had no choice; I would have to go back and take whatever Harry was going to dish out.

When I got back home, he was up and about, looking very sheepish and wasn't saying much. I could hardly bring myself to look at him. I went about putting my bag away, tidying up the bedroom, placing the remnants of his wedding suit in the bin. What was I going to do? What sort of a life was this going to be? Was this what my whole life was destined to be like?

I knew no more till Harry started alisalamin round me. First of all he asked me where I'd been. He could see I'd been crying and he knew I wasn't there in the bed when he woke from his drunken slumber. I didn't answer him at first; I was mortified this was happening to me and now all my family knew about it too. Jesus, what a mess.

Then, before I knew it, he was there putting his arms round my waist. I tried to shrug him off. I had no words to say what I felt. But this just made him hang on tighter. Then he whispered in my ear. 'I'm sorry, Isabelle. It won't happen again. I promise you on my mother's life. I'll get the money back. I swear on *The Bible* itself to keep away from the card school, honest to God.'

Then I started to cry again.

'Why in the name of God, Harry? We have little enough, and then you go and do this? Your wedding suit? Jesus, Mary and Joseph, it's in shreds in the bin. You scared the life out of me. What were you thinking?'

'I said I'm sorry. I meant it. I was drunk and pished off that I didn't win the money back. I didn't mean to take it out on you. I am sure them feckers were cheating. I was so mad about it. I wanted to get you something nice to wear with the winnings, and I had to come home with me pockets empty.'

'Harry, you know it's a mug's game, the road to nowhere. Nobody wins, no one except the bookie himself. Those gambling schools are dangerous too. I've heard those bastards would slit your throat over a pound note, and you know what happened to your da. He ended up six foot under.'

He hung onto me till he convinced me that he would never do his money in or give me cause to be afraid again. I had to believe him; I had no choice. I was stuck fast between the devil and the deep blue sea. Maybe this would be the right time to tell him about what our ones had told me about married relations.

It wasn't long before I felt as sick as a dog and my period hadn't come. Our ones soon confirmed my worst fears: I was pregnant! I didn't want to have any babies yet. I wanted to wait a while to see if Harry meant what he'd said about the money, and hoping we'd get on our feet a wee bit, put a bit bye, maybe even get into a wee place of our own.

The only problem was that if you waited you'd be committing another sin by losing the seed. How could we bring a wee child into the world with the shame of Harry's gambling and hardly a brown penny to live on? I knew that my eternal soul was headed for Hell if Harry or I stopped any babies coming. And there was nothing to stop them even if we knew how to get the hold of French letters.

No good Catholic would be game enough to do it. You'd be confessing it on Saturday and before mass on Sunday, and if Father Flannigan prevented you from taking communion as penance for the sin you had committed, the whole parish would know you'd sinned and would be passing dirty looks.

My whole world was spinning out of control and a deep sadness gripped my heart that nothing could shift. This wasn't how my life was meant to be. I was supposed to have been happily married to Jack, living in Canada, the world at our feet, the streets paved with gold. I walked the streets of Belfast half the night wondering what was going to become of me and I wished the baby inside me would fall out onto the ground.

THE MISSING LETTERS
Isabelle

Months went by and I blossomed with my pregnancy. Harry was delighted about our first baby. He'd often bring his winnings home and always had some toy or clothes for the new baby to give me. Good stuff too—nothing but the best of gear. He whistled to himself a lot; life was okay. One day he'd win the big one and we'd be millionaires. I would be decked out in style, he'd buy me that piano I longed for, and his wee childer would be no goat's toe in the gear. He'd buy them no cheapo stuff, only the best … one day!

I took my usual bus up The Falls road to our house every week. My rounded belly was as big as a football and I gently touched my stomach to feel the wee kicks. I smiled quietly. *I wonder what it is, a wee boy or a wee girl?* Despite the sickness of my pregnancy and my first thoughts about being pregnant, I couldn't wait to see my wee baby. It wouldn't be long now—just four weeks to go. The bus pulled over to let someone off and before it pulled away a fella jumped aboard. 'One full fare to the top of The Falls road please.' Instantly my head shot up. That voice.

I stared at the man getting on and almost fainted as Jack Kennedy walked up the aisle of the bus towards me. 'Isabelle!' he shouted, elated, except when he got closer he saw the huge rounded belly. The smile fell from his face as he took in the full picture of me heavily pregnant.

'Oh my God! Isabelle McKitterick, what have you done?' he gasped.

Embarrassed to death I protectively placed my hands on my belly.

'Don't you dare speak to me like that Jack Kennedy! I'm a married woman. You never came back, you broke your promise, take yourself off and don't ever speak to me again.'

The nerve of him! Coming back here after all this time. What had he come back for anyway? Was it just to make me look like an eejit? I was boiling. How dare he speak to me like that after what he'd done? Jack shook his head and lowered his voice.

He bent down, looked into my eyes and with the saddest face I had ever seen, he said, 'Isabelle McKitterick, that should be my baby you're carrying.'

And with that he turned on his heel, pulled the bell chord and got off the bus. He didn't even look back. I was in such a state when I reached our house. Everyone had come in to see what the commotion was about. Mammy put the teapot on and Daddy sucked on his pipe while I recounted what had just happened on the bus.

'Mammy, you'll never believe it. You were right about Jack Kennedy. The bloody cheek of him, coming back here after all this time, telling me this baby should be his! Why would he say something like that, and me a married woman. Did he think he could just swan back here and I'd be sitting like an aul maid waiting?'

'Aye,' said Mammy, 'I told you more than once that a bird in the hand was worth two in the bush and I was right, wasn't I? I knew the minute I laid eyes on him he was no good, him with that high flatulent way about him, acting like he owns the place, thinking he's better than us here, thinking he could slope round here, then pish off with you to the other side of the fecking world taking us all for a pack of buck eejits. Reckon I did you a big favour. Good job I burnt those letters because it would have led to no good.'

'W-h-a-t … are you talking about, Mammy?' I sunk to the chair grasping the wooden arm as I went because I felt I was going to faint after hearing what Mammy had just said. My whole body felt like it was in a wash tub being dragged about and beaten, and the mangle was coming up, ready to squeeze any bit of my heart that was left through its two rubber rollers.

'Mammy! What letters? What letters?'

I was hysterical. I was up on my feet with my heart beating ten to the dozen. I was so close now Mammy could smell my anger. My God! Oh my God … the awful truth was dawning on me … my ma had done this to me. My own mother. The letters I'd prayed every day to come … Jack 'had' sent for me … he had kept his promise … that's why he said what he said on the bus. Oh my God … we should have been together starting a new life … I knew I hadn't been wrong about what I felt for him.

Jack would never know the truth … he would never know that I had waited … longing to hear from him … that my heart had broken waiting for word. Now wherever he'd go in the world, he'd think the worst of me. He'd think that I just hadn't cared enough to wait. Now it was too late.

My whole life was in tatters and a baby due any time. I hated them all—my ma for wrecking my life and my da for deserting me. If only he'd stuck up for me the day, I'd come back looking for somewhere to stay. There wasn't a baby on the way then. If only they'd let me stay, I would have been there when Jack had come back to get me.

I hated Harry for his gambling, drinking ways that left us without a brown penny to our names, and there was no way out. I was trapped and Jack would be going back to the other side of the world thinking the worst of me. I wished the ground could've opened up and swallowed me. It wasn't the same in those days. Nobody had a telephone like everyone has today, where you could keep in touch with each other. You only got a telegram if somebody died. Letters were all we had and it took weeks to reach you from another country. It really was like the end of the Earth.

Times have changed. Youngsters are worldly and you have a lot more say about your lives than we did. You wouldn't get away with it these days, interfering in someone else's life like that. Well, you could try, but most young ones have more savvy and would tell you to go to Hell. Today's world is a different place alright.

THE REAL GHOST
Isabelle

When Harry and I first got married, it was virtually impossible to get a council house. What houses there were were given to the Prods first. Catholics didn't get a look in and were at the bottom of the pile. Even if you had wee childer, which was supposed to get you a higher place on the list, a house would be given to a Prod first, even if they were weren't married and without a family. People were raging about the injustice of it. We all knew what was going on—that Catholics were being treated like second-class citizens— but you couldn't prove it or do anything about it. There was no use complaining because the fellas in charge of allocations were Prods too, and if you tried to do something, your application would be 'lost' and you'd go to the end of the waiting list again. So Harry and I were on the list since we got married, but until you heard word that you had a house, you had to room in with somebody.

We were renting a room with Willy Spence, a widowed man whose wife Gracie had passed away two years previously. They'd no childer of their own and Willy was glad of the company, and also the bit of rent. I loved keeping the house like a new pin, and Harry got on well with Willy and they would often share a rollie and a tin of baccy in the yard while I got the dinner on. He told me he'd be sad to see us young ones move on when we got a place of our own.

Now Willy was very specific with the chores he gave me to do round the house. There was only one rule of his that I was never to break: Willy's bedroom was out of bounds—no cleaning in there. He had his personal possessions there and Gracie's clothes still hung in the heavy oak wardrobe.

He told me he didn't ever imagine a time when he would be ready to get rid of her things. Somehow, if they were still there, then she wasn't really gone. Many a one thought Willy had 'lost his bap', saying it was creepy the way he hung on to her things. I thought it showed how much Willy loved Gracie and when it was time, he'd come to terms with her loss. Grief is such a personal thing; everyone's different the way they deal with it. All he needed was time.

He could still smell her perfume on her clothes, and when he was in his bedroom he would talk to her as if she was still there. I heard him many a time. I never told anybody or they'd of thought Willy was mad, but I thought his talks to Gracie were lovely; a sign of the devoted couple they were. I thought if I were in that position I'd be the same. I reassured Willy that I would never go into his bedroom no matter what, and nightly when Willy retired to bed, he turned the key in the lock of his bedroom door just to make sure no one came in while he slept.

About three months later, Willy's rheumatism was playing up, so he bade Harry and I goodnight and retired early with a wee rum tottie. A while later we too retired to bed. It had been a long week and a sleep-in on Saturday was on the cards. I went out for the count and Harry was snoring away when suddenly I sat bolt upright in the bed and frantically shook him.

'Harry, quick, get up!'

'What?'

'Harry, get up, there's something wrong with Mister Spence.' Reluctantly he did, while muttering something about having 'married a mad woman'.

We crossed the landing to Willy's bedroom; the door was locked as it always was and we couldn't hear anything. Listening at the door Harry told me that Willy was probably fast asleep as we should both be.

'You know Willy doesn't want us in there. He's okay and probably out for the count.'

I was shaking, my voice now a screech. 'Please, Harry, there's something wrong, I just know it, hurry.'

He let out a long, frustrated sigh, rolled his eyes, then rapped sharply on Willy's door, but there was no answer. He glanced at me again, my eyes widening and I motioned for him to try again.

This time he rapped hard. Still no reply. Harry could sense my rising panic and he was now worried too. He pushed the door hard with his shoulder. It was stuck fast. So with me starting to become hysterical and the door locked, he stood right back and took a run at it. Harry said he hoped to God Willy would understand and not think we'd both gone mad.

When he finally pushed through Willy's bedroom door, Willy was fast asleep alright and his bedclothes were fully alight, the flames almost licking the top of his head. We both screamed Willy's name and began to bash out the flames with our dressing gowns.

That night we pulled Willy Spence from his burning bed and saved his life. The fire brigade was called and the fire put out. The bed was ruined and some of the water from the fire hoses had run through the bare floorboards and cascaded through the ceiling, dripping down the cord of the electric light in the living room.

We were all in shock. The fireman told Willy he was lucky to be alive. He should've known better than to smoke in bed. We were all sitting huddled round, having a cup of tea, trying to get over the shock and Willy asked, 'How did you know to wake me, Harry?'

He explained it was me who thought something was wrong. Then Willy asked me, 'Did you smell smoke, Isabelle? How did you know to wake me up?'

'I got woken up by a lady shaking me by the knee.'

'A lady? What lady?'

'I don't know, Willy. She was standing beside the bed.'

I explained what the lady looked like and very quietly Willy got up from his chair, still hugging the blanket round his shoulders, walked to his room and brought back a photo of Gracie, his dead wife.

When Willy showed the picture to me, I began to cry. 'Jesus, Mary and Joseph,' I sobbed, 'that's her ... that's the lady that shook my knee till I woke up.'

'Well, that's my Gracie. I knew she was here with me, looking over me. She must have known she could tell you what was wrong.'

I felt the hairs on the back of my neck stand up and I started to shake as I looked at Harry to see what he was thinking. At that, he made the sign of the cross on himself because he too knew that something strange had happened that night—something that wasn't of this world.

Willy Spence fell asleep with a lit cigarette in his hand, and I often wondered why Gracie had woken me because twelve months later, Willy stepped off a bus into the path of a cement truck that took his head clean off his shoulders. Harry and I were devastated, but I knew Gracie had saved three lives that night of the fire and that Willy was now with his beloved Gracie in Heaven. If Gracie hadn't woken me up, my childer would never have been born. That's the power of love—it crosses everything, even Earthly boundaries.

THE BIRTH
Isabelle

Gerry's birth was the worst; I didn't know 'B' from a bull's foot about birthing. My waters broke in the middle of the night. I shook Harry to get up and get a taxi to the hospital. He was very excited; he couldn't wait to see his first child. I felt I was in labour too long; something wasn't right. Despite my gut-wrenching attempts to push the baby out, nothing was happening. Panic was spreading in the delivery room.

'Get the doctor quick,' the nurse ordered.

My heart was thumping in my chest. I was shit-scared and nobody told me what was happening. Then the doctor came and told me they'd have to deliver the baby by forceps as it was too late for a caesarean section.

I almost fainted when the doctor applied the forceps; I thought he was tearing me in two, the pain was so bad. I thought my poor baby would be born dead the way he was dragged by his wee head into the world. The doctor and nurses were silent as they cut the cord and wrapped him. The doctor looked at me, placed his hand on my shoulder.

'It's a boy,' he simply said. 'He needs to have some tests and X-rays. We'll let you see him as soon as we can.'

Three days later, when Gerry was placed in my arms, the squeals coming from me were awful. I became hysterical. 'What's wrong with my baby? What's wrong with his wee head?'

'Come, come, Mrs Savage. He's just very bruised from the delivery. It looks much worse than it is.'

My baby looked like a lump of black and blue jelly and his eyes were shut tight with the swelling. It was so bad I didn't want anyone to see him and every time I tried to hold him he screeched out in pain. I knew something wasn't right. My mammy had given birth to seventeen babies, all born at home, and nothing like this had ever happened.

Wasn't it supposed to be safer giving birth in hospital these days? Wasn't that the modern thing to do? Why then had this happened to my wee baby? When Mammy heard about the state of her grandchild, she went stark-raving mad.

'Bloody men had no business with birthing. Doctor or not, midwives knew instinctively when something was wrong. They got the gist quicker than any aul lad, whether he'd been to fecking medical school or not. Standing round there with their two fecking arms the one length, half the time having a good aul gleg at your nether regions. They didn't know everything and should stick to what they knew best and let women get on with the business they had been doing for as long as time had begun.'

Harry was in shock and didn't know what to say to make me feel any better. His first-born son looked like a poor wee monster and I was inconsolable. Nobody had told us this could happen. Weren't babies supposed to be all pink and soft, able to feed from their mother?

Harry made up his mind to speak to the doctor and try and find out what happened. But at each and every turn, he was given the brush off, palmed off with numerous excuses as to why he couldn't speak to the doctor.

'Ah, the doctor is in delivering another baby, Mr Savage. I'm afraid he won't have time to talk to you today.' ... 'Oh the doctor is off on sick leave today. Maybe you can come back next week.' No one was interested.

It seemed that no matter how hard he tried he was up against a brick wall of silence. He couldn't get a straight answer to his questions. The next day I'd be going home and it would be even harder to get answers once we'd left the hospital.

On the day I was due to come home from hospital, the doctor in charge wanted a chat in private. What he told me that day came as a huge shock.

'Mrs Savage, I'm not sure if you realise, but we nearly lost you and the baby,' he told me.

My eyes widened.

'The thing is, my dear, you had a hundred and thirty-one stiches inside your body and out. There is every chance another baby may get stuck in the birth canal as well. I don't believe it would be wise for you to have any more babies, do you understand me?'

'Oh, yes, yes of course, I'll let my husband know.'

'May I ask, are you a Catholic?'

'Yes, I am, doctor.' I wondered why the doctor would ask such a personal question.

'Then you must discuss what I've told you with your parish priest.'

'Of course, doctor, as soon as I'm on my feet.' The answer came soon enough the first time I was able to go to confession.

Back home I did my best to settle Gerry, but he cried constantly and took a long time to feed. I was exhausted and at my wit's end. Harry felt useless; he didn't know what to do to help. So the day we came home from hospital, he cleared off and went down to the pub to 'wet the baby's head' because that's what ye did, you see. Gerry was only weeks old and it was the first time I'd felt myself able enough to go to church. I wished to God later that I hadn't bothered me arse. That aul thumpadonian Father Flanagan was there and I was devastated at what happened next.

'Under no circumstances are you to prevent the planting of the seed.'

'But, Father, the doctor said I mustn't have any more babies. I almost died having this one. Do you need to speak to the doctor?'

I was as green as grass because I really believed when the priest heard the medical side of things he'd understand. How wrong you can be. The aul bastard nearly annihilated me as he rose outa his chair.

Standing over me, he held the crucifix up that he wore round his neck, as if invoking the par of Jesus himself. 'Believe me when I say that your eternal soul is in peril, which is far more important than your life here on Earth. Do you want to commit mortal sin and be damned forever?' I couldn't believe what I was hearing.

'But, Father, the doctor said ...'

'Get out of this holy place!' he yelled, moving closer, spitting out the words. 'Don't come here again with such sinful talk and for your penance do the *Rosary* each day for a month.'

I left the church, silent tears sliding down my face. If it hadn't been for the love I had of Our Blessed Lady, I'd never have darkened the doorstep of another Catholic church again. As I pushed wee Gerry in his pram all the way home, I wondered what I was going to do. I didn't want to go to Hell. I told Harry everything the priest said and because contraception was neither available nor allowed for Catholics, we both knew the only thing we could do was never to have marital relations again. That way there couldn't be any more babies. And so we began a long period of enforced celibacy, until nature could no longer be restrained and shortly after that I was pregnant with you, Berny.

I decided my pregnancy with you would be different. I'll learn all there is to know about birthing. I learned about relaxation and breathing, practising every day. I'd know what to do this time for my baby to be born; there'd be no forceps used. And on the ninth of February 1958, you were born into the world 'Indian style'. I breathed so well the doctor said I looked like I was in a yoga trance. There were no forceps, no stitches and no horrific marks on your wee head. You slipped out of me still half asleep, with the loveliest wee face and fine blonde hair, and you were mine. I'll never forget that day—born within the feast of Saint Bernadette of Lourdes. As I looked out of the hospital window it had just begun to snow.

It's funny, Berny, how every year when it starts to snow, it takes me back to the day and hour you were born.

I was overjoyed—a wee girl. Now I had one of each, exactly what Jack and I said we wanted all those years ago. With this thought, sadness gripped my heart again as I thought about where Jack would be in the world, and how much I longed for him to hold me in his arms, to tell him what really happened, and that I never stopped loving him. But now there wasn't a cat in hell's chance that would ever happen. I was lying in the bed I'd made alright, and the spikes were killing me.

You were only a few hours old when a young nurse picked you out of the cot for a feed. To my horror, she lost her grip on your blanket and you tumbled back into the low cot. The cot had metal mesh sides and the side of your wee head was cut like a cheese grater. I screamed, leaping out of the bed, frantically calling for a doctor. There was blood everywhere and you were squealing. Jesus Mary and Joseph, I couldn't believe what I'd just seen. It was bad enough that Gerry's head was cut to smithereens by forceps, but now this stupid young cowyard had dropped you too.

I was hysterical, you were squealing and the nurse was crying. You can imagine the commotion. Matron was called and the nurse was sacked on the spot. My fear of babies being dropped wasn't just imagined. As I've told you before, I had a friend called Francis Foley who never grew properly. She was a delicate and poor soul, and had a huge hump on her back so she couldn't stand straight. She wasn't born like that; her aul aunty dropped her when she was stocious. No doctor was called and Francis never got any treatment. It was only after the aunty died they found out the truth. So I made a promise to myself years before that nobody would be walking round carrying any babies of mine. So for the nurse in the fecking hospital to drop you was my worst nightmare come true.

Did I ever tell you, Berny, that I had a recurring dream when I was pregnant with you? Almost every night, Padre Pio, one of the rare people ever to carry the stigmata of Christ, appeared to me in my dreams. He held my hand and said he had a message for me. He told me in the dream that

I would have 'one more little boy', so I was quite surprised when you were born because I thought you'd be a wee boy. I was going to ask Mammy to get out her book of dreams to see what it meant, but it went clean outa my head after you were born. I didn't think any more about it as I had no intentions of having any more childer. It was years later when I went to get sterilised that the significance of the dream became clear as day.

JIMMY-PADDY
Isabelle

Again, enforced celibacy was the way your da and I stopped babies coming, Berny. But a year and seven months after you were born, Jimmy–Paddy arrived. It was a very straightforward birth and he was gorgeous.

As you know I had a phobia about anyone walking round holding my babies in case they were dropped. I didn't trust anyone. You always had to sit down when you held a baby, or put the baby in the pram, especially outside. The only exception to this rule was Jimmy-Paddy, who for most of his life was tucked into my left oxter, close to my heart, wrapped in the big shawlie like a baby Indian. This helped soothe him when he cried and doubled up to support my back. I would often say, 'Right, get the big shawlie' because it stopped little moneybox mouth crying for the time he was in it.

The day I was due to leave hospital the paediatrician did her rounds as usual to examine the new babies before going home.

'Mrs Savage, good morning, how are you?'

'Ach, just grand you know, as well as you'd expect.'

'And here's your baby. Let me see him now before he goes home,' and she began to test every inch of him. 'Have you got a name for him, Mrs Savage?'

'Oh yes, this is James-Patrick.'

'Ah, lovely name, lovely little boy, perfectly healthy, perfectly normal. He's a little bit on the skinny side, but I'm sure you'll waste no time fattening him up,' and she moved onto the next new mother, her white starched coat swishing behind her, and a throng of junior doctors and nurses pandering to her every whim because the head doctor was second only to God himself. Jimmy-Paddy was six weeks old and thriving. The doctor was right; my milk was doing him no end of good and he'd a healthy pair of lungs on him. It was Saturday morning and my friend, Rosie, had called in to see if she could get any 'rations' for me from the shop.

'Hiya, Rosie.'

'Hiya, Isabelle. Ach, look at the wee dotes. Where's the new baby? I can't wait to see him!'

'He's asleep. Don't wake him and don't pick him up either. Just duke in and you can hold him when he's awake.'

As Rosie gazed at the baby, she realised quickly something was wrong.

'Jesus, Mary and Joseph, Isabelle! Come quick there's something wrong with the baby.' I dropped the mop and bucket, spilling the soapy water over the floor.

'I only checked him fifteen minutes ago.' When I saw Jimmy-Paddy, his lips were ringed with blue and his eyes were all glassy.

I checked his breathing and within seconds had him out of the pram, wrapped in a blanket and was stuffing my shoes on.

'Rosie, stay with the childer!'

Rosie looked terrified and didn't know what to say. All she kept saying was, 'Ahh, Jesus, not the wee baby!' In seconds I was running as fast my legs could carry me, down the two flights of stairs, along the garden path, up the street and across the road, ducking in-between traffic. My shoe started to come off, nearly tripping me up, so I kicked them both off and ran the rest of the way to the hospital in my bare feet, my heart beating out of my chest, and straight into the emergency department of Belfast's largest hospital, The Royal.

I remember screeching frantically, looking round.

'It's my baby! Please help me! Someone help me! My wee baby's not well!'

The state of me clutching my tiny bundle made everyone jump. A doctor in a white coat grabbed the baby while a nurse made me sit down and take a deep breath. I instinctively made to go after the doctor, but the nurse held me by both shoulders.

'I'm afraid you can't go with him, Mrs Savage. Let the doctors do their job. It could be hours before we know anything.'

'But he's so small. I need to go with him. He's only six weeks old. What about his feed? My milk? He'll be hungry shortly … please … please let me go with him. I'm his mammy. He needs me. Please … he's my wee baby … mine …'

'I suggest you go home, my dear. We will be in touch when we know something.'

I wept long, deep breathless noises as I clung to his wee blanket, burying my head in it. His smell was still there. When I could steady myself to walk, I made my way back to the house trying to figure out what had just happened. *How could my wee baby be alright one minute and so sick the next?* Rosie was waiting. Neither of us spoke. We just clung to each other and cried. It was only when Rosie looked down at my feet that I realised I had no shoes on.

It was a long day and still no news. I told your da when he got home from work. 'He'll be okay, Isabelle, you'll see,' was all he said.

Dr McGee said she'd go to the hospital and see if they would give her any news. I had just got you and Gerry to sleep when Dr McGee returned, her face ashen white. We both looked to her hoping for good news. Neither of us spoke.

'Isabelle, Harry, I need you to sit down. Your baby's very sick. He's got meningitis! The worst kind ... he probably won't make it through the night. You must get on your knees and ask God to take him quickly because if he lives he'll be profoundly handicapped.'

What was she saying? Pray to God that our baby dies? In a heartbeat both of us were on our knees praying that our wee boy would 'live', we prayed.

'Hail Mary, full of grace, the Lord is with thee. Blessed art thou among women and blessed is the fruit of thy womb, Jesus ...' The Holy Mother would save him; we had complete faith.

When Jimmy-Paddy came home from hospital, we thought the doctors were wrong.

'My God, he's beautiful, Harry. Look at his wee face. He looks just the same as before. They must be wrong about the meningitis.'

But it would be only a few weeks before I would realise that something was very wrong with our baby. Weeks went by and even your da was quiet. There were no jokes and he stayed out more, often coming home late, too drunk to be of any use to me.

Again he was at the horses—no wages again this week. He didn't know what to do to make me smile, except try again to win the big one. And weekly I would take you three childer and go down to the loan shark in Smithfield Road who loaned me the money to live on for the next week. The amount of interest we owed that aul lad got bigger and bigger. I felt so alone and filled with shame. I dreaded meeting anyone who might know me, and prayed my family wouldn't find out the way I was living. I wondered what my life would have been like with Jack in Canada. How could I have made such a mistake and marry your da? I survived by throwing myself into motherhood.

I loved my babies. Your smiles and the smell of talcum powder, your laughs, chatter and gorgeous blonde curls. I lived in your world, singing, reading and walking every day out Antrim Road and up the hills with the pram. But despite all the reassurances of the day from your da, I was still worried about Jimmy-Paddy.

Mammy went ballistic when I mentioned the baby's condition. She said if we'd had a house of our own instead of rooming with Dr McGee, the baby wouldn't have been exposed to all the 'aul come all ye of the day,' coughing and spluttering their germs round a wee child.

122

She went mad too because we'd been on the housing list for years and should have been out of there long ago, but Prods got all the houses, families or not. Those bastards cooking the lists had a lot to answer for. Now look what's happened to the wee child.

Mammy was convinced that's what had happened. Babies shouldn't be anywhere near the sick. To be honest I didn't know what to think. We'd been so grateful when Dr McGee had said we could stay in her spare room and what Mammy said just made us feel guilty as if somehow it was our fault too for not getting outa there sooner.

I noticed that no matter how many times I propped the baby up with cushions, he quickly slipped over to one side. Instead of pushing against my knee, his wee legs just dangled. Now I'd had two babies already so I knew he should be pushing against my knee. So I made an appointment at The Royal to see the paediatrician. I hoped it would be the one who had seen him when he was first born. I waited in the long, dark, draughty aul corridor for over an hour.

Jimmy-Paddy was gorgeous in his newly knitted, lemon pram suit I'd done in the new moss stitch, and as usual he was snuggled into my left arm. The wait was tense. I hoped it wouldn't take too long as I'd left Rosie looking after you and Gerry. After what seemed like an eternity, I was called in by the nurse and ushered into the imposing room. It stunk of disinfectant. The doctor sat behind a big, heavy oak desk. He never spoke, the ignorant aul get, just motioned with his hand in an offhand way for me to sit and began to ask me about the baby. I didn't like these places—they had a funny feeling about them—creepy, cold and stark. I told him about the baby contracting meningitis and how the doctors must have got it wrong because he looked just the same as before. But why wasn't he sitting up by now?

The doctor asked me to take off the baby's clothes and lay him on the couch and he then began to examine him, testing his reflexes, going over every inch of him with a fine-tooth comb. He said nothing, but when he was finished he told me I could dress the baby. I was almost finished dressing Jimmy-Paddy and while the doctor was busy writing I asked, 'Well, Dr North, is my baby okay?'

'Take a seat, Mrs Savage,' he said as he peered over his glasses. 'I will be very frank with you. I feel the best thing you can do for both you and your baby is to take him to Muckamore Abbey and forget all about him. These institutions know best how to look after ... uhumm, these kinds of children.'

What ... what did he just say? Did he just tell me to put my child in a home? I couldn't think straight. It was bad enough my friend telling us to pray that our baby would die. But now I was being told to put him in a home and forget about him. What in under God was in people's heads? This was my wee baby they were talking about, my wee child. He was going nowhere except home with me. Clearly they didn't know their arses from their elbows.

My blood ran cold as I looked from the doctor to my tiny bundle, his wee face so perfect, so innocent and so vulnerable. Without finishing dressing him, I wrapped him tight in his rug, tucking him back into my left arm. I then stood bolt upright and, grabbing the heavy wooden doorhandle, looked back towards the doctor.

'Thanks for nothing, you aul bastard!' was all I said.

And the nurse beside him fainted on the spot. I didn't care if they both dropped dead. I vowed from that day on that Jimmy-Paddy would never leave my side.

Our run of enforced celibacy never lasted longer than a few months and before long your three sisters were born. But every time another baby came into the world, I found it more and more difficult to cope with a new baby alongside Jimmy-Paddy who was just like a baby as well.

I hated him having to go into Muckamore Abbey, even if it was only for a week till I was on my feet. Each time I recovered from having my babies, I took the bus to Muckamore Abbey to collect Jimmy-Paddy and bring him home, and my heart broke at the thought of ever having to part with him again.

He had horrific unexplained injuries, which nearly put my head away when I saw them. The first time he came home he'd had half of his wee ear bitten off! The second time he came home with two broken fingers. The last time he ever saw the inside of Muckamore Abbey, he writhed and cried for the next five years, so much so that he had the nickname of wee moneybox mouth, and he had two permanent rivulets down his cheeks from crying morning till night.

Your da was very upset when he saw the state of him when he came back from the home for the handicapped. He tried to hold him to soothe him, but Jimmy-Paddy only cried more. He tried bathing him in a sink full of warm, soapy water to relax his limbs, but that was no good either.

In the end we both decided all we could do was place him on the floor on a soft rug, and let him roll about till he got tired of crying. Your da couldn't stand the distressed cries; he had to do something. He'd heard from somebody at the pub that there was a new treatment being brought out by the Russians, where childer like him would be put through a series of intense physical exercises that could build up the connections in their brains again. There'd even been talk of some childer learning to walk. This was all he needed to hear and within days he found out all he needed to know about the special Russian exercises. If anybody could help Jimmy-Paddy walk it would be him, with his background in physical exercise and his motivation.

The treatment started, and every day we'd take turns placing Jimmy-Paddy on the floor, then moving his limbs over and over again in certain ways to get the nerves in his brain to grow again. The regimen was relentless and he howled and screeched every time we did the exercises till in the end the crying nearly drove me mad and I pleaded with your da to stop—I didn't think it was making a happeth of difference.

Your da was gutted; he would have kept going whatever it took. But he too could see that Jimmy-Paddy hadn't made any improvement and his heart sank to his boots. Even then he couldn't really give up on his boy, so he sat for hours rubbing castor oil into his legs and arms to massage them to keep them from contracting. The last thing he wanted was for his child to end up spastic too.

For me it was like having three sets of twins: the new baby, my other childer and Jimmy-Paddy, whose needs were like that of another baby. The sheer volume of washing was enormous: thirty-six nappies on the line every day. There was no such thing as disposable nappies in those days. I was exhausted and I knew I had to do something or I wouldn't survive. Or worse still, Jimmy-Paddy could be taken off me and put in a home—a home like Muckamore Abbey. I was also worried sick about the rest of you wee childer. What if you were to be taken from me because I had too many babies? Barnardo's homes were full of childer whose mammies and daddies couldn't look after them. Some had just fallen on hard times and I had heard some awful tales about those places.

It was said that sometimes, when the mother or father went back to get the child, they weren't even there—just disappeared off the face of the Earth and there'd been nothing anyone could do to get them back. There was no trace of where the child had been sent. Most of the Barnardo's childer, who you could see being walked to mass each Sunday, looked as if they hadn't eaten for a month; they had big canker sores on their mouths and their faces were painted purple with gentian violet. Poor wee childer, given away to some buck stranger and the tales of cruelty were enough to make your blood run cold.

I made up my mind. There was only one thing I could do to make sure this didn't happen to me or my childer. I had no choice. I had to get sterilised. I told no one outside the house, especially not Father Flanagan. I had to wait ages for the operation because there wasn't a Catholic doctor or nurse who would take part in an operation for sterilisation and preventing the planting of the seed, or they too would be headed for Hell. I knew one thing: if being sterilised meant I could look after my six childer instead of them going into a home, then the God I believed in would surely not send me to Hell.

I was prepped and ready for the operation, but before I went to theatre, I asked if I could see a priest. I explained to him why I wanted to be sterilised and I also told him of my strange recurring dream of Padre Pio telling me I would have one more little boy. I had never been more certain of anything in my whole life. It all made perfect sense now, the meaning of the dream so long ago. I had indeed only had one more little boy, just like Padre Pio had told me I would, and he was always going to need a lot of special care. For me to look after him as God wanted me to, there could be no more babies. I knew in my heart and soul I was doing the right thing.

The priest who came to see me was quite young, with a shock of ginger hair and a kindly face. He couldn't have been any older than me.

'Father, would you give me absolution for what I am about to do?'

When he heard my story, he simply said, 'Mrs Savage, you don't need me to absolve you from anything. You're the most remarkable woman I've ever met.'

My eyes misted over. 'Thank you, Father.'

'Isabelle, let's pray together to keep you safe during your operation.'

And together we prayed. 'Hail Mary, full of grace, the Lord is with thee. Blessed art thou among women and blessed is the fruit of thy womb, Jesus ... '

As I was wheeled into theatre and closed my eyes, I knew there would be no more babies when I woke up. This was one 'sin' I would never have to go to confession for.

Part 2

RATHCOOLE 1960

A GOOD MOVE
Isabelle

As I've said, the shortage of council houses for rent after the war was vast, and it was even worse if you were a Catholic. Couples who couldn't afford to buy a house found it difficult to find a place to rent, and your da and I were no exception.

We longed to have a place of our own, where our names would be on the rent book and where the childer could have a garden to run about. So as soon as we heard of a new estate being built, called 'Rathcoole', we went straight away to put our names down on the list. Our names had been on the housing list for a number of years when we finally got word that we'd been allocated a house in Rathcoole. It wasn't new anymore, it needed attention, but it did have three bedrooms and a garden so we were over the moon.

The new housing estate was built a few miles outside Belfast and what was even more remarkable was that we had heard, on the grapevine, that Catholics and Protestants were living there side by side—something that was almost unheard of. We were delighted to hear this. It didn't bother us one bit living in a mixed area. It was about time; this was the 1960s after all. There would be room for you childer to roam and play and there were Catholic as well as Protestant schools.

So although it was quite a distance from our families and The Falls road, we felt like we had won the pools. While most privately-owned homes didn't even have inside bathrooms, the council houses seemed to have it all—including bathrooms that were inside the house. The council houses also had large gardens and we both said that we would make the garden something to behold. So we moved in with what few possessions we had and set up home.

Daddy often dropped by in his Bedford van to see me and you wee ones, and he always brought a parcel of vegies and some extras he'd got at the market. He knew I was struggling—that I didn't have tuppence to rub together—could see how thin I was, and knew too, that your da was always doing his money in. All this and wee Jimmy-Paddy was still just like a baby. He knew, too, I wasn't happy and deep down inside I know he often blamed himself.

He once told me if he could turn back time, he would.

'Ach, aye, I should never have thrown you out of the bungalow that night after a stupid row about a lousy packet of cigarettes. I should've stopped you going after Harry because you felt sorry for him,' he said. They had found the fecking cigarettes later that night under the table where they'd fallen.

'Oh, aye, it was my fault as much as Maggie's what you are suffering. If I hadn't kicked you out of the farm that night, you'd never have rushed out to get married. Jesus, I'd take it back if I could. It breaks my heart to watch the apple of my eye suffering the way you are.'

I never asked anyone for help. I was so ashamed of having to live that way and I didn't want any of my family to know. I was an excellent house manager. I saved every penny I could. It was almost like watching Jesus himself perform the miracle of the five loaves and two fishes the way I could make a bowl of porridge stretch to feed everyone. I shopped with the co-operative and saved the dividends. And without your da getting haul of the money, I bought you childer your Clarks school shoes. Your wee feet were so important and the way half of you walked inwards, there'd be no second-hand shoes for my childer. As soon as the new Clarks shoes were bought, I took them straight to the almoner's office in the children's hospital, where I could leave them to be 'built up' so that your feet didn't turn in when you walked.

Mrs Granger was one of the Carmeen Drive's well-to-do Protestant neighbours. She lived directly across the street from us and she guessed my plight about your da doing his money in, leaving me without a brown penny. She often spoke to me saying, 'good morning' passing the time of day. She could see I was struggling with four childer, suspecting something was wrong when she saw Jimmy-Paddy in the twin pram and a new baby beside him.

'Poor soul,' Mrs Granger would say. She had rheumatism in her neck that caused her almost constant pain. Even when she wore the collar and a scarf round her neck for support and keeping the cold out, she seemed to feel more sorry for me, especially because I was expecting again. She would wonder what us Catholics were thinking, having so many babies—that we seemed to breed like rabbits! But despite this sentiment, Mrs Granger felt sorry for my troubles as she thought I seemed a decent sort.

She wanted to help me and, as her girls had too many clothes, she wondered if I could use some of them for my childer. She knew it wouldn't be easy, as I seemed like a proud woman; she had to be careful not to offend me. She made up her mind to speak to me the next time our paths crossed and she told me that her girls had outgrown many of their clothes and asked whether I would like to 'buy' some, very cheap of course. This way she'd help me without it looking like charity. With the few coppers that she'd ask for the clothes, she'd buy more wool to knit more cardigans that she'd in turn offer me.

Mrs Granger walked across the road, the brown paper parcel tucked under her oxter so none of the nosey neighbours could see. It was full of jumpers for the childer to try on. It was the best of gear, but I paid for each and every article, no charity, and it felt good. If the jumpers fitted, I paid as much as I could afford. That was the deal.

133

You, Berny, loved to see what the parcels held, carefully tucked under Mrs Granger's cardigan. The knitted jumpers were of no interest to you. You loved the lacy petticoats and fancy knickers she sent. But I always said 'no thank you' to these items. Underwear had to be your own, not second hand. Much to your disgruntlement, they were wrapped back up in the brown paper they came in and sent back, and you were left with the plain cotton underwear that I could afford.

A CHILD'S PLAYGROUND
Isabelle

Life in Rathcoole was great for you childer. You roamed the streets playing rap the door, hopscotch and skipping—the big, heavy rope stretched right across the road with half a dozen childer joining in.

When the dark nights came, the streets became a winter wonderland glittering with ice and snow, the very edges of every leaf on the trees frosted with white, the blanket of snow softening the din of the childer's voices. Aye, I have some great memories of Rathcoole, Berny, … and some not so good … the rest are almost too painful to recall. You loved playing out in the dark nights and playing hide-and-seek. You weren't afraid of the dark at all. You'd look up at the stars trying to see where the Milky Way was. When your da wasn't whistling on the long walks to mass on Sunday nights, he'd be pointing out the stars and you'd try and count them. The dark nights meant Halloween. Everyone dressed up and made lanterns out of turnips. I made lanterns, cutting out triangles for eyes and a crooked mouth with one tooth in its head. It looked really scary when the candle was lit. The middle we ate later, so nothing got wasted.

The right thing to do was to sing a song, which is what we did to make people laugh. The song was the same at each house. 'Halloween's coming on and the goose is getting fat, will you please put a penny in the aul man's hat? If you haven't got a penny, a happney will do, if you haven't got a happney, well God bless you and your aul man too.' Nobody wanted to go home; you childer all wanted to play on the icy paths. Catholic childer made the best slides because your shoes had no grip, making the slides slippery. Up and down the paths you went, sideways, faster and faster till the ice turned clear as glass.

You'd come home freezing, chuffed that your slides were the best that year. Next day you'd wake up, only to find some aul lad had thrown hot ash and cinders from their fire all down the slide, and your magical playground was reduced to a black and grey wasteland. But it didn't stop youse going again as soon as the next frost arrived.

When winter arrived I'd knit you all woollen mittens to keep you warm. The trouble was that they didn't last long in snow before they were wet through, and if that happened, you didn't dare tell me or I would have told you all to come inside.

Snow was the best thing in the whole world. Before it snowed, it got very, very cold and very quiet. You could smell snow in the air before it came. I'd know when this was going to happen and would tell you all to get your coats ready because this meant you could make snowmen and have snowball fights outside.

Sometimes when it started to snow at night, I'd get you out of bed, just to look out of the bedroom window and see the flakes floating from the night sky, soft and gentle, making their way to the ground, slowly covering our street, filling it in like a giant colouring book.

I'd tell you childer it was God's gift to you. I loved it because it made the earth look so peaceful, clean and new. This was exactly how the snow looked in the book you were reading, Berny, called *Narnia*. The word meant 'magic' and I know you wanted magic to happen to us too. You asked me if magic was real, and I remember telling you it would only happen if you believe it. 'Do you believe magic is real, Berny?'

'Oh yes, I believe it with my whole heart.'

I remember one year, Berny, in Rathcoole the snow didn't stop. It snowed every day and every night for almost three weeks. Higher and higher it got till you couldn't even get the front door open without it falling into the house. Every day, your da shovelled the snow away from the path, only to find a couple of hours later it was just as high again.

One morning when we all woke up, the snow was right up to the top of the house window and I said, 'Jesus, Mary and Joseph, when it rains it pours!' This time nobody was happy about it. We couldn't even go outside in case we fell in the snow and couldn't be found.

The pipes in the house froze, so water wouldn't come out of the taps. I filled the teapot with snow and melted it to make the tea. You could hardly get to the coal shed to get the coal for the fire. The milkman couldn't deliver the milk; the baker couldn't deliver any bread. The Co-operative van didn't come on Thursday with the rations for the street. Your da couldn't go to work because the buses had stopped running. I couldn't get to the shops to do the messages, which meant we had to eat porridge three times a day instead of twice, and not even my stories about strong Scottish soldiers marching their way to victory could make it any better.

And you all couldn't go to school; the noise and narration with Jimmy-Paddy crying drove me nuts because I couldn't even get out for a walk with youse. For me, being hemmed in is the worst feeling in the world. It makes me feel trapped and suffocated or something.

This time even I wasn't happy about so much snow. Your da said it was a fucking nuisance, even though I had told him not to say bad words in front of you childer. Not only did it mean he couldn't get to work, but he couldn't get to the bookies either.

I said, 'Snow or no snow, it wouldn't make a happeth of difference to me as either way, it meant there'd be no money coming in.'

I was also starting to get very worried because Jimmy-Paddy had a bad cough, and if I needed a doctor for him, we wouldn't be able to get to the phone box down the street, never mind get a doctor to the house.

Just as wee Jimmy-Paddy's cough got worse, the rain started and the snow started to melt, so the doctor was able to come after all. Good job he did because the poor wee crater might have died in my arms. The doctor told me he was a hare's whisker away from pneumonia.

THE GLORIOUS TWELFTH OF JULY
Isabelle

The glorious twelfth of July signalled the season to celebrate. It was summer time and everyone seemed happier. The nasturtiums, sweet peas and geraniums were a kaleidoscope of colour, creeping over walls and across borders in gardens everywhere. Everyone was so proud of their displays of colour. Neighbours would pass by each other's houses calling out, 'Nice show, missus, where'd ye get your seeds?' Windows were wide open as were people's doors. No one locked their houses—there was just no need.

Bands practised and donned their bright, beautiful uniforms. Banners were unfurled and held aloft, proud and strong. Pipers marched and big base drums boomed out the beat of the victory songs. The leader always twirled the silver mace that shone like something from Heaven itself. Bunting with the Union Jack of England was proudly strung from house to house. Neighbours baked for days, and trestle tables were adorned with all manner of sweets and savoury delights. Even the kerbstones in the street were painted red, white and blue. You childer gathered any aul rubbish and broken furniture youse could find to build the biggest and best bonfire. Collections for the 'boney' went on for weeks. Higher and higher it was built until we thought it would reach the sky.

There were fireworks, bangers, Catherine wheels and rockets. Lots of people joined hands to dance round the boney once it was lit. Childer got begs of sweets; it was better than Christmas, it was so exciting. This show of grandeur, pomp and ceremony was held every year to celebrate the Battle of the Boyne, a triumph of King William of Orange over the Catholics. 'In the year of our lord,' the song started, and was a yearly reminder that it was better to be a Protestant, a superior person, someone with wealth, money and prestige.

I can't remember exactly how old you were when you realised the street party wasn't for us. I think it dawned on you slowly when you asked me why the dummy, which was being burned on top of the boney, had a Bishop's mitre on its head. I told you it was supposed to be the Pope, the person who we prayed for at mass every week. There was no party for the Catholics. We didn't have bands and fine things to decorate the street, and we didn't have a big battle to shout about. We just watched, pulled our childer off the street earlier, and went to bed.

When the parties of the glorious twelfth of July were over, the street returned to normal as if nothing had happened and everyone were friends again. Well … until the day your da got that terrible hiding and we were put out of Rathcoole.

A PROTESTANT STATE FOR A PROTESTANT PEOPLE
Isabelle

Your da never shied away from work. If he lifted a shovel and started digging, it would take a wild man on a galloping horse a week to catch up with him. Where he came from everybody worked hard to earn a crust, and they pulled together when times were tough. Hard work was something to be proud of, and there would be nothing worse than anybody calling you 'work shy' or a 'skiver'.

The women from the streets where he came from were no different to the men. The very concrete steps of each and every house in Sheriff Street would be scrubbed and bleached until they were white as the driven snow. Every windowsill would be painted in the spring and washed weekly, and doorknobs were polished till they gleamed. They were proud people in Sheriff Street and the doors round about. Nobody went hungry because even if ye had nothing, a wee parcel would appear at your door, and you'd never know where it had come from. The glue that bound them in the streets was so strong you could nearly smell it. That's what kind of people they were despite what my daddy said about 'them from the docks area'.

There was only one worm in Sheriff Street and that was the fecker who doled out the money when there was none to be had; Carol Ferguson, the pawn broker. Aye, and that came at a high price. She not only wanted back what she loaned you, but almost twice as much again. And if ye waited a bit too long to go back to buy your gear, your granny's rings would be gone never to be seen again. How in under God any woman could fleece ye like that was a mystery. But none the less it didn't stop the desperate making their way there many a time.

Your da's mother Connie used to say that Carol Ferguson was one dirty louser, preying on the needy, and that she'd never have a day's luck, and funny enough, she was never able to keep a man. Some said she was cursed because she went through three husbands, losing every one to ailments of the damp, and her son ran away with another man, never to be seen again on the streets of Belfast. There were few scourges worse than being a 'fenian bastard' and one of them was being 'queer'. Oh, indeed that was something nobody wanted on either side. It was a well-known fact that there were no queers in Belfast.

There was no excuse to be dirty—soap and water cost a pittance. There was no way Connie would be called 'through other'; she'd die first before she gave that fecker Ferguson a brown penny. She could stick her three golden balls outside her lousy shop up her arse, as far as Connie was concerned. But despite your da's brains and ability, as well as his ingrained work ethic, he often couldn't get a job. Not because there weren't any jobs, but because of what school he went to.

Yeah, I thought it was odd too the first time I heard it. Why on Earth would the school you went to make any difference to what job you got? You see Savage was definitely a Protestant name, inherited when his mother Connie married Billy Savage, a Protestant of Scottish ancestry—a 'mixed marriage' as they called it. As good a difference then, than if one person's skin was white as snow and the other's as black as coal.

It was frowned upon in every circle, rich or poor. The differences were too big to overcome, so ye stuck to your own kind. For those souls brave enough to cross the line, life was troublesome. If it wasn't one lot that tortured you, it was the other. A constant tug of war it was for your heart and soul, and it didn't matter either way because you were headed for the fiery furnace. Being staunch was worn like a badge of honour by both sides. Tolerance didn't come into it.

Your granda Billy was no pushover. Being raised in the docks area of east Belfast, he learnt quickly how to stick up for himself. Known as a hard man, he drank the best under the table and gave many a big mouth a good digging if they started on him about Connie not being of his own kind. That he was killed stone dead in a pub brawl leaving Connie with four wee chider, it's no wonder both sides agreed—no good came of mixed marriages.

The distance between Catholics and Prods was even immortalised in a verse that we all knew. Though, who wrote it, we know not.

The Papisher and the Prod

I was born and reared on Sandy Row, a loyal Orange Prod;
I stood for good King William, that noble man of God!
My motto — No Surrender! My flag — The Union Jack!
And every Twelfth, I proudly march to Finaghy, and back.

A loyal son of Ulster, a true blue, that was me,
Prepared to fight, prepared to die for faith and liberty.
As well as that, a Linfield man as long as I could mind,
And I had no time for Catholics, or any of that kind.

And then one night in Bangor I met wee Rosie Green.
The minute I laid eyes on her, I knew she was my queen;

And when I saw she fancied me, my mind was all a-buzz,
And I clean forgot to ask her what her religion was.

Next time we met I told her, 'I'm a Proddie, staunch and true!'
And she said, 'I'm a Catholic, and just as staunch as you'.
The words were harsh and bitter, but suddenly like this:
Centuries of hatred were forgotten with a kiss.

I knew our love would bring us only trouble and distress.
But nothing in this world would make me love wee Rosie less.
I saved a bit of money, as quickly as I could,
And asked her if she'd marry me — and God, she said she would.

Then the troubles REALLY started! Her folks went ravin' mad,
And then, when mine heard the news, they were twice as bad.
My father said from that day on, he'd hang his head in shame;
And by a strange coincidence, HER father said the same!

My mother cried her eyes out and said I'd rue the day
That I let a Papish hussy steal my loyal heart away.
And Rosie's mother said, when she'd recovered from the blow,
That she'd rather see the devil than a man from Sandy Row!

We were married in a Papish church, the other side of town,
That's how Rosie wanted it and I couldn't let her down.
But the priest was very nice to me and made me feel at home —
I think he pitied both of us — our families didn't come.

The rooms we went to live in had nothin' but the walls,
It was far away from Sandy Row and further from the Falls.
But that's the way we wanted it, for both of us knew well
That back among the crowd we knew our lives would be living hell.

But life out there for Rosie was so lonely, of this I so well knew,
And, of course, we also had our religious differences too:
At dinner time on Friday, when Rosie gave me fish,
I looked at it and then at her, and said, 'thon's not my dish'.

I mind well what she said to me — you've got to pay the price,
'And to eat no meat on Friday is a sacrifice
To make for Christ who died for us one Friday long ago'.
Anyway, I ate the fish — and it wasn't bad, you know.

Then Sunday came and I lay on when she got up at eight.
But Rosie turned to me and said, 'Get up or you'll be late.
You've got a church to go to and there's where you should be,
So up you get this minute — you'll be part o' the road with me.'

We left the house together, but we parted down the line,
And she went off to her church and I went off to mine.
But all throughout the service, although we were apart,
I felt we prayed together, united heart to heart.

The weeks and months went quickly by and then there came the day
When Rosie upped and told me that a child was on the way.

We both went down on our knees that day and asked the Lord above
To give our child two special things alone — tolerance and love.

We wrote and told our families — they never used to call
And we thought the news might soften them, and so it did and all.
My mother, and then Rosie's, said they'd visit us in turn,
And we marvelled at the power of a wee child not yet born.

But we were quickly disillusioned when we found out why they came;
It wasn't to be friendly or to make up with us again.
Rosie's mother came to say the child must be R.C.
And mine said it would have to be a Protestant like me.

The rows before the wedding were infinitely mild
Compared with all the rumpus that was raised about the child.
From both sides of the family, insults and threats were hurled.
Oh, what a way to welcome a wee angel to the world!

The child must be Catholic! The child must be a Prod!
But the last and loudest voice I heard was the mighty voice of God.
And to his awful wisdom I had to bow my head —
Just one hour after he was born, our poor wee child was dead.

That night I sat by Rosie's side and just before the dawn
I kissed her as she left me to join our angel son.
And my loyal heart was broken within thon lonely walls —
Where the hell's Shankhill? Where the hell's The Falls?

But that was many years ago, long years o' grief and pain
When I'd have given all I had to see Rosie's face again.
But my loneliness is waning now; I'll see her soon I know;
The doctor told me yesterday I haven't long to go.

And when I go up thonder they'll let me in, I hope,
But if they ask me who I'm for, King Billy or the Pope?
I'm goin' to take no chances — I'll tell them straight and fair,
I'm a Loyal Ulster Protestant — who loved a Papisher.

And one way or another, I know they'll let me through,
And Rosie will be waitin' there, and our little angel too.
Then the child will lead the two of us, the Papisher and the Prod,
Up the steps together — into the arms of God.

Your da had the right name for a job, but they always asked what school you went to. Once you put St Matthews, Star of the Sea or Christian Brothers, they knew you were a fenian bastard, saying nothing more than, 'I'm sorry, Mr Savage, I'm afraid all applications have been filled.' You couldn't even prove the bigotry was real. It was enough to put your head away and keep you where ye belonged, with no hope of climbing out of the pit you were in.

It was no accident that Catholics weren't employed in positions of politics, power, gas, water or electricity. Those jobs were for Prods only. Anger and resentment was building everywhere, ready to explode. It wasn't right or fair. Catholics didn't even have the right to 'one man, one vote'. We knew in elections there was no chance we'd be fairly represented.

Unfortunately, this just added fuel to the runaway train of your da's low self-worth and made him more determined to 'win' his way out of his shit life and become a 'somebody'. He knew he was smarter than half the fecking eejits who walked into jobs. But the more he gambled to win the big one, the poorer we became and the sadder I got, keeping my distance from him when he was stocious.

Oh your da was great fun when he'd had a few. He wanted everyone to party with him. One night he cajoled a full Irish band into coming to our house. Drums and music blasted out the windows to the whole street that was full of Prods who wouldn't want to hear fenian music.

Times like that, he tortured me to play the piano and reluctantly I would, just to stop any trouble. I became less interested in playing and made plans to get rid of it as soon as I could. That way it would be one less thing I had to worry about. When your da decided the party was over, he kicked the whole shebang out in the street, instruments and all, to make their own way home in the middle of the night. Then he started on me.

Berny, you would remember this well. You would cover your ears trying to drown out the rows and screaming. Some nights, you knew I had to run. You would hear our voices getting louder and you knew to get my coat and purse ready at the bottom of your bed so I could escape through the back bedroom window. You were always terrified I wouldn't come back and tried to climb out the window with me.

You'd say, 'Mammy, take me too. I don't want to stay here. What if Daddy comes in here? What'll we do? He might hit us too, Mammy. Don't go.' But I promised your da wouldn't hurt you; that it was just me he was after and that I'd be home in the morning when he was sober. I couldn't risk another black eye. I don't know how many times you got my coat and purse ready and prayed for me to come back quick. Sometimes I didn't go anywhere—just into the coal shed where I'd sleep on the coal sacks. Ah Jesus, Berny, I'm so sorry love. No wee child should have gone through that. It wasn't what I wanted for my family. Somehow it was true, though, that he wasn't mad with youse. I think now that he never could forgive me for loving somebody else, no matter how many boxes of Black Magic chocolates he bought when he was drunk. He knew I loved Jack Kennedy and there was nothing he could do to change that, and when he couldn't win the big one and get rich, he got drunk and mad. It's something I have no control over. Jack is in my soul. I often sit and wonder where he is and what he's doing, if he's married, happy ... I hope he is. I wonder if he ever gives me a second thought. I wouldn't blame him if he didn't. He still thinks I did the dirty on him and never waited. If only he knew the truth, eh? But it's too late. It's that, more than anything else, that breaks my heart.

I'm not sure how exactly, but your da landed a job at ICI (Imperial Chemical Industries). Somebody clearly hadn't done the usual school checks. We went to the firm's Christmas party; it was the best party we'd ever been to. He insisted youse were all dolled up in your Sunday best. We'd never seen that much food in our whole lives.

Now as I've said before, your da was very good at mental arithmetic, which helped him calculate the odds at the bookies. As he settled into his new job at ICI, he got to know about an employee scheme that could earn him quite a bit of money—enough to become rich beyond our wildest dreams. I never took it underneath my notice really as I thought it was just another of his 'get rich quick' schemes, a bit like the penny coins he made us all collect, driving us mad looking at all the dates from morning till night.

There was an employee suggestion box at the company and if any suggestions were found innovative and implemented into the processing at the plant, the worker whose idea had been used would be given a certificate stating it was his property. Depending on how big the innovation was, the money paid to the employee would rise accordingly. At the end of the year, when the company knew if they had profited, a lump sum of money would be paid to the worker on presentation of the certificate.

Now your da, as wily as he was, cottoned on to this very quickly and for the next few months drove me crazy with all the designs and plans that he drew, to make the chemical processing more efficient at ICI. Week after week he brought home 'suggestion certificates' proudly displaying his name and before long he had a big brown envelope full of them.

He told me all our money troubles were over and that by Christmas we'd have more money than the Vatican. He was ecstatic and I couldn't believe it. Was this the end of all my worries about money? The certificates were worth a fortune. They were kept in a brown box, beside the fireplace in the front room, and nobody went near them. Or so I thought, Miss B-E-R-N-Y.

I don't know whether to laugh or cry. I remember it like it was yesterday. When nobody was looking you'd sneak into the cupboard. You wanted to see what was going to make us rich. What did 'rich' look like and feel like? You thought that at last we were going to look and feel like Protestants. We'd have fancy curtains at our windows and go on holidays to Blackpool and Butlins. You'd get the pink plastic Cinderella slippers you'd always dreamed of having at Christmas, instead of a school beg. You'd hold the certificates in your hands when nobody was about, turning them over, and before anyone came back, you'd carefully put them back exactly where they were and dream of being rich. Your da was doing a late shift at ICI and I was at the shops. There was a knock at the door. You opened it to a big man wearing an overcoat and a trilby hat. He asked you, 'Is your daddy in?' You explained that your da was at work and he'd be back about nine o'clock.

The man seemed uneasy, shifting from one foot to another, and then suddenly he bent down, rubbed his chin and smiled.

'Listen, love, your daddy has something that belongs to me and I'm here to pick it up. It's a package of big brown envelopes, about twenty of them, and they have "ICI" stamped on them. Would you know where they are?' Immediately you knew what he meant, and where the envelopes were.

'Oh yes, I'll get them for you,' you replied.

'Good girl,' he said as he let out a deep sigh. Off you skipped to get them and handed them over.

'Is this what you're looking for, Mister?' As he checked the contents his eyes lit up like the boney on the twelfth of July.

'Oh, yes ... indeed it is ... these are mine.' He then hot footed it down the path and was gone.

When I returned from the shops you explained what had happened and my face turned ashen white. I put the baby down, grabbed you by the shoulders, and with hardly any breath I said, 'What did you do? Please tell me you didn't give them to him? Jesus, Mary and holy Saint Joseph, please no, don't say you handed all your da's suggestions out the door to a buck stranger? Your da'll kill you when he gets in! Jesus, Mary and Joseph, the money, our fortune, gone out the door. There'll be open murder!'

You started to cry and said, 'The man said they belonged to him. He said they were his.'

'In under God, I just leave the house for an hour and this happens. What am I going to do? Harry will be crazy,' I responded.

By this time I was beyond mad and scared to death. 'We'll have to hide you; I'll take you to Mrs Granger's over the road before he gets in. Maybe we can somehow get them back. This will be the longest day you ever live, wee girl. Never ever open that door again to a buck stranger. Do ye hear me?'

'I won't, Mammy,' you replied.

I remember, your biggest fear was that you were going to Barnardo's, the home for bold girls, and that you'd never see me again.

You weren't at the house when your da got in from ICI that night and it turned out the man was right. The suggestions did belong to him. It seemed your da had wagered the whole lot in a card game at the factory, losing everything. The man had come to collect his winnings that your da had been hanging on to, to see if he could somehow raise the money to pay his debts without giving our fortune away. Isn't that right, Berny? But it was a long time before you found out the real reason why you didn't get a good hiding that night or why you weren't sent to Barnardo's. All you knew was that we weren't going to be rich, we'd never go to Blackpool or Butlins or live like a rich Protestant, and you thought somehow it was entirely your fault. Jesus, Mary and Joseph, Berny. That's one day I wouldn't like to relive in hurry. I thought your da was going to have a stroke when I told him what happened. Of course he knew he was in the wrong, hanging on to them certificates. He should have paid his debt, the greedy fucker. That's why you didn't get a good hiding; you were saved by the skin of yer teeth.

151

CHURCH-GOING PEOPLE
Isabelle

Life was either work or church for your da and me; we were true believers in our faith. We had been raised to believe every word that was preached at mass and school. We believed in Heaven and Hell and in mortal and venial sin. Of course, we were both indoctrinated by the biggest sword possible—Catholic guilt. It would have put yer head away.

Priests were regarded as heavenly beings, and nuns not far behind them. They were seen as the guides of your mortal life and eternal soul—making decisions for yourself wasn't on the agenda. We were taught to believe that when something couldn't be logically explained, like the virgin birth, that it too was a mystery of faith and more holy than that which was plausible.

You weren't encouraged to ask questions about your faith. Having faith itself was seen as a quality of miraculous proportions. The doctrine of the Catholic Church was seen as more important than the written word of God, whereas Protestants put more emphasis on *The Bible*. So basically you were kept in line by your faith, and didn't step out of it on peril of your life and yer soul being lost for eternity.

This was the same for people rich or poor, which is why even doctors and nurses were afraid to step out of line. But somehow the poor did it tougher because we were the ones who kept making babies, even if there wasn't enough money to feed and clothe them. We too paid our tithe to the church no matter how little money we had.

So it was a sin to do almost everything including being born. Born with original sin, the sin of Adam and Eve stamped on your soul, was a great start to life. Along with being born a sinner and being riddled with guilt, you then spent the rest of your life trying to repent for it, just to make it to the pearly gates, unless you stepped out of line along the way. It was a lifelong spiritual game of Snakes and Ladders, with Satan waiting at every turn if you slipped up, ready to take you to Hell.

One of the biggest sins was having sex before marriage. 'Sex' was a dirty word, never talked about, unless it was in the context of making babies—even then it was called 'marital relations'. To have sex before marriage was a mortal, as well as moral, sin. Only loose women, dirty mares, whores, the gullible and easily led, and Prods would put their souls at risk, by committing this sin.

It was said by some that Prods had loose ways, due to the fact that they knew where to get French letters, and were known to be doing it from morning till night. Good Catholic girls had to be pure when they got married—untouched like the blessed virgin. Some poor souls ended up in institutions for the handicapped or insane for the rest of their lives; their only crime consisting of having a bastard baby.

It was odd, though, that from time to time some Catholic girls, like Mariead Dooley down the street as well as Di Fitzgerald who worked alongside me in the Belfast Swiss, would suddenly go to work in England or go to look after a sick aunty in the country, only to come back again nine months later and carry on as if they had never been away at all.

Nobody was game to question it, talk about it, or change it. To be an unmarried mother in those days was to bring incredible shame on yourself and your family. It was no surprise then that there were no shortage of babies at children's homes, orphanages and convents ready for adoption. You know, Berny, most of the time it was the poor girls who copped the burden of it all. They bore the brunt of the ridicule and shame. They were the ones sent off somewhere to have the babies, and they endured the heartbreak of having to give them away, even when it wasn't what they wanted to do. Imagine the emotional torture. It was enough to put yer head away. It would be years and years before the crusty, humiliating, demoralising bullshit would begin to change. Aye, the aul thumpadonian reprobates who kept us all in those moral chains have a lot to answer for alright, God forgive them.

We prayed lots—morning, noon and night—trying to keep our souls safe.

'Now I lay me down to sleep, I pray the Lord my soul to keep. Matthew, Mark, Luke and John, God bless this bed that I lie on. If I die before I wake, I pray the lord my soul to take. Jesus, Mary and Joseph, I give you my heart and soul. Jesus, Mary and Joseph, assist me now and in my last agony. Jesus, Mary and Joseph, may I breathe forth my soul in peace with you, Amen.'

We made the sign of the cross with holy water before we left the house.

'In the name of the Father, and of the Son, and of the Holy Ghost, Amen.'

I waited for the angelus to ring out at lunchtime. I went to benediction if I could make it and said the *Rosary* at night.

Confession and mass was once a week for everyone except for you, Berny, who had to go to mass twice on Sundays due to the fact that you spent more time fainting from hunger and from the smell of incense, and so missed a lot of the blessings you should have had. Your da wouldn't walk to mass on his own at night in case the wild dogs in Rathcoole ate the arse off him.

You were never sure why your da thought it would make a difference, you going with him. You thought the dogs would have eaten you too. I guess he thought there would be safety in numbers. Besides, you were the only one who could keep up with his fast stride.

'It never did you any harm, Berny. Sunday mass was compulsory for everyone. Only the sick or mad were excused because you couldn't have anybody who was a nutter disrupting the mass, or anybody sick vomiting on the nice, clean carpet you knelt on in the highly-polished pews. Now yer da and I had a problem; Jimmy-Paddy was such a handful, it was impossible for us to go to mass at the same time. So I took all the children except Jimmy-Paddy to mass on Sunday morning, and in the evening your da would go while I stayed at home. Do you remember?'

Sunday morning mass was a grand affair with your best second-hand clothes from Mrs Granger on, shoes polished and your hat on. It was also a sin not to have your head covered in a Catholic Church. Ladies like me didn't wear a hat. We wore a small lace triangle, called a mantilla, which clipped onto your hair. You couldn't wait to be old enough to wear a mantilla, not only because your hat made your head itchy and reminded you of walkers, but you loved anything made of lace. I was so proud of the way you childer turned out, and done on a sixpence too.

The walk to church took about an hour, if you remember. Now you liked the music and all that, but standing, sitting and kneeling for an hour, listening to Latin you couldn't understand and without any breakfast (because that too was a sin, to eat before you received the body of Christ) left you feeling faint. You used to last about halfway through until you smelt the incense, which went straight to your head, and you'd keel over like a dead duck.

When we left the church and got into the fresh air, your colour came back. Another hour later we were back home to get our dinner of soup and floury potatoes with some beef if we were lucky.

Sunday afternoons I allowed youse to play. And then it was your da's turn to go to mass and I'd call you in to go with him. 'Get yourself ready and go with yer da. He likes the company. You've got the best legs for walking. The wee ones are too small and ye can tell yer da all about the dancing. Make sure yer coat's clean and yer shoes polished. Ye know what yer da's like, and another good walk never killed anyone.'

You later told me there was one benefit to going to mass with your da at night. He never waited till the end, God forgive him, setting a bad example like that. He gave you the nudge and you scarpered before the priest gave out the Holy Communion. He always said, 'Don't tell yer ma we left early,' the crafty bugger.

'Ma, why were we all just a couple of weeks old when we were baptised? What was the rush?' you asked me one day. Babies were always baptised as soon as they could be. Usually two to three weeks after they were born because babies born with original sin on their soul, who died before they could be baptised, would spend eternity in limbo. This meant neither in Heaven or Hell and that was something all mothers dreaded—babies not being able to enter the gates of Heaven—before they had the chance to be cleansed of the sin of being born. You also asked one day, 'If we really were the chosen people, and said all the prayers and did all that repenting in the eyes of God, then why were we so poor? And why do the Prods in our street have such lovely lives, with nice lace curtains at their windows and good clothes to wear? They even had marching bands all to themselves, and holidays and cars.'

'Aye, Berny, that should have been us too. There's no excuse for your da's gambling, keeping his own wee family destitute. Everytime I think about it, I could run a knife clean through him. Thank God, I threw them all in the bin,' I'd reply.

'Ah, Ma, would you really have done it?'

'That's the thing, Berny: push a human being beyond endurance and they can just fecking snap. I couldn't take the chance.'

When you were a wee girl you used to wonder about stuff like that too. And you often wondered what the inside of the Proddy churches looked like. You wondered if they had statues of Our Blessed Lady with her sad face, white gown and blue sash dropping down to her feet, where she stood on a red rose. You wondered too if they had the Stations of the Cross and if the Proddy childer cried with their mammies when they felt the suffering of Jesus on the cross at Calvary.

'Do they have a crib at Christmas with the baby Jesus in it? And three wise men bring gifts of gold, frankincense and myrrh to a Protestant baby Jesus?' you'd ask.

You also wondered how come it was okay for Prods to have a Christmas tree in their church when our priest told us it was nothing but a sign of the heathens they were, bringing down the sanctity of the church and bringing pagan falsities into God's holy house.

NEVER CROSS A GYPSY
Isabelle

There were lots of different people who used to call round the doors in Rathcoole; some were travelling salesmen selling their wares from a suitcase, like shoelaces, polish, needles and threads. Others sold bread and rations, and there were even 'rag-and-bone men', who drove their horse and cart along the streets calling out, 'A-N-Y AUL R-E-G and B-O-Nesssss?' The rag-and-bone men didn't talk like us and I told you they were gypsy men, just out doing a hard day's work. They'd pick up any aul furniture and washing machines, even if they were broken, and aul clothes for rags if you had any. But they were particularly interested in any aul copper you might have laying about the house, and if they couldn't beg it, they'd steal it off yer roof because it was worth a fortune.

Every time they came round the streets, they'd have something to give you back if you had anything for them. Needless to say, we never had anything to give them like the Prods in the street did who were always throwing things out; it nearly put my head away looking at all the waste. They'd even throw out aul prams, not a thing the matter with them except a spoke or two missing in a wheel. In return their childer got something nice, like free balloons. I wished I had something to give them for youse, but the stuff we had was worse than what the Prods threw out.

It broke my bloody heart them all prancing about with balloons and youse not.

Other people weren't so welcome—the gypsy women. Most people were afraid that if they didn't give them something, they'd be cursed. This was always a problem and sometimes people would hide out in the back and pretend they weren't in, just so they didn't have to talk to them. It's fair to say that I was pretty in tune with the psychic elements of the world. I believe in powers that can't be seen, and I especially believed in a gypsy's ability to curse you if you ever wronged her. Gypos, as they were called, roamed the streets selling haberdashery and bunches of heather for good luck.

One day a gypsy lady appeared in our front yard asking for 'Mama Lady'. They always followed their sentences with 'Lady' or 'Mister'. You, Berny, ran in like a scalded cat to tell me she was coming up the front path. Jesus, I wondered what I was going to do because I knew I didn't have a brass razoo to buy lace or heather due to your da doing his money in.

The gypsy carried a large suitcase full of combs, lace and bundles of heather, and as soon as she saw me at the front door, she began to talk quickly, running her hand over the suitcase of trinkets and treasures. The case was full and heavy to carry, and the gypsy looked rattled. It was a hot day and from the look of the suitcase, she hadn't sold much. I listened patiently to her as she ran her hands through her thick, coarse, grey hair and I began to feel sorry for her. I wasn't sure how old she was, but from the grey of her hair I gathered she must be near seventy. Her hands were gnarled and if she'd had a pointy hat and broomstick she'd have looked like a witch at Halloween!

The gypsy scanned me from head to toe. She must've understood from the look of you childer that we didn't have much of the world's goods. I was very respectful and explained that unfortunately I couldn't buy anything, but since she looked hot and tired, I asked if she'd like to come in and have a cup of tea. I didn't usually ask strangers into our house, but the gypsy must have recognised my kindness because she put the suitcase down on the step and came in. To be honest I was shitting myself; the last fecking thing I needed was for us to be cursed on top of everything else!

159

I couldn't take my eyes off the curious stranger; her clothes were different from what we wore, even if our clothes did come from social services. Her skirt was very long and she wore sandals with coloured beads on them. I made her a cup of tea and offered her some porridge with stewed apple in it. She silently scanned our living room and saw Jimmy-Paddy in his wheelchair and you childer playing about while she slurped her tea. She didn't have the porridge. I didn't blame her; I was sick of eating it too. I wished the gypsy all the best and hoped she'd be lucky with selling her wares to the wealthy Prods down the road. The gypsy nodded her head as she tipped a drop of the tea into the saucer, while still looking at all of us. She then told me she must go. Before she left, she touched Jimmy-Paddy's head and made a sign of the cross, which told me she was blessing him. As she stepped over the suitcase at the front door, she stopped, opened the suitcase and picked out a bunch of heather and handed it to me saying, 'Good luck, lady, good luck', and then she was gone.

You couldn't wait to ask why I'd brought the gypsy into our house.

'Never cross a gypsy,' I said. They have special powers that can bless or curse you. You should always cross their palms with silver for luck, but if you don't have any silver, it's okay to give them something to show you're not stingy or mean. You can show them the 'silver of kindness', which is a gift you can't buy.

It's the act of 'giving' the gypsy wants to see, not how much lace you could buy, because if you buy from a gypsy with a bad heart, as in not wanting to really give anything, then they'll curse you anyway because gypsies can read your soul. And besides, I said, 'I couldn't afford to bring any more bad luck round us. I already had enough with yer da doing his money and leaving me without a brown penny.'

'Now,' I said when we went back inside the house, 'just check if anything's missing.'

'Why, Mammy?'

'Because gypos can also be thieves!'

GETTING THE RATIONS
Isabelle

Gerry was the only one of youse to be issued with a rations book. But it was never used because the government stopped it just after he was born. It was 1956 and supplies of food and all kinds of commodities were now easy to get. Everyone was getting used to shops having full shelves and times were becoming easier, that is, if you didn't have a husband who was always doing his money in trying to get rich.

Not many people had a car, so getting the rations was still hard because you could only get what would fit under the baby's pram or what you could carry in yer arms. I thanked God for the milkman and his wee book. Everyday milk was delivered to my doorstep icy cold because the milkman always came early, winter or summer, rain or shine. The glass bottles were placed on the front step, closed at the top with shiny silver foil tops, which were embossed with writing, and at Christmas time, the milk bottle had green Christmas trees or robins on the foil so you always knew what time of year it was. The milk had thick cream at the top, and if you weren't quick enough bringing your milk in, the birds would steal the cream. I never worried about it; they only stole the cream when the ground was too hard for them to dig for worms. They too were God's little creatures.

Sometimes in winter when it snowed, the milk would have little piles of snow on top of the lids and be frozen solid. I'd have to boil a pan of water on the stove and stand the milk bottle in the hot water to defrost it before you all could have your porridge. The milkman was always kind to me. Even when I didn't have enough money to pay him, he left the milk anyway.

The baker's van came round too, stopping every few houses. The other mothers and I would make a line behind the baker's van and wait to be served. The baker's van was lined with shelves and loaded to the top with bread, like wheaten farls, barnbrack and soda bread, and cakes and scones too. Every Saturday the order was the same: 'four pan and two plain loaves please.' I wished that just once I could get the cakes that everyone else got. I cursed yer Da, seeing the disappointed look on yer wee faces every week when I came back out of the baker's van with the same thing, week in and week out.

Each night when youse got ready for bed, you'd ask me if you could get your 'bed piece'. You told me, Berny, that this was the best bread of the day because you got a whole piece of bread to yourself. And it was slathered with butter and jam so that you didn't go to bed hungry, as it was too hard to go to sleep if your stomach was empty. Youse always wanted your bed piece made of the plain bread that lasted longer. Jesus, Berny, it broke my fecking heart that it was all I had to give youse, and youse never complained once, God love youse.

The Co-op van came round on Thursdays. I was glad to see them not only for the rations, but also because I could save the dividends. This was how I bought all your shoes. Very rarely there'd be enough money to buy a packet of Rowntrees Fruit Gums between you all. It felt so mingy handing one packet out for youse all to share while all the other childer in the street could get a packet each. I saw some of the aul ladies getting a good skeg, looking down their noses at me as if to say, 'Is that all you can get, missus—a bag of spuds, a tin of green peas and a box of porridge oats again?' I wanted to push them down the back steps of the fecking van, and

I cursed your da again for putting me in that position in the first place when there was no need.

The butcher didn't come round the streets to sell meat. He had a proper shop down at the 'Diamond'. The butcher was miles away and I used to send you to get the meat I needed for dinner. We had a bike, a three-wheeler, which you all shared. It was saved from the boney on the glorious twelfth of July, and so, instead of helping to 'burn the pope', it did you childer nicely to play on and to go to the butchers. But the bike had no chain so you couldn't ride it like a real bike. Instead you had to run alongside it, then jump on the seat as fast as you could while it was going fast, until it slowed down and stopped, and when you got tired of running alongside it, you could use it like a scooter, standing on one pedal, using your other leg to push it till you got tired of that too.

I'd tell you to get the bike ready and go to the butchers for me, and you didn't mind because Carmeen Drive was on a hill and you could get a good sail down the hill to the end of the street before you had to do the running thing past the blue painted Protestant Church, through the alleyway, across the fields and towards the Diamond.

Minced steak was all I could afford, but when I counted the change I looked at you.

'Was this all the change ye got?' I asked. Nodding yer head as quick as you could to say yes, I let out a big sigh.

'The dirty lousy dog! The robbing get! He'll never have a day's luck. What was anyone supposed to do, prices going up and down like that?'

And again I cursed your da for leaving me so short that all I could afford was half a pound of mince to go round us all.

BURNT HAIR AND GETTING THE CANE
Berny

Now it was bad enough being born stupid with two left feet and eyes that couldn't see past the end of my arm, as well as wishing I was a rich Protestant, but I also had to contend with 'skinny hair'. I was as bald as a badger until the age of eighteen months when finally some hair did start to grow. When it did, it was fine and flyaway, as wispy as the fine, fluffy head of a dandelion ball with the bits blowing away on a windy day. Regularly I'd ask you to check my hair, especially if our Grainne had been playing with Susan Craig, who was always lousey, and you'd say, 'If you had walkers I'd be able to spot them from the end of the street, that hair is so fine.'

It didn't matter; I sat on the stool anyway and got you to check. You would part each strand and look for the unwanted creepy crawlers, working your way round my head like a monkey checking its mate. All of a sudden you'd stop and take a sharp intake of breath and I'd say, 'What is it, Mammy?' You would gasp as if you'd seen a walker and that would send me into hysterics thinking you had seen something crawling in my hair. You see it wasn't so bad if Grainne got scalped with the scissors if she

164

had walkers because she had hair like Da's, which was as black as the ace of spades and thick as a bull's lug. So it wasn't long in growing again, but me, I feared I'd be a baldy all my life if you took the scissors to me.

Can you remember you tried all roads to thicken my hair? It was put in rags to make ringlets and brushed out the next day to fluff it up, but one day you told me you had the answer to 'thickening' of the hair. You sat me down on a stool, rolled up a newspaper tightly, lit the end of it with a match and I had to sit still while you singed the ends of my hair, all the way round my head, the ends of the hair stinking like a cat on fire. It was hard to sit as still as I could while seeing the lighted flame coming round my shoulders. The stink of the smoke as my fine hair sizzled went right up my nose. And more than once you clouted me with the newspaper as my hair went up in flames. But Bina Lamb, who lived next door to us, swore she'd seen it work—because her sister's childer were also afflicted with skinny hair—and that results would come with regular singeing.

The singeing made my hair look thicker, mainly due to the ends of each strand of hair being donned with a melted blob of hair and frizzed into a ball like you'd just stuck yer finger in an electric socket. It couldn't be brushed for days because no brush could cope with all those burnt ends and frizz. I'm not sure how old I was when you decided that singeing wasn't working, but thank God you did or I'd have stunk like a cat on fire my entire childhood.

Most of my primary school life was spent sitting at the back of the classroom, reading to Gerry, keeping out of trouble and not drawing any unwanted attention from anyone including the teacher. That was a big part of my day at school. Keeping quiet when we were told, lining up when we were told, reciting daily prayers when we were told, and collecting our milk at break time when we were told. I made sure Gerry and I never got into trouble. When other childer in the class were pulling each other's pigtails, passing notes to each other, sticking chewing gum under their desks, kicking their feet under the desks, not paying attention, looking out the classroom windows and even falling asleep, Gerry and I just sat quiet as mice. I'd wait till the teacher started to talk before I started to turn the pages of the book I was reading to Gerry, just so he'd be quiet.

The only time Gerry and I carried on was on the long walk home at lunchtime. This was the time we pulled each other's coats, raced each other and talked. Well, I talked and Gerry listened. We raced home every day to eat the meagre lunch you'd made; it was almost always the same as breakfast—porridge!

Sometimes if you'd got hold of some cooking apples, there might be some stewed apple in it. I didn't want it. I didn't like porridge, but you somehow cajoled us both into eating it. You had to; there was nothing else. You raved about what good childer we were, showing us the Scottish soldier with his red tartan kilt on the box, telling us stories about the armies who marched and won mighty battles eating the Scot's oat porridge, and that we'd be strong like them too.

'And, sure, wasn't it delicious and creamy made up with a drop of milk this time and the stewed apples?' you'd say.

And so we ate it to please you, Ma, and you never scolded us for not liking the porridge. You just made up better stories to take our minds off eating it. And then it was time for the long walk back to school, ready for the afternoon classes.

On one occasion, I accidentally spilled the porridge all over my school uniform during lunchtime. I was beside myself. The uniform was stripped off me and wiped, but I couldn't wear it back to school. You told me I'd have to wear something else. I began to cry. It wasn't the fact that I'd have to go back to school in a bright pink crimplene dress that came from Social Services that bothered me, but the fact that I'd stick out looking like a tube. The teacher would notice me, sitting like two black coal eyes on a snowman's head. I was terrified of standing out in the crowd, of not blending in, of our cover being blown. But you'd have none of it. The more I protested and tried to faint, like when the incense from church wafted up my nose, the more you insisted I'd be alright and to stop making such a fuss about a piggin uniform.

I walked back to school with dread and everybody did look. I knew they would. People pointed me out and shouted, 'Hey, marshmallow, where's yer uniform?' Oh God, I was going to die of shame. I was so glad to hear the bell for home; home to see you; home to make sure my uniform would be ready for tomorrow; home to get out and play before it got dark. The cloakrooms at school were divided up into box-shaped sections with metal hooks for the hats and coats. Under the bench there were metal cages for shoes. It was very hard to tell which coat was your own because there were no name tags or numbers on the metal hooks, and nearly everyone had the same sort of duffle coat.

When the bell went, it felt like a million childer crammed the hallways, grabbing for their coats in the cloakroom, pushing and shoving each other. They trailed the hats off their hooks and kicked the school begs round on the ground. I was careful to wait until the masses had gone, then I'd pick up mine and Gerry's coats and school begs. I stepped into the cloakroom when out of nowhere I felt a piercing pain across the back of my legs, again and again. I fell onto my knees grabbing the metal cage. Still the lashing pain kept coming; I couldn't even tell what was happening. Gerry just stood beside me, trying to pull me up on my feet. I was terrified and crying. The big, ginger tachara teacher from the classroom next door had whacked me till I couldn't stand up because she said I stood on a coat and should've picked it up. I was in too much shock to even speak. I knew I hadn't stood on anyone's coat; I'd waited till the cloakroom was clear. But the ginger tachara had it in for someone that day and me, wearing a bright pink crimplene dress, was an easy target. I was only eight years old.

As I walked home with Gerry he tried to cheer me up and, of course, you can't really see the backs of yer legs so I'd almost forgotten about what had happened on the long walk home. That was until you saw the huge, red, raised welts across the back of both my legs and shrieked, 'Jesus, Mary and Joseph, what has happened to your legs?'

In the time it had taken to walk home, the welts had turned purple. I couldn't sit down. When you heard what had happened, I knew no more till you'd dressed the baby and Jimmy-Paddy, put our coats back on and marched us back to the school. You said you'd 'tear the cowyard's head off' for beating me for nothing and that you'd 'take the fecking cane and cane her, teacher or not.'

Gerry and I held tightly to the handles of the big coach pram, either side. We had to almost run to keep up. You walked so fast and my duffle coat was banging against the backs of my legs again, which just made the stinging worse. To make matters even worse it started to rain, so by the time we all got to the school, we were hungry and soaked to the skin. The rain made you all the madder because you had no way of drying our clothes when we would get back home, and tomorrow we would need them again.

You didn't even go to the head teacher's office; you pushed the coach pram through the school front doors, down the corridor, past the assembly hall and right into the classroom where the big tachara teacher was still giving her lesson. In a flash you trailed the tachara by her jumper across the floor and shoved her up against the wall.

'Where's the cane, you fecking big ugly mare, because I'm going to leave welts on you the way you've marked my wee child.'

The teacher said that there must've been a mistake and that she was sorry for what she'd done and offered me some sweets, which, much to my dismay, you didn't allow me to have. You looked the tachara straight in the eye and told her, 'If ye ever lay a finger on any of my wee childer again, I'll pull every one of them fecking ginger hairs of out of yer ugly head by the roots. Is that clear?'

'Oh yes, Mrs Savage, I'm very sorry, it won't happen again!' And at that you gave the teacher a look that would have turned milk sour, turned the big pram round, gathered us together and marched right on out of that classroom and along the road home in the rain. It was dark when we got home; we were all hungry and soaked to the skin. It was the sixth time I'd done that walk in one day, the last two times with legs that I couldn't sit down with. I was never caned again, though, especially for something I didn't do. I remember that day alright. You were boiling, Ma. The teacher was lucky you didn't break her neck. It was such a desolate feeling walking back that day in all the rain. You said you had nowhere to dry all our wee clothes ready for school the next day, and there was very little in the cupboard for us to eat. Jimmy-Paddy started the crying again and there was no pacifying him, poor wee soul. Worst of all there was no dinner ready for Da coming in from work. It didn't take much for him to start. No dinner was enough; no matter what had happened. You went to bed that night with another swollen cheek and black eye where you'd 'walked into another door'.

I wasn't sure exactly when the hopelessness hit you. It sort of crept up on you when you weren't looking. Da's probably the blame for most of it, but it wasn't only that. There was an awful feeling of doom sweeping the world too. You couldn't walk down a street in Belfast without some aul lad wearing a billboard sign on his back and front preaching the end of the world was near. There was talk in America of a nuclear war and it came very close to the end of the world with the Cuban missile crisis in 1961. If it hadn't been for the humanity of President Kennedy and Mr Khrushchev, the world could have been blown to smithereens.

If that wasn't bad enough, the Vietnam War started—the whole world aghast at the atrocities that happened there, and the feeling that America and its allies were fighting a losing battle. Most of the youngsters who were recruited were hardly nineteen themselves and had no idea what they were getting into. More than most of them came back scarred for life in one way or another, and what was worse was that many of them weren't seen as heroes because half the people in the world were against the war in the first place.

Then President Kennedy was shot dead in November 1963. I was only five years old. He was a good man who had just saved the world from destruction and who was going to do great things for his people. They say he was cursed. They said there would never be a Catholic or a black man in power, and there you go, he was shot stone dead. It was awful. You cried for days.

Then in 1964, the civil rights movement in Northern Ireland started to try and get some basic rights in place for Catholics. They protested against the discrimination we all knew existed if you were Catholic by a unionist government. They wanted to end discrimination in the workplace, which Da had experienced firsthand, and in the allocation of public housing, which up until then, favoured Prods. They also wanted to get 'one man, one vote' passed to make elections fair for Catholics. People were sick of it all—the gerrymandering of borders and the fecking 'B specials' who were the only armed police force in Britain. They hated Catholics and were renowned for their brutality.

Then in April 1968, with the Vietnam War still raging, Dr Martin Luther King Jr was also killed stone dead and that poor soul was only sticking up for what was right. It looked as if the world had gone crazy. It was said, too, that the Pope had opened one of the messages given to the children of Fatima and fainted with the shock. Even our priest said he thought the message was about the end of the world. That's why you took us all to the monastery for a special blessing. You wanted us all to be together if it happened.

Then the troubles really started. It was 1968, I would have been about ten, and the government had banned a peaceful civil rights' march that had been planned in favour of a Proddie march. Obviously there was a huen outcry and over a hundred marchers were injured. It was terrible. A few days later a couple of thousand students from Queens University tried to march to Belfast City Hall in protest of the police brutality, and they too were shut down. As soon as Catholics tried to get some justice they were squashed like flies.

I don't know where all the dope-smoking, re-lax-ed hippy days of free love were in the 1960s, or the liberation of women who burnt their bras and took the pill. We saw none of it. The Catholic Church and a unionist government made sure we weren't even in control of our lives, from the jobs we got to the very houses we lived in and how many babies we had. We were trapped in a time capsule consisting of a teddy bears head wrapped in a Union Jack. When I look back now, it's no wonder your emotional health became a ticking time bomb, Ma.

All you ever wanted to do was rear your wee childer in peace, be holy, happy and be a lady. You constantly thought about Jack and how lucky he was being in Canada. That's where you should have been. That's where your life was meant to have been, with him. But there was nobody you could tell about it and you knew it was all too late anyway, just a pipe dream of a life that should have been.

God almighty, Ma, you must have been terrified and broken-hearted.

BUNK BEDS
Isabelle

Sometimes your da won at the races and he'd often get me a big box of Black Magic chocolates. 'Only the best,' he'd say. I told him I'd rather he came home with his wages, or gave me the money so I could put it to better use than eating chocolate. This particular day, I couldn't believe it when he handed me some cash after a big win. I knew I'd have to spend it quickly on something I really needed because if I didn't, he'd be looking for it the next day to put on another horse.

Until then, you'd all slept in two big double beds in the back bedroom. Jimmy-Paddy always slept between you and Gerry because it would stop him rolling out of the bed at night. You see if he fell out of bed, he couldn't get up and climb back in again. And if he hurt himself, he couldn't tell anyone where he was hurt. Lying between you and Gerry also made sure he was kept toasty warm.

He didn't know how to keep 'hapt up' at night and I always worried that he might lay all night with no bedclothes round him and get a 'foundering'. The only problem was that even though I put thick tights on him at night to keep his legs warm, he would stick his big toe out straight and rub his big toe up and down your leg for hours and hours, and you used to complain that you couldn't get to sleep.

I knew you were all getting bigger and should have your own beds. Of course there wasn't enough room to put four single beds in the one bedroom, but I knew that bunk beds were all the rage because Bina MacMaster had got three sets of them. She said they were a God send and I'd be able to put four beds in one room. So everybody was going to have a bed to call their own. You were very excited because you wanted the very top bunk. I also said this would be a good way of keeping your heads clean, too. So if one of you got the walkers, it wouldn't spread between you all. Walkers were just interested in staying in warm hair, not going for long, cold walks up bedposts and that would be one less worry I'd have.

Not only did we get new bunk beds with the money your da won at the horses, but we also got new yellow and orange brushed nylon sheets from Brentford Nylons. The new sheets were all the rage too. I was delighted because they'd dry in no time. Jimmy-Paddy's sheets got washed every day because even though he had a nappy on with plastic pants and red, thick tights to keep his legs warm, he'd often be saturated or done his numbers.

Do you remember that day, Berny, when the new bunk beds came into the house? You thought we were so posh, didn't you? The top bunk all to yerself. And I'd tell you all bedtime stories that I made up for you. *Little Wanda* and *The Pencil Factory*? I should write them down one day and make my own childer's storybook. My stories always had a happy ending, even if they were about witches or wicked stepmothers. And I always ended the stories with prayers.

'Now I lay me down to sleep, I pray the Lord my soul to keep. Matthew, Mark, Luke and John, God bless this bed that I lie on. If I die before I wake, I pray the lord my soul to take. Jesus, Mary and Joseph, I give you my heart and soul. Jesus, Mary and Joseph, assist me now and in my last agony. Jesus, Mary and Joseph, may I breathe forth my soul in peace with you, Amen.'

A WOLF IN SHEEP'S CLOTHING
Isabelle

Every child in the neighbourhood played out, Berny, not just youse; that's just how it was. No good hanging round inside the house when there was too much to do outside. Summer, winter, rain or hail, there was no such thing as bad weather, just the wrong clothes. I said the word 'bored' was made up by somebody who needed a good kick up the 'durbeg', and that if I could get hold of them, I'd show them. There was just no excuse for somebody saying they didn't have enough to do. Imagination was endless, so childer should never be bored.

You were twelve before you did actually look up the word 'bored' in the dictionary because Enid Tooney said it a lot. It was never a word used in our house. You thought she was so grown up. All the childer in the street crowded round her listening to what she said. While you were still playing with dolls, Enid had other things on her mind. You were all sitting on the pavement, chalking and playing hopscotch one day, when Enid told you she knew where babies came from.

You were curious because you thought you already knew babies grew in the mammy's tummy. But when Enid said you had to get naked to make babies because she'd seen her mammy and daddy do it, you shrieked in disbelief.

You raced home and recounted the story. I just smiled and didn't really say either way or you didn't ask. 'Naked? No clothes on? That just couldn't be true. Nobody got naked in our house. You and Daddy always had your clothes on, even in bed,' you shrieked at me. You were sure if that were true, you would've been told.

One day you and Maeve were playing out and she wanted to call for Meg Smith, her best friend. You went down the alley beside Meg's house and headed into the back garden to call for her.

Her da was sitting on the backdoor step. Maeve asked for Meg and he said she was inside the house and we should go in and get her. Maeve squeezed through beside Mr Smith and went into the house to call for Meg.

You waited outside. You didn't like Mr Smith. Something about him made your blood run cold. Maeve was still inside, and you were wishing she'd hurry up, when Mr Smith got up off the step and came over to you and tried to grab your wrist. You moved like lightning, pulling away, just in time to feel the vice-like grip slip off your wrist. He looked like a wolf out of your storybooks because his mouth was smiling but his eyes weren't. You were very scared.

You never went near that house again. I remember you telling me what happened and it wasn't long before several mothers in the street became aware of Mr Smith's unhealthy interest in their childer. Maeve told her mammy that Mr Smith had done things to her and the police were called. It was then you realised that you'd been right to feel afraid, and that if he'd got hold of your wrist, he would have pulled you into the house as well. You knew you'd had a lucky escape.

The police came and went, but the next day the street awoke to find he'd done a moonlight flit, disappearing off the face of the Earth. Two years later the Six O'clock News was on the telly and the news broke that a sniper had been shot by the British army; the man was named as T.M. Smith. I stood stock-still. There was his photo, the dirty bastard, for all to see. He'd disappeared alright and joined a paramilitary group. Now this 'hero' was to be given a burial with full military honours, the tricolour

175

draped across the coffin. Hundreds of mourners walked The Falls road to Milltown Cemetery, except a scuffle broke out in the crowd and a woman had tried to pull the Republican tricolour flag from the coffin.

It was a total disgrace, the paramilitaries vowing they'd find who'd been so disrespectful to one of Ireland's heroes. It wasn't long after that Mrs McQuaid was in our house having a cuppa tea when a huge, black, shiny car pulled up outside. There were very few people in our street who had cars, never mind big, black, shiny ones. Three men knocked on the door and you were all sent to the back bedroom and told not to come out until you were told. The three men had come to find the woman who had tried to pull the flag off the coffin. Mrs McQuaid and I told them that it certainly wasn't us. But I asked if they had a minute to listen, then told the men that Mr Smith was nothing but a dirty baste and a child molester and that it was said by some that he'd even molested his own wee girl.

He was no hero of Ireland that was for sure. The men in the big, black, shiny car were shocked and very upset to hear what one of theirs had really been up to and they were boiling about it. They then told us that they wished the fucker was alive because they'd be able to kick the shite outa him, then hand him over to the parents of the childer he'd interfered with. They said the plaque in Milltown Cemetery may have his name on it, but that his body would be dug up out of that grave before another day rose and placed in a pauper's grave. There'd be no child molester sleeping with Ireland's heroes, not on their watch. Aye, Berny, that bastard got his comeuppance the day the British soldiers put a bullet in his head. Half the poor wee childer in the street were interfered with and him, with a wife and childer of his own, masquerading about the place like an ordinary family man. There we all were believing the street was a safe place for youse all to play, and that bad things only happened to childer in England. All the while that preying fecker was right across the road on our very doorsteps. It turned a time of innocence and trust into a hellhole of evil and degradation. Nothing was ever the same again. I had

176

believed as sure as God that Ireland was the safest place in the world to raise childer and now, as if I didn't have enough to worry about, I couldn't even let youse out to play in our own street. I hope the bastard rots in Hell for eternity.

ANGELS WATCHING
Isabelle

It was Friday night and again six o'clock had come and gone. I had counted down to the angelus and began to pray. Pray that yer da would come home with his wages and not head straight for the bookies and the pub. Jesus, all I wanted was a man who'd meet me halfway in life and we'd fly. I was such a good manager with what little I had that we'd soon have all we desired.

We could pay off the loan shark, whose greed and interest just kept going up beyond belief, and I'd be able to go into Elizabeth West's clothing store and buy what I needed for the childer outright, instead of having a club card and not getting the clothes till Christmas. I'd be able to buy your white ankle socks for dancing, and I would be able to tell Mrs Granger that I could buy my own wool and knit your jumpers, instead of always having to get them as hand-me-downs in brown paper parcels. Oh, aye, if your da would have just met me halfway.

Most importantly, I could hold my head up respectable-like, knowing that I owed nobody a thing. This was no way to live; the shame of it all brought me to tears. What had I ever done to deserve this? I told no one what my life was like, not even our ones who all had good men. The shame of living like this was just too great to admit because everyone have said that I didn't have 2ds' worth of sense to marry a man like that in the first place. And at this my mind wandered again to the only man I'd loved, still loved and would only ever love, my beloved Jack. And I cried again because I knew what a terrible mistake I'd made marrying your da.

I made the childer their tea and got them ready for bed.

'Get yer bedclothes on kids and two pairs of socks tonight, it's freezin outside. I think it might be cold enough to snow.'

'S-N-O-W,' you all exclaimed at once, huge grins rising on all your faces. When youse got ready for bed you didn't get undressed and put pyjamas on—youse didn't have pyjamas—you had bedclothes which were often heavier and thicker than the clothes you wore during the day. You had wooly jumpers, too, which went on over the top of everything else and, although you had blankets on the beds, on nights like this one, the big, black, thick woollen overcoats were also spread across the beds for warmth.

The weight of all the extra clothes and big overcoats made it hard to move about in bed, which was okay because you weren't supposed to move about in bed, but go to sleep. Often when youse woke you were in the exact spot you'd been put to bed because all the clothes and overcoats kept you that way.

I was very worried now. The later your da came home, the more likely he was not only to have lost his wages, but also to be stocious drunk. And if I didn't have his dinner fresh for him, or wouldn't play the piano, he'd fire the dinner up against the wall and then start fighting with me, gulldering and yelling, demanding I do as he bade. I felt like some class of performing monkey having to play under duress.

I was very scared this night. It was very late and his dinner was long spoiled but I was trying to keep it warm in the oven. I was terrified of the state he'd come home in, as when it got this late, he didn't need an excuse to thump me. Jesus, Mary and Joseph, I was so tired of being used as a punching bag. He was always sorry the next day and swore in front of the Sacred Heart picture and you childer that it would never happen again, but that was only true till the next time he did his money in at the horses.

It was round this time you really began to realise what was going on—that your da was hurting me, and you didn't like him one bit. You didn't want to walk to church with him on a Sunday anymore, even if it meant you missed out on the extra blessings I wanted you to have. Even if it meant your da might get his arse eaten off by a pack of wild dogs in Rathcoole. You didn't want to tell him about the dancing anymore, or what happened at school. You didn't want to skip along holding his arm as he whistled a tune. You didn't want him to take you to the dancing Feis, even if it meant you didn't get to see Granny and big Joe and have fish fingers and tomato sauce.

Everyone talked about you when your da picked you up from the Feis; he was so drunk he couldn't walk straight. The girls whispered behind their hands pointing at you. So you persuaded me to let you go by yourself on the bus to Belfast. Often the conductor wouldn't take your fare, which left a whole sixpence to spend. I knew the conductor must have been a Catholic because he could see your dancing costume sticking out from under your coat.

Eleven o'clock came, Berny, and you were all in bed when I heard the drunken patriot songs stop outside our house. I'd locked the door and yer da started banging and thumping when he realised it was locked. I was terrified and came running barefoot into the back bedroom where you childer were asleep and immediately your eyes flew open. You were ready—you had my coat at the end of the bed with my purse stuffed in the pocket, and my shoes too. You frantically forced up the frozen leaver of the window as I pulled on my coat and leapt onto the window ledge, dropping into the garden outside.

'Mammy, don't go. Hide under the bed instead. Where will you go?' you pleaded. 'Don't worry. I'll be back in the morning. Yer da will sleep it off. I just can't take another hiding tonight. Now close the window behind me and get back into bed. Yer da will probably fall asleep on the porch, he's so drunk.'

You told me later, Berny, that your heart was beating so fast you couldn't think.

'Yeah, I remember, Ma. As you ran into the night, I closed the bedroom window, folded the latch, pulled the curtains across and climbed back under the overcoat as you'd told me to do. And even though my eyes were shut tight, I was wide-awake. I knew I'd stay awake till you came back. I was scared for you, Ma.'

'I know, Berny. In your mind you thought if you went to sleep, I might never come back and that would be your fault because you weren't watching for me.' My poor childer.

But this night your da's shouts got louder. He was really angry thinking I wouldn't let him in his own house and saying how dare I, it was his name on that rent book. He started shouting for me to open the door, and you were terrified he'd start on you if you did let him in because you felt he knew you helped me with my coat and purse.

The shouting and screaming got louder; you thought he'd break the door down. He called you till you felt you couldn't stay in bed anymore pretending to be asleep. You got out of bed, walking barefoot towards the front door and, as you glanced round the corner, you could see his shadow outside the glass door.

'I'm coming, Daddy!' you shouted but he didn't hear you because he was so angry and still yelling. As you ran towards the door, he started to kick in all the glass in the door. Crash! Smash! The sound echoed as the glass fell into the hallway, sliding across the tiled floor, smashing to smithereens and making the hallway floor look like a million crooked diamonds.

You kept running in your bare feet, over the glass, trying desperately to open the door. He was still shouting like a mad man. The latch was really high up and you were on your tiptoes trying to open it. As the last of the glass was smashed in, the door swung open and he fell into the hallway. As he got up off the floor he looked at you, covered in shards of glass and shaking like a leaf. 'Where's yer ma?' was all he said.

'I don't know, Daddy,' you said and he told you to get back to bed.

You walked back across the river of broken glass, down the hallway, climbed back into bed, shut your eyes tight and stayed awake till I came home the next morning. The next day when I came home and saw the devastation, I looked at you and asked what had happened. You told me the story of running across the hallway that was covered in glass and being showered with the last three panes of glass as they broke. I turned you round, looked at you from head to feet, searched your bed, then sank down on my hunkers clutching my head with my hands and began to cry.

'I'm alright, Mammy, why are ye crying? I'm not even cut anywhere,' you said.

'I know, love, I know. It's just the angels. I asked them to watch over you when I jumped out of the window last night. There's not a scratch on you and not a piece of glass in your bed. The angels were watching.'

To this day, you couldn't remember your feet touching the ground that night. You felt like you were floating to the door to let your da in. If it wasn't for you having my coat and purse ready to run, love, I don't know what would have happened. Jesus, what an awful thing for a wee child to have to do.

BUTTERCUPS AND DAISIES
Isabelle

'How did you ever manage to stay sane, Ma, with all that going on?' you asked me once.

'Well, Berny, I felt like I constantly walked a tightrope, and either way I tripped I would land in shit and trouble. I was worried about wee Jimmy-Paddy; he was so sick with the fits and the stinking medication, phenobarbitone that was rotting his wee teeth. I wondered what would happen if he couldn't chew his food. I worried even more about our poor Gerry. He wasn't fitting in anywhere. I knew something wasn't right with him, every mother knows her own, but them stupid bastards at the health centre told me I was worrying about nothing. Your da, and the rest of it all, I tried daily to put to the back of my mind and live in the world of you childer and your innocence. And in our world, we walked.'

Walking was just a normal part of our day; there was no car and no money for buses, so we walked everywhere. We walked to school, walked to church, walked to get the messages in, and for fun we walked too; away down to the road that led to the beach.

All the seasons brought their different gifts, so even if it was raining, I would get youse all ready, wellies and all. And with Jimmy-Paddy's special big, blue pram loaded to the gunnels with everything that was needed, we'd set off on an adventure. There was often another child in the street begging to come with us and that wasn't a problem to me either.

'You wished I didn't, Berny. You said it was your magical time with me and you didn't want any other child sharing my stories because they were for you.' With every season there were delights. In autumn there were a million leaves, the colours of burnt orange to lime green with patchy brown dots to kick up in the air, jump through and throw at each other. There were pine cones and conkers to pick up and put in the basket under the pram, and at Christmas I bought glue and glitter so on days that were too cold to play out, I'd help youse make paper chains and decorations.

We must've looked like the flight in Egypt with the big, blue pram loaded up with bags, tarls, bread and jam to eat, and a flurry of childer hanging on to the handles or skipping ahead. I would holler at you all to stop at the roadside, do the 'green cross code' and cross together.

'Now look right ... look left ... look right again ... and into the middle and stop.'

My instructions were always the same, safety first, because you never knew what eejit might come round the bend too fast and kill you stone dead.

'Right, kids, walk on,' I'd say when it was safe to cross, and you'd all skip ahead.

It was on these walks I'd explain why the seasons changed and what every cloud meant from cumulonimbus to wispy cirrus. I explained what happened when the Earth went to sleep, and how bears in Canada also did the same thing. I explained why berries were on the holly tree at Christmas time, why the squirrels hoarded the nuts they found ready for winter, and where the cold north winds came from—a place called Siberia, the coldest place on Earth where nothing much could live.

'It was so cold even the trees didn't grow past a place called the Tundra,' I told youse childer, and how we needed the cold to kill germs in the winter. I always carried an empty knitted beg, and as we walked along, I'd stop and pick up broken glass from the pavement and say, 'If a wee child fell on that they'd cut the legs off themselves.' Banana skins were also picked up because if a poor aul soul slipped on that, they'd break their hip or cut their skull open. So that would go in the beg too.

Silver milk-bottle tops were collected separately, do you remember? They were brought home, washed in the sink and taken to mass every Sunday for charity, as the silver foil could be used again and sold for a good cause. But it was mainly to feed the poor black babies in the African missions; God love them.

I told youse childer how we must look after the outside world as well as the inside of our house, as it was God's playground for us. The outside belongs to everybody and we all have to look after it for the future.

These days I'd have a degree to my name for Environmental-Sustainability Studies, majoring in Eco-Friendly Waste Management and Recycling, ha-ha.

But eco-friendly me arse, it was just a pinch of common sense mixed with a handful of gumption really. Often I found a brown penny, a sixpence or a shilling just lying there on the pavement.

'Jesus, Mary and Joseph, pennies from Heaven; find one and pick it up and all the day you'd have good luck!'

Any man who wouldn't stop and pick up a penny had too much pride, and what came before pride was a fall as that penny was worth a lot to some poor soul.

Our adventures took us past the church where we went to mass. Reverently, and hushing youse into respectful quietness, I'd whisper youse could take the money I'd found and light a candle for the repose of souls.

The church felt so different with just us in it, with the soft light streaming through the stained glass windows and the hundreds of votive candles flickering away on the candle stand, wax dripping down the sides of the stand making blobs in the sand tray below.

'Do you remember those visits to church, Berny? You'd ask me, "With all the hundreds of candles being offered up for the repose of souls

185

or even special requests, how would God not get mixed up with which candle was for who? How could you be sure God would know which candle I'd lit?"' Smiling gently I'd whisper, 'Ach, God knows everything, love.' You thought how smart God must be.

This was also when I explained who all the holy statues and pictures in the church were, especially the Stations of the Cross. One by one I explained and I'd begin the stations by saying, 'We adore thee, O Christ, and praise thee,' and then youse would have to say, 'Because by thy holy cross thou hast redeemed the world.'

The first station of the cross was bad enough; Jesus is condemned to death. What a terrible thing to happen to anybody and for nothing. The second station; Jesus carries his cross.

'We adore thee, O Christ, and we praise thee ... because by thy holy cross thou hast redeemed the world.'

You were a funny wee child, Berny, always asking so many questions and taking it all in and to heart. You told me your chest was feeling heavy and you understood why Jesus's mammy would be crying if she saw her son carrying a big, heavy cross and falling down, knowing the bad people were going to kill him at Calvary. The fifth station, Simon helps Jesus.

'We adore thee, O Christ, and we praise thee ... because by thy holy cross thou hast redeemed the world.'

'Oh, that's good,' you'd say, Berny. 'Someone is helping Jesus with the cross.'

It's funny the things that you feel as a child, eh? You thought it was just so sad, all that suffering. You didn't think you'd feel happy again thinking about the suffering Jesus walking with the heavy cross to Calvary. By the time Jesus had fallen for a third time at the ninth station of the cross, you were heaving heavy sobs and I said that you could go and kneel at the altar rails and look at the beautiful tabernacle, and to picture in your mind Jesus resting inside.

This too was a mystery to you—how a big man that hung on the

186

cross could possibly fit inside the tabernacle, which was only the size of our potato box. Maybe you thought he was really good at curling up small like a baby inside his mammy's stomach.

I'd go on and finish the rest of the fourteen Stations of the Cross. When I came out of the church and headed for Beach Road, we'd all feel happy. You couldn't understand why it didn't make me cry, all the suffering and falling down that Jesus did. After visiting the church we headed on down to the beach, which was always littered with treasures that I encouraged youse to pick up, like pine cones, silver milk-bottle tops and, if we were lucky, maybe a brown penny. The only thing I didn't allow youse to pick up were feathers because birds carried diseases. You really wanted to pick up the feathers because they looked just like the fancy quills kings and queens wrote with in storybooks of places faraway, like Persia and Siam. As I said, you were a funny wee thing, full of imagination.

I allowed youse to pick any of the wild flowers you saw in the fields as we walked along. Buttercups of bright yellow were gathered by the handful and held up under yer chin to see if the colour was reflected on yer Adam's apple. That meant you liked butter. Daises with white petals and bright yellow centres were also gathered, and there was always a competition between youse childer as to who could make the longest daisy chain without it breaking.

Dandelions didn't count for the competitions, because they were weeds, but when the head of the dandelion was covered in white fluff, youse could pick that too and see how many puffs of breath it took you to blow all the fluff away.

Spring was the time when wild snowdrops pushed their heads up through the earth to tilt towards the weakened spring sunshine. It was a glorious sign of new life. I'd often stop as we walked, bending down to gently cup in my hands the delicate white bells with their thin green lines. I always told you childer how I admired these perfect little flowers who bravely pushed their tiny heads though the hard earth every year, despite the harsh spring weather and tough ground.

'See how tiny and perfect they are, but how strong they must be to be the very first flowers of springtime like God's little miracles. They don't care if it's a frosty morning or if they're surrounded by ice and snow. They stand up anyway bobbing their tiny heads in the spring breeze.' I always gave youse plenty of time to look and feel them, standing for ages to look right inside.

'We'll see them again next year God spares us to live,' I'd say. And off we'd walk again until another miracle of nature crossed our path.

I never minded how many puddles youse splashed in, or how dirty your hands or clothes got rummaging in the leaves and grass. And I loved the pink rosy hue on your cheeks from all the fresh air; I knew you'd all sleep well that night. I pointed out the robin redbreasts, their chests puffed out proudly in the winter light, and the starlings flying away to warmer places; countries like Africa. I also explained that when they flew, if one starling got sick and fell to the ground, another healthy bird would go with them to keep them company until they got better or went to Heaven. Ach, sure, the wee birds could teach human banes a thing or two about compassion.

Along with the snowdrops came clumps of bluebells, taller and stronger than the snowdrops, their colour almost an indigo blue that made my heart skip a beat.

'Ach, just look at that display in God's garden.'

'Can we pick some, Mammy?' you'd ask.

'Ach, go on, sure God won't mind. There must be thousands.' And so again we'd stop to gather as many bluebells as our fists could clench.

I encouraged youse to take the flowers to church and leave some at the feet of Our Blessed Lady's statue to give thanks. The tall statue stood serene in her flowing white robe with pale blue sash. It was especially important to bring flowers to Our Blessed Lady in May because that was 'her month'. There was even a special procession where Our Lady's statue was carried round the outside of the church while we all sang songs in praise of her because she was Jesus's mammy.

'Bring flowers of the rarest, bring blossoms the fairest, from garden and woodland and hillside and dale; our full hearts are swelling, our glad voices telling, the praise of the loveliest flower of the vale! O Mary, we crown thee with blossoms today, Queen of the angels and Queen of the May. O Mary, we crown thee with blossoms today, Queen of the angels and queen of the May.'

As spring gave way to summer, our world changed again. I was up at the scrake o' dawn, with the washing out early on the line, nearly before sunrise, the promise of sunshine lifting any clouds of doom and worry about your da's gambling and drinking ways, at least for a while. You didn't have to wear the thick liberty bodices that kept out the winter chills and protected your chests from the consumption or pneumonia, but the green sacred scapulars were still pinned to your vests to protect youse from anything bad, no matter what season of the year it was.

You couldn't understand how a piece of green cloth was meant to keep you safe, even if it did come from a holy person's robe. But I told you it wasn't just any aul cloth, no. The scapulars were made from a person's robes that were very holy and I believed if you wore the holy relics, you'd have the same divine protection. Summertime meant more long walks to the beach and, although there was never any money to spend when we got there, I always had a new game I'd invent to keep youse occupied and I joined in too. We played chasey or hide-and-seek, and I'd often pretend I was hiding even though I was just behind Jimmy-Paddy's shawlie or big, blue pram shouting, 'One, two, three, now I'm invisible. You can't see me.'

Youse were brown as berries. God, it did my heart good just looking at youse, with arms glowing with the sun—skin that stung when you got washed that night. At night when youse hopped into bed, I'd tell the story again of *Little Wanda*. 'Poor little Wanda!' I'd start as you all snuggled down to listen ...

'Once upon a time there lived a little girl called Wanda. She lived with her daddy and a very wicked stepmother. You see the wicked stepmother was jealous of Wanda, and she was always trying to make her life very hard.

'The wicked stepmother gave Wanda all the hard tasks in the house to do, and she never let her play with her friends. She was always asking little Wanda to do things that she knew she couldn't, so little Wanda would look stupid and feel very sad. One day when her daddy had gone to work, the wicked stepmother sent little Wanda into the woods to bring her back a bunch of bluebells. She shouted at little Wanda with a hateful voice, "Don't come back until you find them." Now everybody knows that bluebells only grow in the springtime, and it was November so little Wanda knew the Earth was fast asleep. It would be months before the woods would be carpeted in bluebells. Poor little Wanda …

"Woe is me," she said to herself. "What am I going to do? Boohoo." As she began to cry, she made her way into the deep, dark woods.

'Little Wanda was so afraid of the creatures that roamed the woods, especially the hungry wolves with their piercing blue eyes and saliva that drooled down the sides of their jaws whenever they saw a tasty little girl to eat. And there were no bluebells anywhere.

'The deeper and deeper into the forest little Wanda went, the darker and darker the forest became, until there was practically no light at all. Now she was lost in the woods too. Little Wanda didn't know what to do; she was so scared that the bears and the wolves would gobble her up, and then she would never see her daddy again.

'She sat down on a big log and she began to sob, boohoo. But in the distance little Wanda thought she could hear voices. Faintly at first, but yes, they were there and they were laughing too. As she looked up, she also saw a light glowing in the distance. So she set off to follow it and when little Wanda followed the light, it grew brighter and brighter, until she found herself at the edge of a clearing in the woods.

'Low and behold, she found herself looking at a crowd of very tall elderly men sitting in a circle, all huddled round a camp fire, right in the middle of the forest. She dried her eyes and started to count how many men there were; one, two, there, four, five, six, seven, eight, nine, … little Wanda took a breath … ten, eleven … there were twelve in total and each of them had a very long beard.

'Round their shoulders were draped the finest cloaks of silver and gold that little Wanda had ever seen. What could all those men be doing in the middle of the forest on a cold November day? Maybe they were lost too, little Wanda thought. All of a sudden one of the elderly bearded men turned round and saw little Wanda and slowly he stood up, sweeping his shimmering golden cloak up to one side as he stood. His eyes were twinkling and kind.

'"My, my, my, little Wanda, what may I ask are you doing here in the middle of the forest in the middle of winter? Come closer to the fire, child, you must be frozen."

'"Oh, how do you know my name?" asked little Wanda.

'"Oh, my dear, that's easy. We are the creators of all living and sleeping things in the forest." Little Wanda wasn't sure what the elderly gentleman meant, but she understood he was kind and meant her no harm.

'"Please, sir, I'm lost and afraid and I can't find my way home. My stepmother has sent me to the woods to find her a basket of bluebells, but it's November and there are no bluebells in the woods." The other eleven gentlemen began to whisper among themselves. This was indeed a terrible predicament for little Wanda.

'"Little Wanda, maybe we can help you," said the tallest of the gentlemen. "Let me introduce my brothers."

'One by one each of them stood up from their wooden log bench, taking turns as they introduced themselves. The first bowed his head to Wanda.

'"Good afternoon, little Wanda, I'm January," he said and then he sat back down. The second gentleman stood up.

'"Nice to meet you, my dear, I'm February." Then the third said, "And I'm March," as his eyes twinkled like stars. The fourth gentleman said, "I'm April." One by one they stood in turn, each one of them the very months of the year. Little Wanda was astounded. She had never met anyone like these gentlemen in her whole life.

'Then the tallest gentleman began to speak again to Wanda. "We are the keepers of the seasons, little Wanda, and your wish is our command."

'"Oh, do you mean you can make the forest turn into springtime?"

'"Indeed, my dear, that is so."

'"Thank you, sir," she said. Little Wanda couldn't believe it and clapped her hands with glee. With that, the gentleman who was the month of May clicked his fingers and, low and behold, the forest floor began to change … right before little Wanda's eyes. There were bluebells, hundreds and thousands of them—so many it would fill ten of little Wanda's baskets.

'"Gather them quickly, my dear," May chided. "You must hurry, my dear, before the day is gone or the magic will disappear."

'Little Wanda gathered as many of the bluebells as she could carry, quickly filling her basket to the very top. Then the elderly men altogether blew a huge puff of breath on the embers of the forest fire, which made it burst into life again, lighting the forest up all the way back to the edge of the woods so that little Wanda could find her way back home.

'As little Wanda reached the edge of the woods and looked back, she waved to the twelve months of the year and she shouted, "Goodbye everyone and thank you" as the twelve gentlemen vanished one by one, leaving behind nothing but twelve giant Celtic stones in a perfect circle, right in the middle of the woods.

'Now when the wicked stepmother saw the bluebells that little Wanda had brought back from the woods, she clenched her fists with rage until her eyeballs fell out onto the cheeks of her face. She stamped her foot, until the wooden floorboards in the house shook and the ornaments crashed from the mantelpiece onto the floor, smashing everywhere. She was furious that little Wanda had managed to complete the hard task she had set for her because now she felt like a fool.

'"Where did you get these bluebells from? How could you do this?"

she demanded to know. "Bluebells only bloom in springtime and it's the middle of winter." But then she thought … umm … maybe little Wanda had magical powers she didn't know about. And what if she uses the par to turn me into an ugly aul toad? So the wicked stepmother never asked little Wanda to do anything again that was too hard for a little girl, and little Wanda lived happily ever after.'

And by this time youse were all fast asleep.

Other nights when I tucked youse into bed, I'd sing the songs Molly and I sang in the dance halls of Belfast when we were young; those American songs like *Tallahassee* and *Waiting For The Robert E. Lee*. And I'd tell youse about the prizes we won of fancy clothes. If not songs or stories, I'd recite poetry. I knew songs about everything from how to count to five, to twins in a pram having twenty tiny fingers and twenty tiny toes. I sang that song a lot because for many years there were always two babies in our pram, just like twins.

'Twenty tiny fingers, twenty tiny toes, two angel faces, each with a turned-up nose. One looks like Mammy, with a cute little curl on top, while the other one's got a big bald spot, exactly like his pop, pop, pop, poppity-pop.' *My Aunt Jane* was another song I sang.

'My Aunt Jane she called me in, she gave me sweeties out of her wee tin; half a bap with sugar on the top, and three wee sweeties outa her wee shop.'

Another song was about Mister Moon who comes out too early, like what happens in the summertime even before it gets dark.

'Mister Moon, mister moon, you're out too soon, the sun is in the sky. Get back to bed and cover up your head, and wait till the day goes by, goes by, and wait till the day goes by.' My favourite poem of all time made you shiver and you always asked me to stop so you could cover your ears. I'd laugh and tell you there was nothing to be scared of, as the poem was just about a traveller out in the middle of the night. But the way I started the poem sent shivers down your spine because it was also about ghosts of which you were terrified. And so I would begin …

'"Is there anybody there?" said the traveller, knocking on the moonlit door, and his horse in the silence champed the grasses of the forest's ferny floor.' All you could picture in your head was the figure of a highwayman, a big black cloak, a wild white horse, with its warm puffy breath pouring out its nostrils like a dragon, and a forest like the one in the Hansel and Gretel storybook. You'd duck right under the coats on the bed and try not to listen to the rest of the scary poem, but on I would go, with you being a scaredy-cat, and sticking my hand under the coat pretending to catch you, which made you squeal harder. The poem was *The Listeners* by Walter De La Mare, and I knew every word. '"Is there anybody there?" said the Traveller, *Knocking on the moonlit door;*

> *And his horse in the silence champed the grasses of the forest's ferny floor:*
> *And a bird flew up out of the turret, above the Traveller's head:*
> *And he smote upon the door again a second time; "Is there anybody there?" he said.*
> *But no one descended to the Traveller; No head from the leaf-fringed sill*
> *Leaned over and looked into his grey eyes, where he stood perplexed and still.*
> *But only a host of phantom listeners that dwelt in the lone house then*
> *Stood listening in the quiet of the moonlight to that voice from the world of men:*
> *Stood thronging the faint moonbeams on the dark stair, that goes down to the empty hall,*
> *Hearkening in an air stirred and shaken by the lonely Traveller's call.*
> *And he felt in his heart their strangeness, their stillness answering his cry,*
> *While his horse moved, cropping the dark turf, 'neath the starred and leafy sky;*
> *For he suddenly smote on the door, even louder, and lifted his head: —*

"Tell them I came, and no one answered, that I kept my word," he said.
Never the least stir made the listeners, though every word he spoke
Fell echoing through the shadowiness of the still house from the one
    man left awake:
Ay, they heard his foot upon the stirrup, and the sound of iron on stone,
And how the silence surged softly backward, when the plunging hoofs
    were gone.'

By the end of the poem, scared or not, you were sound asleep anyway.

The next day we would be out walking again. I used to speak to everyone I met in the street when we were out.

'Hello, Mrs Morris, fine morning it is and what about yourself?'

'Oh, grand, Mrs Savage, and what about the wee boy? How's he doing today? Any sign of him walking yet?' would often come the reply.

Every few feet we went there was another person I knew. I knew most of the people because they lived in our street, but when we walked further outside Rathcoole, I still spoke to those people too, even if I didn't know them.

People always said hello back. There was one particular poor aul lady who I never failed to stop and greet. The lady looked very old indeed. She had a long coat on, right down to her ankles, even in the summertime, and she walked along, bending to the right as if she couldn't stand up straight. She also wore a very large hat, which flopped right down over her face. Her voice was barely a whisper when she spoke to me, and she stooped so low when she spoke that you couldn't really see her face at all. I would stop, take her hand and cover it with my other hand telling the aul lady to take care of herself.

'Mammy, who's that lady and why does she hide her face?' you'd ask.

'Ach, sure, the poor soul has awful scars. Her whole face is melted off her like chewing gum from falling into a fire when she was a wee girl.

She keeps her hat low so the sight of her terrible scars doesn't scare you childer. When you see a person like that you should always say "Hello". You should say "There but for the grace of God go I" and "God bless the mark", because you never know what's in front of you and Jesus knows if it was us that looked like that, we'd want people to pass the time of day with us too, now wouldn't we?'

'Yes, Mammy, tell the lady next time you see her that I'm not scared of her face and that she can take her hat off when she talks to us.' I just smiled at your response and never did say anything to the poor aul lady because I knew if you'd seen the full horror of her scars, you wouldn't have slept for a month.

THE SECRET DRAWER
Isabelle

It was a wild, bitter winter with winds that came straight from the depths of the Siberian wasteland of Russia, and too cold for youse to play out. Trying to keep six childer entertained in the house was a job and a half. Jimmy-Paddy was in his pram and the rest of you childer were playing anywhere you could. Youse were under the table, and pulling out the pots and pans. I didn't mind, I knew where you all were and youse were happy.

On one particular day, you were standing on top of a chair, ferreting through old boxes in the cupboard, looking for treasure—aul earrings, maybe even a sixpence. The aul Singer sewing machine was heavy and you couldn't move it, but your small fingers searched round and suddenly the bobbin drawer opened. You peeked inside and started rummaging round. 'Yes, got it!' I heard. A handful of money—you were rich, you thought. You pulled out the treasure of money to find it all had lovely patterns on it, Celtic patterns and a loop on top like the holy medals you wore pinned to your vests. But they were silver so maybe they were still money, you thought.

As you turned the treasure over in your hands you began to read what was inscribed on the back: Jack Kennedy, 1st Place, Belfast Championship 1952. The second and third medals you had in your hands also had the same name: Jack Kennedy. 'Oh damn!' you said as you realised it wasn't money after all. But you turned to me anyway and casually asked, 'Mammy, who's Jack Kennedy?' I almost collapsed across the ironing board, tripping as I ran over to you, frantically grabbing the treasure from your hands.

'Oh Jesus, Mary and Joseph, give me those quick. Where did you get them from? Don't tell your daddy, for God's sake.'

I realised you were really shocked to see me in such a state and couldn't understand why some silver medals had made me so frantic. I carefully wrapped the precious medals back in the tissue paper they'd been wrapped in and tucked them into my apron, trying not to let on what happened. But as I tucked you into bed that night, after we'd said our prayers, you whispered, 'Mammy, I'll keep your secret about the medals. Don't worry, I won't tell anyone.'

'Okay, love. When you're older, I promise I'll tell you the whole story. Those medals are all I've got of him. It would break my heart if your da found out about them; he'd probably throw them in the fire. Now promise me, Berny, not a word, not to a living soul.'

'I promise, Mammy.'

THE BIG ONE
Isabelle

Your da's mathematical mind never stopped ticking. He was always thinking of ways to make money—and quick. He truly believed he could win the jackpot at the horses if he studied the form carefully enough. He listened to tips that came from the stable jockeys he drank with. He'd then calculate the odds, which in his mind was a cinch. He felt it in his bones. If he just kept betting, one more time, he would win the big one. It wasn't luck; it was a mathematical certainty, according to him. The drive to win the 'big one' was what kept him going back to the bookies, despite our decline into abject poverty. He was convinced it was only a matter of time and we would be rich beyond our wildest dreams.

He headed out early one summer morning; he'd had some red-hot tips for the races and he felt lucky. Today was the day all his luck was about to change. When he wasn't back home by teatime, I knew well where he'd be. God only knows how much money would be wasted that day, putting another extension on the bookie's house—money that could have put food on the table and shoes on the childers' feet. A deep fear gripped me. What if he lost badly? He'd be like a bear with a sore head. He'd be stocious and it wouldn't take much for him to start. Oh Jesus, not another night like the one a fortnight ago. I still had the bruises where I hadn't ducked quickly enough.

I'd been too slow that night and my ribs still ached from where he'd pushed me up against the sideboard. This coupled with the shame and degradation was enough to put your head away. I was worried. Daddy had dropped by with some vegies a few days earlier and I hadn't even time to cover up the bruises. Oh I was so ashamed. Still, I thought Daddy bought the story of me walking into the back door. Little did I know that he knew well that I hadn't walked into any back door, and when he'd got home, he rounded up my brothers again telling them to get over to our place as soon as they could and 'teach that bastard a lesson he'd never forget'—and to make sure this time they didn't come back telling him they were too late and that your da had fled. He was sick of seeing the apple of his eye suffer like this and it had to stop. I prayed that if your da was drunk there'd be nobody with him trying to start a party, and that he'd go straight to his bed and sleep it off. I'd kip with one of the childer and leave him to it. I didn't want you childer hearing any gulldering and fighting, not like I'd endured when I was a wee girl. All I wanted was to be holy, happy and a lady. I desperately didn't want to make the same mistake with my wee childer. I'd make sure you were bathed early, stories told, prayers said, and off to sleep long before he'd be back.

I'd start a pan of stew; that would be something he could have no matter what time he landed. It could be reheated and wouldn't spoil if it was left on the stovetop, and it wouldn't get fired up against the wall. It wasn't unusual for him to roll home stocious, laughing and singing with a tribe of some 'come all ye' whom I'd never met in my life, trailing after him while he acted like the goose that laid the golden egg. The trouble was they'd all be as drunk as him from the drinks he'd splashed out on them buck strangers after a win at the horses, and they'd want to party too. Why couldn't he just bring some of that money home to me? And as often as not, he would insist I play the piano, which was the last thing I wanted to do. I could hardly bear to think about that piano now. I hated the thought of even striking a key and I made up my mind to get rid of it. That way there'd be one less thing I'd have to contend with. It was never too long anyway before he took umbrage at something one of them said, and then he'd empty them all out to fuck, no matter what time of the night, and they'd have to make their way home from Rathcoole, the last bus having long gone.

Suddenly I heard the car pull up outside. I ducked out to see the big, black taxi stop, its engine still running. *Christ, here he is!* But I couldn't tell if there was anybody with him. I took a deep breath and waited nervously and then the door was knocked. When I answered it, there was our Tom, my youngest brother, with your da draped round his neck.

'Oh my God, Tom, what in under Jesus are ye doing here?'

'Oh, Isabelle, I'm so sorry. He knocked at me door, asking me to grab me guitar and told me he was throwing a party.'

'For God's sake, Tom, did ye not realise he was stocious?' I was getting rattled as if I didn't have enough to contend with. It was bad enough that your da was in a drunken stupor with no money again, but now I had to endure the embarrassment of one of my very own family seeing this.

'Isabelle, I really am sorry! It wasn't till I got in the flaming taxi that I realised he was "full" or I'd never have got in with him. He's had me singing *Hey Jude* all the way from Belfast. And then he had the cheek to fall asleep on me.' By this time your da was swaying on one leg, and when I saw our Tom's face, I felt sorry for him too. I knew your da's way of cajoling people into doing things. Tom had felt beholden, as your da always made a fuss of him as a youngster. He even took him to the circus when he was wee, and taught him how to lift a hurling ball with only the stick at Falls Park. And hadn't your da been a good friend to Tom? Extending the hand of friendship that was rarely felt anywhere else? So Tom hadn't wanted to offend him by refusing his open invitation to a party.

'Well, come in for Heaven's sake and bring him with ye. The childer are in bed. Can ye help get him onto the bed because there's no party here tonight?'

'Oh aye, yes, of course, right away, Isabelle,' said Tom as he heaved your da's near-dead weight down the hall and into the bedroom. When

Tom came back into the hallway, he looked outside hoping to get the same taxi home, but the taxi had waited long enough and had taken off into the night.

'God almighty, what am I going to do?' He looked distraught. But he quickly regained composure and made it seem like it was just the fact that he hadn't time to lift his wallet when he'd left home that worried him, even though I could tell there was much more to it than that. He hardly had the change in his pocket to get another taxi, but it was enough to get him close enough and then he could walk the rest of the way. He'd have to wait for another taxi, though. The taxi ride back to Belfast had been a much quieter one. There was no singing *Hey Jude* or strumming the guitar. Tom had just sat with his head in his hands. He didn't know what to do, whether to say something or keep shtum.

You see, unbeknown to me when your da had picked him up from his house earlier that night, he'd opened a big, brown bag to show Tom. There, before Tom's eyes, was the biggest bag of money he'd ever seen in his life, and your da was grinning like a Cheshire cat from ear to ear. 'Holy mother of God, Harry! Have ye robbed a bloody bank?' The bag of money was full to the top with tight wads of high notes—fifty and one hundred pound notes. There must have been thousands of pounds.

'I did it son,' your da declared to his friend and confidante, his words drawling as he wiped his mouth. 'I won the big one. We're rich. We'll live like lords.' Your da's eyes glazed as he looked at Tom, with a mixture of drunken cockiness and pride.

'Jesus, bless us,' said Tom as he made the sign of the cross on himself.

'I'll see you right, young fella, you've been a good friend to me,' your da had said, but as Tom arrived back in Belfast, outside his own house again, his legs could hardly carry him he was so shaken. He had got distracted helping your da out of the taxi, and then taken too long at the door explaining to me why he was there, and then helping your da into bed, that he'd forgotten about the big, brown bag of money ... still on the back seat of the taxi! It sped off afore he realised it with your da's big win and our future sitting right there on the bloody back seat. He was sick to his stomach.

Tom prayed your da would never remember. And he prayed that, if your da didn't remember, he'd never have to tell a soul about what had just happened. Because news like that could break my heart even more than he knew it already was, sending me to Purdysburn Asylum. He knew he wouldn't be able to live with himself if that happened, so he thought it was better to say nothing to anybody ... ever!

THE DANCING YEARS
Berny

'Hey, Ma, do you remember me driving you mad wanting to go to dancing classes when I was wee?'

I drove you crazy for years wanting to go, but you'd no money to send me, which broke your heart. I don't know where I got the yearning for it. It certainly wasn't from you or Da. When I was born my feet didn't sit straight. Instead they were turned in the wrong way. So for the first eighteen months, I spent a lot of time in special boots held together with a rigid metal bar, which turned both my feet out the right way. It seemed to do the trick and, even though I still tripped a lot, special exercises strengthened the muscles to keep them turned out the right way. I didn't even need my Clarks shoes built up at the almoner's office at the Royal like all the other childer. I'd been cured.

'Mammy, where are all those childer going?' I'd ask.

'Ach, they're going to learn Irish dancing,' you'd say.

'Let me go. I want to go too.'

I must've driven you crazy for years pleading with you to let me go with the others on Friday nights. But if I did, you didn't say, you just told me 'maybe next week' or 'maybe when you're a wee bit older'. You had two worries: the first was the worry of whether the other childer would look after me right; the second was money.

But, by some miracle, when I was seven you agreed I could go with the others and join the Johnson School of Irish Dancing. The same school that Jack Kennedy had been a head dancer. Ely Mulligan knew you well. She'd watched the love story of Belfast unfold before her eyes. She'd known how close you and Jack had been, and she'd been shocked when she heard that you had married me da, leaving her head dancer's heart broken. She'd heard on the grapevine that he still hadn't looked at another woman, and that must have been almost ten years ago. So Ely Mulligan also knew very well who I was the minute I walked into my first dancing class.

It was many years later that you told me Ely blamed you for Jack Kennedy leaving Belfast, leaving her dancing school in tatters without its leading man, because she knew that you were supposed to have got engaged and instead something dreadful had happened that put an end to that. Then Jack had taken off for Canada, never to be heard of again. That was until the day Jack had come back to get you, and apparently he'd found you alright, the size of a house, ready to have a baby … somebody else's baby.

A bright, shiny sixpence was pressed into my hand to give to Miss Mulligan for the dancing lesson. Miss Mulligan was standing with the other childer in the aul school hall. She looked very busy, putting on the double jig record and shooing the childer in the class to the back of the room, ready to start the steps. Suddenly Ely Mulligan asked me to come over to her. She gently took my face in both her chubby hands.

'My dear, I've waited a very long time for you to join me,' she said to me. I had no idea what she meant; I just knew that it felt good.

Life revolved round getting to Ely Mulligan's dancing classes every Friday night. Da thought the dancing was great, and when it came to competing in the local Feis, well, he volunteered to take me as you couldn't with all the other childer to look after. Da would stride along, proud as punch, whistling away, me hopping alongside of him, my arm hooked in his, keeping up a constant drone of childish chatter. He just kept whistling and never said a word. He'd drop me off at the hall where the Feis was being held, and then head off somewhere telling me he'd be back to get me later. He didn't stay to watch like the other daddies; he'd go straight to the bookies and the pub.

Da would come back and he'd be staggering as he pushed open the door to the big hall. Other parents glared at him and talked about us. It must have looked disgraceful—a drunken father here to pick up his child … again. But to me, Daddy was back just like he said he would be and he was happy. He must have had a 'win'.

I didn't care what anyone thought as long as I got to dance. Ely Mulligan was always very kind to me. She knew the predicament well, looking at the state of Daddy when he came to pick me up, and she shared her sandwich with me. It was always a long day and I had no money for food or a drink. You must have thought he would do the 'neatful', but instead he headed for the bookies. I never told you in case you wouldn't let me go back to the Feis, and eating nothing was better than eating porridge twice a day anyway.

The first time I ever won a medal for the dancing, I couldn't believe it. And then when I won a second one on the same day, I thought all my dreams had come at once. Da was delighted when he picked me up that night, and instead of going straight home, he took me to Granny's house to show her what I'd won. I held the medals so tight in my hands, afraid to let them sit in my pocket in case I lost them. They were just like the medals I'd found in the secret drawer that had the name 'Jack Kennedy' on them. Da said he'd have them engraved with my name, which he did.

When I was eleven, I won the chance to compete at the Oireachtas in Dublin. I couldn't believe it. 'Mammy, Ely Mulligan said she'd take me. Can I go please?'

'Away to Dublin without me? Jesus, what if you aren't looked after properly?' you had said.

But I begged, 'Oh, Mammy, please? I promise I'll not leave Miss Mulligan's side.' And again, like a miracle, you got me a little, checked, royal blue and navy bag and a beautiful pink trench coat from Elizabeth West's shop at the Diamond. I had a funny feeling the coat and bag came from the same place as our bunk beds and my Stella Maris girls' school uniform.

I was going to Dublin on the train and we were staying at Maloney's Boarding House right in the middle of Dublin. I'd seen the steam trains and waved to them many times as we'd all walked to the beach with you, but never in my wildest dreams did I ever think I would get to go on one. I gazed round the dancing hall in Dublin, reading the names of the competing countries—England, Australia, America and Canada. The costumes, the colours, the smells and the live music striking up for each dancer—I was in Heaven.

I was sitting transfixed, mesmerised by the flying feet of the dancers when Ely Mulligan tapped me on the shoulder and told me there was somebody she would like me to meet. She didn't say who it was, but obediently I walked over with her to the part of the hall where the Canadian dancers were assembled.

I couldn't believe my eyes. The dancers' costumes were a brilliant white with purple and yellow embroidery round the hems and all along the edge of their shawls. Each dancer also had a purple waistcoat that had a fancy Celtic 'K' emblazoned on the right side of them. The dresses had a flared skirt, which came above the dancer's knee, and when they practised their steps it burled round, and you could see their matching white knickers underneath. They all had proper ringlets, too, which bounced up and down when they moved, and a Tara Brooch that held their shawls in place on their shoulders.

I knew I'd never have a beautiful dancing costume like the ones the Canadian dancers wore, but I made up my mind that I'd ask Santa Claus to bring me a Tara Brooch for Christmas, which I too could pin on my shoulder, even if I did have to borrow a dress from Ely Mulligan.

The dancers' shoes were the most delicate shoes I'd ever seen. They had proper laces in them that crisscrossed all the way up their feet. They had white bobby socks that were the proper ones you were supposed to wear, not like mine that came from Elizabeth West's at the Diamond, 'but did the neatful' as you would say. I was standing in the dark-green pleated costume that Ellie Mulligan had lent me, and my dancing shoes had elastic instead of fancy laces.

I was still drinking in the resplendent colours of the Canadian dancers' costumes when a tall man with red hair approached us. He continued to talk to dancers at his right, and then left, until he was right beside us both. He greeted Ely Mulligan with a big hug, so I knew he must be someone she knew. She was standing, holding my hand, waiting for the man to join us.

The tall man wore a very smart navy suit, and he had a kind face. Ely looked at the man and simply said, 'This is Isabelle's little girl.' The man smiled at me, but didn't speak; he just kept looking at me, which made me go bright red. Ely Mulligan talked away to him about our train ride down from Belfast and what the boarding house was like that we were staying in. She said the place was a 'cold rife hole' and that the aul wooden sash window wouldn't shut, making the room feel as 'cold as the arctic', which was true.

She went on to say that it had been the coldest Easter she'd known for a long time, and she hoped none of us would get a foundering because we only had light clothes with us, and that you 'shouldn't cast a clout till May was out'. After what seemed like a long time, Miss Mulligan simply told me to go back to my seat. As I walked back, I turned round to see if the man was still looking at me. He watched me until I sat down and then he went off to talk to another one of the Canadian dancers. Who was that tall stranger? How did he know Mammy's name? And why did Ely Mulligan want me to meet him?

All too soon the trip to Dublin was over and we were on the train back to Belfast. I couldn't wait to tell you all about the trip—what I'd seen, how I'd danced, and of course I told you about meeting the tall stranger with the red hair and what Miss Mulligan had said to him about me being 'Isabelle's little girl'. You started to cry.

'What's wrong? Why are you crying? Don't cry.'

But you knew exactly who I'd been introduced to. Who else would be standing beside the Canadian contingent at the Feis with his aul dancing teacher but your beloved Jack? He was in Dublin—on the same strip of land. All you said to me was, 'He said he'd have his own dancing school one day.' Oh God, if only things had been different, you'd be there with him in Dublin. If only you'd known what your mammy had done with Jack's letters. If only you hadn't made the worst mistake of your life and married my da. Your life should have been so different; you should have been in Canada with the only man you ever loved. You wouldn't be poor; you wouldn't have to live a life you were ashamed to tell anybody about. That day another piece of your heart died inside because you knew you were trapped, with no way out, and there wasn't a thing you could do about it. And I knew too, that this was not the first time I carried a secret that made you sad, which nobody else knew about.

UNEARTHLY WARNINGS
Isabelle

As you know, Berny, your da had got the job at ICI not because of his brains or work ethic, but because 'Savage' was a Protestant name. The man who gave him the job forgot to ask him what school he went to, so nobody knew he was a Catholic. He loved his job. It gave him a sense of pride working for an important company, and hard work never killed anyone. He didn't even mind the shift work because that meant he would earn more money and so have more chances to win the 'big one'. I never understood why someone as supposedly brainy as your da couldn't see that it was a mug's game.

Your da's quick mind and opportunistic nature soon meant that he was looking for ways to make even more money. The only problem was he didn't tell me. I found out exactly how much money he was earning when I bumped into Mary McCourt, whose husband worked the same line as him. She was bumming and blowing about the new car they'd just bought and the holiday they were going on.

I couldn't believe how Mary could buy a car or go on holiday when your da had told me he wasn't making much yet. But all the while he was flying, rolling in it. I nearly died when I heard this, and here's me waiting patiently for things to get better like a bloody eejit, while all along he was playing me for a fool. Jesus, how could he keep me down like this? I never asked for much and now this, too—the humiliation, being shown up in front of some nosey aul cowyard in the street. There were my wee childer running about having to eat porridge twice a day because there was nothing else, and he was out there putting it all on a horse. I couldn't believe it! God forgive him, the lousy bastard. All he was good for was putting another extension on the fecking bookie's mansion, while I tried to survive on a pauper's pittance. I was furious that he'd kept me so short. All that scrimping and scraping I did to make ends meet and there was no need for it. What was even worse was that now Mary McCourt knew my business and the shameful way I had to live. I'd never be able to hold my head up again in the street because she had the biggest mouth in Rathcoole.

But every time I plucked up the courage to front your da about the money, he'd come home stocious with nothing in his pockets except for bookies dockets. Oh he'd promise me all the fine things of the day, and one day he brought home a box of Black Magic chocolates that was so big it filled half the table. I told him what use were chocolates when what I needed was shoes on the childers' feet? He got mad, calling me all the ungrateful cowyards under the sun, and the fighting began again.

Many a time I paid the price for opening my mouth when your da took the head staggers—my head being bounced off the bathroom floor and my ribs black and blue. I was sick and tired of it all—having to do a runner, my coat and purse ready at the end of the bed, ready to leap out of the window in my bare feet, running like a scalded cat into the night. But the more money he made, the less money I saw.

One night he was late again and I knew what this meant. No money and a hiding for good measure. I was filled with dread. He stounced into the house in a very bad mood and fired his dinner to the floor—dinner I'd been keeping warm for him.

He had started to look for something in the cupboard when he came across an aul biscuit tin full of photographs from when I was younger—photos of my youth hostelling days with all of my friends. In one fell swoop he opened the glass-fronted fire and emptied all my memories into the fire. I was devastated. There were hundreds of photos—a lot with my best friend Siobhan and I, some of our ones when we were all wee, and all the ones your Granda took of me when I was growing up. They were all gone, melting as if they'd never existed. He went off to do another shift at ICI that night and I cried myself to sleep. Thank God you childer hadn't witnessed that night.

What I didn't know, Berny, was that you heard every word of it Later that night I was suddenly woken from my sleep. *What was that?* Something had woken me up, and I had exactly the same feeling on me as the night I had been woken by Gracie's ghost. There it was again. I knew I wasn't dreaming. Tap ... tap ... tap ... coming from the wall, moving, going right round the middle of the wall.

Was it the central heating? We hadn't long had it put in. I sat bolt upright in bed, pulling the covers tightly round me. Jesus, Mary and Joseph, the whole house was freezing. How could that happen? The fire was still glowing in the grate. I could see my breath in front of me in white puffs. I was wide-awake, trying to take in what I was hearing and there it was again. Tap ... tap ... tap. I made the sign of the cross on myself. I knew instantly this was a warning—a premonition of trouble, terrible trouble.

Oh Jesus, I was so scared. *Please, God, make it stop.* But the tapping continued right round every inch of the house that night, even into the bedrooms where youse childer were asleep. Then, just as I thought the tapping had stopped, my heart missed a beat because there in front of my very own eyes was the wrath of your da passing straight through the wall in the hallway. 'Ahhh, Holy Mother of God, protect us all.' What in under God did this mean? 'Harry?' Sure he was at ICI doing the night shift.

It was bad enough that I had to put up with him during the day, but now he was fecking haunting me when he wasn't even there. I slowly reached over to grab my rosary beads and, trembling, I began to say the *Rosary*, the most powerful prayer of all.

'Hail Mary, full of grace, our lord is with thee. Blessed art thou among women, and blessed is the fruit of thy womb, Jesus. Holy Mary, Mother of God, pray for us sinners, now and at the hour of our death. Amen.'

Light was just coming through the slit in the curtains when your da came in the door at seven o'clock the next morning. I breathed a sigh of relief until I heard him, roaring mad, and I leapt out of bed to see what all the commotion was. He was in the kitchen with his trousers in tatters, and blood running down his leg where half a dozen wild dogs that roamed the streets in Rathcoole had near ate the arse off him as he walked home from the bus stop.

'Wild fucking dogs, five or six of them. I'll have to get that hawthorn stick your da made to take with me to work. The fuckers near ate me alive. If I get the chance to get the boot in first, I'll kick their melt in. I hate fucking dogs and as long as I live there'll never be one in this house.'

Well, underneath my serious face I didn't know if I was going to laugh because I couldn't help thinking he deserved all he got for what he put us through.

As I made a cup of tea I remembered what had happened the night before. I told him the tale about seeing his wrath walk right through the wall.

'It's a sign ... a sign of bad trouble coming. It's what Mammy used to say ... the tapping's the worst of all.'

But he took no notice. He was too busy licking his wounds thinking about how he was going to get to work that night, and where the feck he could find a big enough stick to bate the skulls off the wild dogs. It wasn't long after I heard that warning that your da was half kicked to death and left in the gutter, and we were put out of Rathcoole.

I was shit-scared, but I couldn't tell anybody. What could they have done about it anyway? If I had, they'd have said I must have been drunk or nuts, and in them days I never even touched a drink.

THE DAY THE DANCING STOPPED
Isabelle

What happened to us in Rathcoole should never have happened in a million years. We weren't involved in anything and your da's only allegiance was to the bookies. I had trouble keeping my head above water on a daily basis, just trying to get above the poverty line and raise you six childer. And with poor Jimmy-Paddy so sick all the time too, I was lucky to get time to scratch myself.

'But, Mammy, why can't we go and help light the boney for the twelfth? Mrs Greene said there'd be fireworks and everything. Can we go?' you'd ask, Berny.

'For the last time, you can watch from the window. You're not going outside to join in that "Orange" party anymore, and that's the end of it!' I'd say.

Things were changing in Rathcoole; there was talk of trouble between Catholics and Protestants. Neighbours retreated behind their doors and were mixing only with their own kind. No more parcels arrived from Mrs Granger with knitted jumpers or fancy underwear, and people became afraid to talk to each other. Worst of all youse were all kept in at night—no playing outside especially after dark. The troubles in Belfast were getting worse and often we heard the bombs going off. With every bomb we heard explode, your da and I became very scared.

'It'll never reach us. There are good people here; we'll be safe. The peelers will catch the troublemakers soon. Don't be worried. If I've said it once, I'll say it again—British bobbies are the best in the world. They'll catch the hallions causing the trouble. You'll see, Isabelle,' your da said reassuringly.

We stepped up the prayers at home. We believed that if we prayed hard enough, the cloak of divine protection would be enough to shield us from any troubles. We would say the *Rosary* together because not only was that the most powerful prayer of all, but the family that prayed together, stayed together.

Every evening, no one was allowed out to play; we all had to kneel down in a circle in the living room. That is, everyone except Jimmy-Paddy. He was allowed to sit because he couldn't walk or talk. I handed out the rosary beads; we all had our own, which, when they weren't being used were draped over the corner of the Sacred Heart picture that hung on the living room wall. These rosary beads were special because they had been blessed by Lourdes water. Your rosary beads were pale blue, Gerry's were brown, your da's were black and mine were mother of pearl. Even your da knelt down on the floor and leaned on his chair with his elbows, and I'd lead the *Rosary*.

You always asked me how long the *Rosary* would take, Berny, and I always said the same thing; about an hour. But you knew it would be longer if you didn't say the prayers properly because I would make you all start right back at the beginning if you did it too fast. I had to kiss the crucifix as I started the prayers, bless myself and then I would begin. God, Berny, that brings back memories alright. 'I believe in God, the Father Almighty, creator of Heaven and Earth, and in Jesus Christ, his only Son, our Lord, who was conceived by the Holy Ghost, born of the Virgin Mary, suffered under Pontius Pilate, was crucified, died and was buried. He descended into Hell. On the third day he arose again, he ascended into Heaven and sitteth at the right hand of God, the Father Almighty; from thence he shall come to judge the living and the dead. I believe in the Holy Ghost, the

Holy Catholic Church, the communion of saints, the forgiveness of sins, the resurrection of the body, and life everlasting. Amen.'

Now the prayers in the *Rosary* were the same every night, but what you had to think about as you said the *Rosary* changed depending on what day it was. On Mondays and Saturdays I'd tell you we would be praying about the joyful mysteries of faith.

You didn't mind thinking about those because they were about happy things like the angel of the Lord telling Mary she was going to have a baby, and Mary going to visit her cousin Elizabeth, who was having a baby too, who turned out to be John the Baptist. The third joyful mystery was all about Christmas, when the new baby Jesus was born, and you definitely didn't mind thinking all about that as you were praying.

The fourth joyful mystery was all about Jesus being taken to the temple when he was a baby, because that's what you did with baby boys in those days. And the fifth joyful mystery was all about finding Jesus at the temple when he was older, when his mammy thought he was lost, but really he wasn't. He was just trying to be a big boy by preaching to the holy men, who all thought this was amazing that a young boy knew as much about holy things as they did, because he was only twelve.

We all had to take a turn to say a decade of the *Rosary* each. I went first, your da second, Gerry third because he was older than you, and you went last, which meant I always said an extra decade because all the other childer were too young to say the *Rosary* on their knees. When all the decades of the *Rosary* had been said, I'd say the *Hail, Holy Queen.* You liked this prayer because it was all about Our Lady, who was Jesus' mammy. And it seemed to you that if Jesus wasn't listening to your prayers, you had a second chance at it because if you prayed to his mammy, she could put a good word in with her son. And because he loved his mammy, he would listen to her and grant your prayers.

'Hail, holy Queen, Mother of Mercy, our life, our sweetness and our hope. To thee do we cry, poor banished children of Eve, to thee do we send up our sighs, mourning and weeping in this valley of tears. Turn, then, most gracious advocate, thine eyes of mercy toward us, and after this our exile show unto us the blessed fruit of thy womb, Jesus. O clement, O loving, O sweet Virgin Mary. Pray for us, O holy Mother of God.'

And you would all say, 'That we may be made worthy of the promises of Christ. Amen.' So the only nights you really paid any attention when we were saying the *Rosary* was Mondays and Saturdays because you didn't want to think about things that were sorrowful or too hard to understand.

I told you prayers, especially children's prayers, were very powerful and would do you all no end of good. I was very pleased that your da was joining in, too, because it was a good example for you all. You had an idea that the quicker you said the prayers of the *Rosary*, the quicker you'd get back out to play before it was time to come in. But I knew better. Any time you tried to hurry the prayers, I'd look at you and remind you of the power of prayer.

'Now, Berny,' I would say, 'children's prayers are even more powerful than adult's. God listens especially to those ones so you better say them right or God'll know that you don't mean them.' You did try to say the *Rosary* right, but on all the other days of the week, when you were supposed to be paying attention and not dillydallying in your mind, all you could hear were childer having fun out in the street, and you wished again you were a rich Protestant who could be out playing outside and not have to be worried all the time about what God thought. One night, as your da got off the bus after finishing work, he was jumped by a gang of hooded men and was half kicked to death. They left him lying in the gutter. Hours later, he was found by the minister who lived in the manse as he put out his bins. He thought someone had dumped a sack of rubbish when he saw the bundle in the gutter. That was until his eyes focused in the misty light of the street, and realised that the bundle was a person. As he bent over to take a closer look, he thought the person was dead.

There was frantic rapping at our door. 'Isabelle, can I come in?' said Mrs Greene. 'I have some awful news. Harry is at our house. He's been badly beaten. We need to call the police.'

'Jesus, Mary and Joseph, why? Why would anyone do that? He's done nothing wrong.'

'Ach, it's probably been some young hallions.'

When your da was carried into our house on a blanket, I thought he was going to die. He was moaning and all limp; his face was covered with blood. He couldn't walk; he just kept saying, 'Ah Jesus, ah Jesus!'

'Get the childer out of here. They shouldn't be seeing this,' said Mrs Greene, and youse did as you were bid. But it was too late; youse had seen everything.

You were all crying with fright.

'What was happening? Was Daddy alright? Was he going to die? And what were the police going to do?'

Your da took months recovering from his injuries and he was never able to return to work at ICI. He became very depressed losing the best job he ever had. He couldn't lift a shovel of coal his back was so bad. They'd broken almost every rib he had, and to make things worse there was little or no money coming in anymore, which made him even grumpier than usual.

He hated the fact that he had to take handouts from social services because he was too sick to work. 'Fuck them and fuck them over again,' he said. Life was in a downward spiral, with a sense of doom looming closer every day. Just when we thought things were returning to normality, another gang got hold of our poor Gerry, him that couldn't defend himself, but he managed to run and fell into the house scared to death. He'd seen what had happened to his da and they nearly got him too. We were terrified.

One night the TV news was on, telling the usual stories of unrest and trouble in Derry and Belfast. Wee Jimmy-Paddy was propped up in his wheelchair, looking at the cars going up and down the street, when we heard an almighty crash followed by a thump. Our front window had just been put in and a huge rock with a note attached lay in the middle of the living room floor.

'Jesus Christ!' your da exclaimed. There was glass everywhere.

I screamed, 'Stand still! Don't move or your feet will be cut to ribbons!'

Your da grabbed Jimmy-Paddy. He was covered in shards of glass, but seemed to be unhurt. We put youse under our oxters, lifting youse up and into the back kitchen. Everyone was hysterical. I was shaking. Your da was saying, 'The fucking bastards, I'll kill them,' and then the shock set in. Jimmy-Paddy could have been killed. He was at the window. The poor wee soul, who couldn't even walk or talk, could have been killed for nothing. Jesus, when was all of this going to end?

The note that was wrapped round the brick said, 'You've got twenty-four hours to get out or your dead!'

Your da called the police. The police knew we were in grave danger. People who had ignored such notices had been burned out by Molotov cocktails—this was our first and last warning. There was only one thing we could do, and that was to let the police take us somewhere safe till things got sorted out.

'What? Leave our house, Mammy?' you said. 'Tonight? But … but … it's bedtime. What about our clothes? What about school? I told Bernie Dugan I'd call for her on the way. And we've got cookery tomorrow. What about dancing class Friday night? And the Feis … on Saturday? Mammy?'

Panic was rising in your voice. 'Whose going to tell Perry McDaid that I can't do the two-hand reel with her? Can I still go? Please, can I?' Your voice was now a crumbly sob. 'How … how will anybody know where we've gone?'

There were no answers that night, just a numb quietness as we all tried to take in what was happening. So in the middle of the night, with only the clothes we stood up in and one packet of Jimmy-Paddy's paper nappies shoved into a plastic bin bag, we were spirited away like ghosts—no flashing lights to tell people something bad was happening to us. 'Just get your clothes on. Take nothing else. We'll be back for the rest.'

'Where are we going, Mammy?'

'I don't know, love, just somewhere safe.' That night, two police cars drove us miles into the countryside to a caravan park. A place that your da later found out was a safe house for police informers.

When he discovered this he was terrified people would get the wrong idea and think we were informers too. That would be all we'd need; some bastards getting the wrong idea and we'd be in danger again.

His brain worked overtime trying to figure a way out. He believed the troubles were the road to nowhere—innocent people and families being crucified for nothing. As I've said before, his loyalties lay with no one except himself and the bookies, and he wished the fuck the troubles would disappear so that he could get back to the racetrack.

He was right to be worried, though. It didn't take long for the rumour mill to start spinning. Even some of our own families began thinking that your da must be an informer. Why else would we have been put out, then taken to a safe house in the middle of the night? The rumour grew even bigger. Some said he informed to pay off some huge gambling debt; a rumour that seemed plausible to all who knew his addiction to the horses. They even said your da had been paid thousands—then where the hell was he hiding it? I couldn't believe what I was hearing on the grapevine. I made him get on his hands and knees in front of the Sacred Heart picture to swear on his mother's life and *The Holy Bible* it wasn't true, which he did. I believed him, Berny. He was many a thing, but a thief or a liar he wasn't. If he'd come into money, he'd have disappeared to the bookies with it; he wouldn't have been able to resist splashing out on boxes of Black Magic. I knew him inside out. He may have been a foolish gambling fecker, but he was no turncoat or informer.

You had a deep fear, Berny, that we wouldn't go back to Rathcoole, so before you got into the police car, you grabbed your dancing medals and Portia, Jimmy-Paddy's teddy bear. As you looked out of the window of the police car, you knew you'd never see our house again. You wondered why this was happening to us, even though we'd said the *Rosary*, the most powerful prayer of all, on our knees to protect us. 'Maybe we just hadn't said enough rosaries to stop the trouble coming,' you said. You also thought it was your fault the prayers hadn't worked because you only paid attention on Mondays and Saturdays, you said the *Hail Mary* too quick, and you wished you were a rich Protestant who lived in a fancy house and went on holiday to Blackpool and Butlins.

But the thing that made you feel really sad was that the second-chance prayer hadn't worked, and you wondered why. You were sure Jesus would have heard us reciting the *Rosary*, as we said it every day for a whole hour. But you weren't sure if Our Lady had followed it up with her son and told him how important the prayers were, or if Jesus just wasn't listening to his mammy when she told him about us. You decided I was right ... if you didn't say the prayers correctly they just didn't work. Not even the second-chance ones, not even if God was supposed to listen to childer more. We never said the *Rosary* again on our knees. There was no point. It didn't work and the troubles came anyway. We were exhausted and scared half to death. Jesus, Mary and Joseph, and that's a prayer, if you'd get that warning for nothing, what else could happen? Despite the awful situation, childer have an amazing ability to live in the present. I told youse we were on a wee holiday because there were swings and a slide in the caravan park. Maybe things weren't going to be too bad after all. So with me feeding you childer and all of us crammed into the caravan, I suggested your da take himself off to get out from under my feet, and go to the pub for a pint.

I was hoping he'd keep himself right. He knew our situation was serious and I didn't need any more trouble, least of all from him getting one over the eight or even worse, stocious. I knew he was as worried as me. He was pacing the floor like a bloody cat on a hot tin roof, but having him hang round the tiny cramped space of the caravan was making things worse because he would start chiming in with my business with you childer.

He agreed that a pint might help him relax, so he set off that evening and walked the couple of miles to the village pub. When he came out of Tobernaveen many months later, he told me he walked along the seashore that night looking at the rippled sand. The tide was out for miles and the smell of the sea filled his nostrils. Big clumps of stringy seaweed lay flat along the rippled sands, like discarded toys. He felt in his pocket for his baccy and lit the last rollie he had in his tin, deeply inhaling the sweet taste.

He just stood looking out at the channel, Berny, his hands thrust as far into his overcoat as he could push them, and he shivered. Not a sign of any trouble here, not a soul about. Was this really the same country? It was almost hard to believe. There was just the twinkle of cottage lights as homes lit up along the seashore like a necklace about a giant's neck. He wondered how the hell we were even there, how this could have happened. What was going to become of us all, and what the hell could he do about it?

The thatched pub with its whitewashed, thickset stone walls had stood for hundreds of years, welcoming locals and travellers alike. Even dogs were welcome if they slithered under the table of their masters and kept a low profile. He flipped up the latch and was immediately hit with the loud rumble of voices, banter and country craic. He sidled his way to the bar and ordered a Carlsberg Special.

Gingerly he glanced round, watching to see if anyone was looking his way, but no one was. They were all engrossed in their own company and he told me he felt relieved for a minute. Here alone at the bar, he had time to get his head showered, time to think about what the hell he was going to do. Where would we live if we couldn't go back to Rathcoole? It was still so hard to get a council house and we'd waited years for the bungalow so that we didn't have to keep carrying wee Jimmy-Paddy up and down the stairs.

We'd put our heart and soul into that house, as if we owned every brick. All the years of hard work to get it looking half decent; diverting the stream that ran under the house, clearing the garden of all the rubbish and rocks, and planting flowers. And now it was all gone, with every stick of furniture and piece of clothing we owned. Where would youse childer go to school? And would we be able to find another special-care unit for Jimmy-Paddy? Would we have to change our names? Would anyone believe us that we weren't involved in anything?

Why the hell did we have to scarper like rats into the night? Why hadn't the peelers arrested the fuckers who had caused this mess? Were the peelers scared too? Then a dreaded fear filled him: if the peelers had no say in what was happening, then the law of the land couldn't protect us. And if it took nothing to get us put out of Rathcoole, then what would somebody make of us staying in a safe house? The stupid, stupid fuckers, bringing us there … of all the places in the world they could have taken us. Some bastards could say there was no smoke without fire, and that could be enough for us all to be riddled. People were getting intimidated left, right and centre.

He said he had never felt so alone or helpless. There wasn't anybody who could help us or take us in. They were all in the same boat; everyone was afraid and not a room to spare. He was certain only of one thing, there was no way out. As last orders were called at the pub, he shuffled out into the darkness, back along the seashore, the seaweed all covered now by the incoming tide. Moonlight was dancing on the silvery waves as they crept closer to the shore. Every footstep he took felt so heavy. How did everything look so normal when in reality it was anything but? As he crunched the sandy beach, his chest felt as if it was made of lead. He couldn't breathe and he said he wouldn't have given a soul a penny for his thoughts because they weren't even worth a penny that night. He said it was the longest walk of his life and every soul in the caravan park looked like they were now asleep. He was stocious, staggering and swaying so much he fell over the childer's seesaw in the playground. Without a word he opened the caravan door.

Do you remember what happened next, Berny? I probably don't have to tell you. We were in bed; you were sitting up talking to me. Your da staggered in and pulled the door firmly shut behind him. He locked it with the key and then without a word reached over and threw the key out of the caravan window. We didn't know what was happening. He bent down, turned on the gas and announced, 'If we're going to die, then we're all going to die together.' Then he collapsed unconscious across the fire, cutting his head open as he went down. The panic and confusion was instant. The baby started to cry, you were hysterical, and I knew I'd have to move his body to get near the gas switch to turn it off. You leapt out of bed and, with me, tried your hardest to shift his dead weight. It was no good. We couldn't move him. The caravan was so small and the blood from his cut head was now all over our hands and your petticoat. He was wedged tight against the gas fire and up against the table. The smell of gas was quickly filling the caravan and you were all crying. I looked at you and said, 'Quick, Berny, I'll push you through the window. Find the key and open the door.' Next thing, I was pushing and squeezing you, shoving you out of the caravan window. Oh my God, you were caught.

'I can't move, Mammy. I'm caught on something.' You were dangling upside down, half out of the caravan window, all the blood rushing to your head.

'Mammy! I'm caught!' You tumbled, head first out onto the damp, dark grass and onto your hands and knees. Your petticoat was torn. It was pitch black and freezing. You swept your hands round, left then right, turning around and doing the same motion—no key. You couldn't find the key! Panic set in. I could see your hands shaking and you weren't thinking straight. The gas! This was really bad. Mrs MacNulty had taken the head staggers in Rathcoole when her husband went off with a woman from White Rock, and she was so ashamed she put her head in the gas oven and was killed stone dead.

If you wanted to do away with yourself this was the way to do it. John Riley who lived in the flats next to the Diamond shops did it— head in the gas oven—and he was only twenty-three. He left a note to his mammy that nobody talked about. It was a terrible shame for his family. Mrs Lamb next door told me that the note he left said he was queer, and if he couldn't live with the person he loved, he'd rather be dead. You didn't know what it meant to be queer, but you knew it made John Riley so sad he killed himself with his head in the gas oven, and his mammy cried every day for the rest of her life.

You were outside in the dark and everybody else was inside the caravan. If we all died you'd be on your own! You couldn't find it. My heart beat faster and you had started to cry more. Suddenly you found it. 'Mammy, I've got it!'

'Good girl! Now open the door, quick! Hurry, Berny! Put the key in the lock.' But the key slipped out of your hands again, you were shaking so much. *Oh God! Please help her.* You couldn't see anything in the pitch-black night. But this time you felt it and clutched it tight, holding your right hand with your left to stop shaking. You felt for the lock, turned the key and the door opened.

We all ran out onto the damp grass. I grabbed Jimmy-Paddy, you grabbed the baby, and the other childer huddled together sobbing. As I looked up, Gerry wasn't crying. He was standing motionless, as a big dark stain began to spread down his legs where he'd wet himself in fear, while the rest of us began to vomit from the gas fumes. The police were called and your da was arrested, and when they heard that he'd taken the head staggers and tried to kill us all, they committed him and took him to Holywell Mental Hospital. It would be many months before we saw him again. I thought to myself again, what I had ever done to deserve all this. As if it wasn't bad enough being put out by those dirty lousers and cowards who called themselves an army, but I had to contend with your da going nuts and nearly killing us all too.

And this was all due to making one lousy mistake in my life and marrying the wrong man. I shivered as I felt the spirit of someone walking over my grave. My silent tears were unstoppable because all I could think about was Jack Kennedy and what his arms would feel like round me right now, and if youse had been his wee childer, this would never have happened. Do you know, Berny, what scared me most of all? If I'd lit up a cigarette to calm my nerves, we would all have been blown to kingdom come. This was the day the dancing stopped according to you, Berny, and our lives were changed forever. You'd never see your dancing teacher or your best friend or Stella Maris ever again. Worst of all, you had said, Teresa Wright would step into your place at the dancing championships, performing the dance you'd made up. She'd get the trophy. You weren't sure what broke your heart more: the fact we'd been put out of our house leaving our life behind forever; that your da had just tried to kill us all; or that this was simply the day the dancing stopped. Nothing would ever be the same again and crying about it would just cause more trouble. And that was at least one thing we could do something about. Berny, for years I wanted to kick your da's melt in I was so angry with him and that's the truth. We were all shit-scared, nobody more so than me, but to take it into his fecking head to take us all with him? I couldn't comprehend it. I was boiling; the audacity of him to think it was alright to take our lives too. I understood his fear, of course I did, especially after everything that had happened, but his actions? I never forgave him for that. No one has the right to do that to another human being.

PART 3

ANTRIM 1971

STARTING OVER
Isabelle

Now, the government tried desperately to quell the rapidly escalating unrest. The British army had been called in to protect Catholics who were in danger of intimidation. Families were being burnt out or put out nearly every night of the week, and as soon as they were out, Prods moved in. But even the army couldn't stop what was happening, and things got worse. After the caravan park we got the house in Antrim. We had nothing to speak of—the house was bare as most of what we had was left behind in Rathcoole.

It wasn't just the furniture, clothes and toys that were left behind, but our lives, memories, friends, schools and neighbours. And your da was still locked up in Tobernaveen. But for the rest of us, some semblance of normality returned for a short while, and I began to believe we would be alright. I set about getting youse into schools and making the house as homely as possible.

I was terrified of the day your da would be discharged from Tobernaveen. I didn't know how he'd be. Would he take the head staggers again? And would we all be safe? He'd lost his bap once and we were all lucky to be alive. God, I didn't know who to be more scared of—the fecker's causing the troubles or him. Many months later he was discharged with reassurances from the doctors that he was well enough to come home. And so, having no choice in the matter, he came back to live with us in Antrim. You childer were all pretty reserved round him, especially you, Berny.

The troubles in Belfast were getting worse. Your da and I were still afraid we'd be targeted again. Many people were intimidated or lifted from their beds by the British soldiers and interned without trial in Long Kesh. Armed bandits could kick your door in during the night for no reason other than what religion you were and empty a machine gun into you, or just take you away into the night never to be seen again. They didn't care who was watching, women or childer. There were tit-for-tat killings and reprisals. One night a Catholic would be killed, and the next a Protestant. Even young teenagers weren't safe, especially the boys.

We heard nightly on the news about yet another sectarian murder. We were terrified. We decided the only thing to do was to take turns nightly watching the bedroom window, in case any suspicious car pulled up outside. We slept in relays, always one of us on guard. This continued for eighteen months. The front and back doors were bolted from the top to the bottom. One morning I went out to get the milk from the front door step. As I stood up and turned round, I dropped the milk bottles, the glass crashing all round me. There right in front of me was a huge white cross, painted on our door. I started to tremble, and when I glanced down the street, all the Catholic houses had the white cross of death, too.

Oh my God, it was happening again. I leapt over the glass and spilt milk and rushed to tell your da what had happened. We didn't even hear the car pull up that night, we were so exhausted from lack of sleep. We knew too well this was a serious warning to get out again and we were both beside ourselves with worry. *Where could we go? To Dublin? Across the border?* We had no money, no car, and Dublin wouldn't accept Jimmy-Paddy because he was born in Belfast as a British subject.

He needed so much extra medical care; he wouldn't get that in the Free State. We made the decision that your da would have to look for work in England and see if he could rent a house. So off he went, using what little money we had, but there was no luck. There was plenty of work, but no houses. So he returned, defeated and even more depressed because it looked like there was no way out again. I took on child minding, along with my own six (there were often one or two other childer to mind) just so I could make a bit of extra money for our escape.

You'd remember this story, Berny. I thought maybe I would have forgotten a lot of it, but it's as if it happened yesterday. Our move to Antrim was a huge change in so many ways. Your da was still in the mental hospital and we weren't allowed to visit him. We knew nobody, had no friends and, of course, it also meant you had to start at a new school.

Saint Olcan's High School was a bus ride away. Even though there was a school nearby, you weren't allowed to go there because we were Catholics. For the first time in your secondary schooling, you had to contend with boys. You didn't know where to begin, how to talk to them, and what to say without going bright red. The school was so different, too. You thought the childer talked funny because you could hardly understand the thick country brogue. Saint Olcan's wasn't as strict as Stella Maris, where you had to have indoor and outdoor shoes.

The St Olcan's childer barely wore uniforms at all. If you looked hard enough, you could see a few of them had grey pleated skirts and blue jumpers. You thought you stuck out like a sore thumb because the only uniform you had was the one you stood up in and it came complete with a navy-blue gym frock, shirt, tie, blazer and beret with matching blue ribbons. There was no money to buy another whole uniform, but at least it was something to wear. Fitting in was the least of our worries, especially for me who was focused on keeping us safe and finding the money to feed us all. It wasn't long before the class you were assigned to were laughing behind their hands, talking about the stranger with the odd uniform, and, to make matters worse, these childer all said their prayers in Irish and you didn't have a clue what they were saying.

Then you found a friend.

231

'I remember, Ma, that day at school when someone nudged me in the back and, as I turned round, a girl with hair as black as coal and skin like a gypsy smiled and said, "Hello, I'm Freya O'Hare." *Freya*, I thought. *What sort of name was that?* But Freya let me follow her round the school, into the classrooms, round the schoolyard, and gave me the lowdown on all the teachers—who was nice and who wasn't, who to say hello to and who to steer clear of. By the end of the week Freya and I were inseparable, which was great because I didn't have to speak to the boys. Freya got free dinners at school like me. I got them because we were poor, and Freya got them because there were so many childer in her house they qualified anyway. So at least I wasn't standing in the free dinner line by myself because that was worse than wearing a different uniform. It felt shameful. It was as bad as having a sign round my neck saying, "I am poor".'

The school bus to St Olcan's made a thousand stops, picking up all the Catholic country childer along its route. You were on the bus to school one day when a crowd of childer got on and right in front of you were two teenage boys exactly the same—twins, with long golden curls that fell to their shoulders, denim jackets and the nicest smiles. You tried so hard not to look, but the sight was amazing—the two of them so gorgeous and they were exactly the same. Each day you'd wait to see if the twins got on the bus and stared at them as much as you could, without them catching on. You couldn't tell them apart. 'Who's that?' you asked Freya. 'I mean, who are they?'

'They're the Magonnical twins, Sean and Jerry. Why, do ye fancy them?' Denying it all roads, you nudged Freya back and swore her to secrecy.

You were on a mission to rid yourself of your Stella Maris uniform and so, bit by bit, I managed to buy you another uniform, which meant you looked the same as the other childer at school. The skirt was bought first and then the jumper, and finally the tie. No blazer or beret was required—sure you didn't even have to tie your hair back.

Another glorious thing happened to you: your teachers believed you when you told them you were in the 'B' stream of Stella Maris. They didn't even ring me to check, so you were able to avoid the plague of maths and science you'd had to endure previously. You never attended another science lesson again. Mr McBaine taught English and you couldn't wait for those classes every day. You were spellbound by the words of Keats and Wordsworth, even when you didn't really understand them.

Freya's family was much bigger than ours. There was no way you could remember all their names. They seemed to be everywhere at lunchtime. Freya was always bumping into someone she knew.

The bomb scares happened almost daily, and you spent a lot of time just sitting on the grass on the hurling pitch until it was time to go back in. You always prayed it wouldn't happen in Mr McBaine's classes or you'd never learn to recite the poetry. It's strange, you know, because even though we were in the middle of the country, the number of armoured cars, soldiers with riffles and tanks grew as the British army patrolled the streets more and more every day.

Sometimes they stopped you as you were walking to the school bus, their guns pointed as you boarded. Sometimes the soldiers ran alongside the tanks and they would suddenly lie down on their bellies, behind hedges or on the grass verges while still pointing their guns, and some walked backwards covering each other. They shouted to each other through mouthpieces. I told you never to look at the soldiers or talk to them. You never spoke to the soldiers, like you were told, but you had desperate trouble trying not to look at them because some of them were black, and you hadn't seen a black person in real life, never mind ones with English and Scottish accents. You'd only ever seen pictures of black babies in the missions in church magazines, and those people lived in Africa.

One day you couldn't keep your eyes off a soldier who was patrolling alongside your bus, because his skin was so black it almost looked blue. When you came home you asked me why the only black people you'd seen were soldiers, and how come there were no black people living in Northern Ireland. I told you I'd never seen a black person live in Belfast in my life, and it wasn't only Catholics that 'Orange men' didn't like. They wanted a 'white Protestant state' as well.

I told you that our skin may as well be black because it was the same prejudice and bigotry that went on towards us. People were not only judged on what they believed, but also because of the colour of their skin. And you were still trying to work out in your brain what it meant to be queer because that too was something that wasn't wanted in Northern Ireland and it made people very sad—sad enough to put their heads in the gas oven. I said maybe one day we'd live in a world where it didn't matter what you believed, what colour your skin was or if you were queer.

I went mad when you told me what the soldiers were doing on your way to school, but it wasn't because of the colour of their skin. It was because I knew the soldiers were using you as a protective shield against snipers who were hiding in bushes and fields, figuring they wouldn't be shot if they were in among the school childer.

Jesus, Mary and Joseph, why can't they leave the childer alone? They're supposed to protect you, not use childer as protective shields. Look at what's just happened last night. A poor girl, pushing her pram and seven months pregnant, lost her wee unborn baby when the bastards fired rubber bullets into a crowd. When's it all gonna end?' But there was nothing that we could do about it. Everybody was in the same boat and there was nobody to tell; it was happening everywhere and you still had to go to school.

It wasn't surprising that not much work got done in school on the days the soldiers were round. The teachers found it difficult to control the childer and to get them settled. Even when they did, the alarms would sound for yet another bomb scare and you'd be running out to the hurling field again and again. Your prayers to Our Lady must have worked because you never missed one of Mr McBaine's English classes, even with the bomb scares.

There was no dillydallying on your way home. Anyone talking to the soldiers would be tarred and feathered, a sign of a traitor. One morning you'd just got off the school bus and were walking to the school gates about fifty yards away. You didn't even notice the armoured car pull alongside you. You were trying hard to get a skeg at the twins. Within seconds the soldiers were pouring out of the armoured car round you all, shouting at the top of their voices and pointing their guns at you. You didn't know what to do, and Finn Kelly wet himself when they looked at him and called him a little fenian bastard. His da had been lifted the night before and he thought he was next.

They grabbed both the Fitzgerald brothers, who were in the class above you, their older sister screaming to let them go. They were thrown with brute force into the armoured car with the soldiers (who had faces covered in black stripes that looked like coal) still pointing their rifles at them. As the armoured car sped away with the boys in the back, you later told me that you saw the soldier in the back pishing all over them. They'd been lifted on their way to school. They were fourteen years old. By the time you all ran screaming into the safety of the school to tell the teachers, the soldiers were gone. You never saw the twins at school again.

SUNDAY BLOODY SUNDAY
Berny

When the government moved us to Antrim, Da wasn't with us because he was still locked up in Tobernaveen. You tried your best, Ma, to make the house homely. And because Da was locked up and couldn't work, we got free bus fares and free school dinners, which I hated and complained about constantly because only 'poor people' got free dinners. You were just glad we had a decent meal in our bellies. Looking poor was the very least of your worries. We didn't know when Da would be let out of Tobernaveen, and we weren't allowed to visit because the place was full of lunatics.

You know, Ma, I remember thinking if Da was a lunatic, then how would he get home again because lunatics were never allowed out? I clung to the hope that Da had just taken the head staggers because people sometimes did that and it didn't mean they were a lunatic. Being a lunatic was a big disgrace and if you had one in your family, you didn't tell anybody about it. So we didn't tell anybody round the doors where Da was all those months and, funny enough, nobody asked. It just looked like I didn't have a daddy. With him locked away, we existed in peace and there was no fighting in the house. Jesus, it was great.

I had a lot more time to think about things, like how nice Donny Osmond was and what life would be like if we lived in America. And so it was about this time I remember talking with an American accent and telling everyone in Antrim I'd just moved from there. That sounded much more interesting than my real life, as did walking with a limp and trying to dye my legs brown with leftover tea.

Of course, you couldn't make head nor tail of why I suddenly developed a limp and a strange Yankee accent, but you were so busy with all the other childer and had enough to worry about without taking any notice of my imaginings. So my imagination got to run riot for a while until the day David Gillespie, who sat at the back of the school bus, set fire to the ends of my plaits with a cigarette lighter, which he stole from his mother's handbag. He did it because he said I walked and talked like a tube.

It was the smell that I noticed first—the same singeing smell from when I was wee when you tried to thicken my skinny hair. At first I didn't realise it was me who was on fire. David Gillespie had run to hide at the back of the bus where all the naughty childer sat, and he started shouting, 'Look at the tube; the tube's on fire!' When I turned round to see who he was shouting at, my plaits flicked round and the burning ribbons smacked me in the face. I was up like a shot running up and down the school bus squealing. I didn't know what to do and the flames were getting closer to my face. The bus driver heard all the commotion and stopped the bus quickly, which made me fly down the aisle on my hands and knees, putting a big hole in my new black tights.

The bus driver took David by the scruff of his neck and threw him off the bus telling him he was a 'little bastard' and that he'd be walking to school from now on. He then picked me up off the floor of the bus and checked the fiery plaits were out, and told me to tell my mammy when I got home what had happened. I was devastated. It had taken me four years to grow the skinny hair long enough to put in plaits. Now it was all gone.

This abruptly ended my affair with wanting to look interesting. It also made me want to stay away from boys. It was a year later that Tony O'Neal asked me if I would go to the pictures with him. My first date! So I said yes, although I wondered why Tony O'Neal would ask me out as my face had more acne spots than the whole school put together and I flushed scarlet every time he spoke to me.

The reason soon dawned on me for Tony's romantic dalliance. As the lights dimmed in the picture house and his arm slipped around my shoulders, his hand slid down the opening of my shirt to grab anything he could. The dirty bastard! All he wanted was a touch up.

'Get off me ye creep!' I said, but undeterred he leaned over to kiss me, grabbing my bottom lip, sucking it nearly off me chin, and declaring that's how to French kiss. French kiss me arse! All I could think of was how I'd ever talk again with a lip that felt the size of a balloon. When I told Freya at school about what happened, she agreed boys were dirty bastes and good for nothing.

The day came when you told us childer that Da was finally coming home from the mental hospital. You didn't want him to come back because you'd had a bit of peace while he was locked up. There were no rows, you had no trouble with money because he hadn't been able to do it in at the bookies, and you were afraid of trouble starting all over again. You told him you didn't want him back, and that you couldn't live with no money and just wanted some peace. It was bad enough that we'd been put out of our home in Rathcoole. We even got a dog while he was away in the mental hospital, which he wasn't one bit pleased about; he was shit-scared of dogs.

You said the dog was staying and that he could go; it was up to him. You told him you'd trained the dog and you would only need to give the command to Judy and he'd be a goner. But there was nowhere else he could go. Everybody else's house was full and nobody really wanted somebody living with them who'd been in the nut house. He pleaded with you on his hands and knees to take him back. He had to because by now it was your name on the rent book and you didn't have to run anywhere. This time the shoe was on the other foot, and it gave you some hope that, at last, you had the power in your own home. He swore in front of the Sacred Heart picture that he'd never do his money in again—that is, if he was ever able to get a job again. I must admit he was a pitiful sight. You felt sorry for him, and nobody deserved what he got, for nothing. He looked pathetic and he still had a bad back that needed Belladonna plasters put on him every night. So reluctantly you said he could come back as long as there was no more trouble. He said he'd live with the dog but that, if it so much as looked sideways at him, he'd wring its fucking neck. And after what happened to us in the caravan, we believed him.

The peace in Antrim didn't last long. The troubles started getting much worse. The nightly news reports of people being lifted and interned for nothing were widespread. You could be taken from your bed and imprisoned without trial by the *Special Powers Act* that had been passed, and everybody was terrified it could happen to them.

Da said we'd all be safer in the lunatic asylum up the road. What had been bad troubles turned worse again, and people were getting riddled in their homes or at work. One time a Catholic would be shot dead and then days later there would be retaliation and a Protestant would be shot dead. Nobody knew who'd be next, so a baseball bat was kept under your bed and again you took turns staying up at night and peering through the windows, in case a strange car pulled up at the door. In the time we lived together in Antrim, you didn't get one night's sleep—both of you at the same time. Armoured cars with soldiers patrolled the streets round us, even at night, but even that didn't stop people getting riddled. We were terrified all the time, and you were glad we had an electric fire and cooker in case Da took the head staggers with worry and tried to kill us all again.

You both made a plan to try to escape to somewhere safe and England was the only option due to wee Jimmy-Paddy's condition. But Da couldn't work because his nerves and back were bad after him being half kicked to death, being put out of Rathcoole, and for being locked up all that time with the lunatics. So you had to go out to find work and try to save enough money to get us out of Northern Ireland so we could live in peace.

You saved enough money for each trip to England for him to look for work because you took a night job at British Enkalon, a factory in Antrim, and you took in more childer during the day to mind. But each time Da came back from England with no house and no job, the feeling in the house got worse. Not even Da was telling any jokes and the news we listened to every hour of the day, told us how bad the troubles were getting.

Sunday 30th January 1972 was so cold—you could imagine the fur-clad people in Siberia, the wind was that bad. We'd all gone to eleven o'clock mass. Well, all of us except Da who said he'd mind Jimmy-Paddy because it was so cold, but really it was because his nerves were still wrecked and he was afraid to go out of the house in case he was lifted, riddled, given another good hiding for nothing, or his arse eaten off by wild fecking dogs.

You had made a big pot of soup the night before and we were looking forward to our Sunday dinner. Da didn't complain this time about the potatoes not being floury enough because there were worse things to worry about than floury potatoes, and he wouldn't have dared fire it up against the wall. I think he knew that any trouble from him and the men in white coats would get him and he'd be back to Tobernaveen, and that was one place he wasn't going back to again if he could help it.

Sunday afternoon was quiet in the house as we watched a film on TV while you busied yourself getting washing folded and clothes and uniforms ready for school. The six o'clock news began its usual theme tune, and us childer knew to be quiet while you and Da listened carefully to updates about the troubles.

Da walked over to turn the volume up on the TV as the news began to report a massacre of unarmed people in Derry. People were shown dead on the ground, blood all over the pavements, and a priest trying to help by holding a white hankie. Nobody knew how many people were dead or wounded.

People were running everywhere and screaming, some trying to waken up the dead who were lying on the pavements covered with people's coats. It showed the British army everywhere, pointing their guns and shouting at people. Except this wasn't a film. This was on the news and it was real.

'Isabelle, Jesus, come quick!' Da called. As you rushed in from the scullery you saw the TV and people lying dead on the streets of Derry. You fell to your knees, the tea tarl covering your mouth.

'Jesus, Mary and Joseph! Harry what's happened? What's going on? Are people dead?'

'The army's opened fire and just kept shooting. They haven't counted the dead yet. Jesus, what's going to happen next?'

We were terrified. You could have heard a pin drop; none of us childer spoke.

'The fucking bastards! They were sent here to protect us and they're murdering innocent people in broad daylight. How in the name of Jesus can this happen? It's 1973, not the fucking dark ages!' Da raged at the TV. But no answer came that day, only fear. Fear that not even the police or army could protect us, and there was nowhere to run or hide. Even if we'd had a place to run to, we had no way of getting there. You were both shaking as you lit cigarettes to calm your nerves, and us childer stood motionless and pale.

I don't mind telling you, Ma, it's another day I'll not forget. I was shit-scared, the knot in my stomach getting bigger and tighter. I knew there were gangs who could kill us. I knew, too, that Da had tried to do the same thing in the caravan.

Now in front of my eyes on the TV, the army was also shooting people dead in the streets. My legs were turning to jelly and my head felt like it did when the altar boy at mass swung the incense that made me faint. I wanted to run away from Da in case he tried to kill us again, and away from Northern Ireland where death seemed to be inevitable. I reached out to grip your arm and looked up at you.

'Mammy, I don't want to die.' Seeing the impact on us pulled you back from the despair you felt and you got angry. You were angry with the 'arseholes' who had nothing better to do than terrorise ordinary people; angry with the British army who were sent in to protect us and instead were shooting the very people they were there to help; angry that we'd lost everything we'd had in Rathcoole; and angry with Da whose feckless, gambling, foolish ways hadn't even left us an escape route, just a slippery slope into poverty.

You knew you had to do something immediately to reassure us or there'd be more than one person in the house headed to the lunatic asylum. You dried your eyes, steadied your hands and first of all you boomed at Da. 'Harry Savage, as God is my witness, you'd better pack your beg and head to England, and don't come back until you have a job and a house for us. I've worked my fingers to the bone to make it happen and you need to do your bit. And if you so much as raise a hand to harm a hair on our heads, I'll set the fucking dog on you.'

Eh, Da had never seen you so mad and he knew that you meant every word.

'Now, pack your beg for England.'

And like a child, and to our astonishment, he got up and started packing his beg, and the shawl he had round his shoulders slipped to the floor. The black Belladonna plaster was sticking out from under his jersey as he dragged himself off the chair, making his way up the stairs to pack his beg. All I could think of was who would put the next plaster on his back if he was in England because it would be too awkward to do it himself.

'Right! Childer, listen to me. There's nobody going to be dying in this house, do ye hear me? Daddy and I have got a plan and I need you all to be good and help me.' We all nodded frantically, willing to do anything so we wouldn't die.

It was another long year before Da got a job in England and a house for us to live in, but your complete belief in our escape plan, and your extraordinary strength for working extra shifts in the factory night after night to get the money we needed to get out of war-torn Northern Ireland was what kept us going. I was able to believe there was a chance to stay alive because at least there was no one inside the house that was going to kill us because you told Da you'd do him in if he tried anything again.

It was that day, Ma, that you took every sharp knife out of our kitchen drawers and put them in the bin because you were afraid that if Da started, you'd run a knife straight through his gut and out the other side. You knew that if that happened we'd have no Mammy or Daddy, and your worst fear was that we would all end up in Dr Barnardo's. You said there was no way you were going to let that happen, not for some no-good dirty louser who gambled all his money and left us poverty-stricken.

So for the rest of our lives we had to peel the potatoes with a butter knife that had no sharp edge, but you said you didn't mind that the peelings were as thick as your finger, and that it was a small price to pay for peace of mind and making sure you wouldn't be done for murder.

'Hey, Ma, would Judy really bite the arse off Da if you gave her the command?' I asked.

'Ach, Berny, that dog is afraid of its own fecking shadow. It was all a bluff and blow, but he doesn't know that and I had to try something and bluff is all I have left.'

On Sunday 30th January 1972, British soldiers shot dead twenty-six unarmed men during a peaceful civil rights demonstration in the Bogside area of Derry. Thirteen men died immediately; seven of them were only teenagers. Many were shot in the back as they tried to run away. It took the British government two major investigations to find out what happened that day and why. It wasn't until 2010 that the British Prime Minister made a formal apology to the victims and their families who died on Bloody Sunday.

From that day on, there was no walking to church. No one walked anywhere, especially after dark. By this stage Da was back home and you were both walking a fine line with your health, and were desperate to escape to somewhere safe, when one night a TV program was shown on BBC Two about a company needing key workers for their factory in Durham in England, and that accommodation would be offered if applicants were suitable. You both looked at each other and knew you had to give it one last go. So with the last fifty pounds that you had saved, Da returned again to England to apply for the job and this time, bingo!

He got the job and the house. Even us childer were dancing, we were so excited because at last we knew we could escape. All the arrangements were made in secret. We couldn't tell anyone where we were going. We weren't allowed to say goodbye to any of our friends, and our dog Judy was given away, much to your dismay and Da's relief.

Our begs were packed and the plane tickets bought. We were going to England! The day before we were due to fly, one of our neighbours got into his car, turned the ignition key and had both his legs blown off. And we really believed we were next.

PART 4

ENGLAND 1973

WE ARRIVE IN ENGLAND
Berny

Season of mists and mellow fruitfulness,

Close bosom-friend of the maturing sun ...

Until they think warm day will never cease,

For Summer has o'erbrimmed their clammy cells ...

Where are the songs of Spring? Ay, where are they?

Think not of them, thou hast thy music too ...

Hedge crickets sing; and now with treble soft

The redbreast whistles from a garden-croft;

And gathering swallows twitter in the skies.

Keats, John: *Ode to Autumn* (Extract)

We couldn't leave for the airport quick enough. The taxi was called and we all piled in. We childer were so scared of something really bad happening. The plane took off for Newcastle, England. I'll never forget the feeling of fear and disbelief—fear that the plane would be blown up, and disbelief that we were really escaping. I also felt panic that even though we were on a plane, it wasn't going fast enough to get us away. And I was scared because I couldn't see who the enemy was. They didn't have a face or a uniform. I just knew they were out to get us.

As the plane flew over the Lake District, the cartwheel of mountains and lakes became more and more visible. The pilot announced we were flying over a national park. As I gazed out of the window of the plane, I couldn't match the picture I was seeing with my eyes to Mr McBaine's English lessons at St Olcan's. Was this really going to be the place of daffodils as far as the eye could see? Maybe it would as long as we landed in Newcastle. And just as long as nobody blew up the plane, maybe I would get to see where Wordsworth had written his poems.

'I wandered lonely as a cloud that floats on high o'er vales and hill, when all at once I saw a crowd, a host of golden daffodils.'

I remember trying to make sense of the muddled thoughts in my head, Ma. Suddenly I turned, 'Mammy, look, it's just the same colour as Ireland.'

I felt so desperate to find something, anything that looked familiar; something that would tell me not everything in our lives had changed. The only thing I could think of was that at least the ground we were about to land on was the same colour.

It's not a long plane ride from Belfast to Newcastle. The journey was so fast it was hard to imagine we were really in a different country. Da met us all at Newcastle airport and I didn't understand why you were crying. Weren't you glad we didn't get blown up? Weren't you pleased we'd get a house and all our troubles would be over? Later you told me you cried because of what Da said when he saw you. He told you that he'd make sure you never saw your family again. He said you'd pay the price for him spending all those months in the nuthouse. You cried because you were now in a country with no sisters, brothers, mother or father, so there'd be no more visits from your daddy and no sisters to visit. It wasn't a great start.

We may not have been killed by bullets or bombs, but Da had just stomped all over your heart. And the new rent book was now in his name so he could treat you whatever way he wanted, and you'd be on the run again. The black dog descended, seeping into every crevice of your heart and soul.

We were waiting at Newcastle train station and it was getting late. Fog had set in, making everything seem colder. We childer were all tired and getting hungry. Jimmy-Paddy was hapt up in his buggy, which was a new invention and easier to move around than a wheelchair. No one saw the tramp move up beside us as we stood waiting for the train. Before anyone could stop him, the tramp with his brown paper bag and torn clothes, leaned over and kissed Jimmy-Paddy on the cheek.

Da yelled at the aul tramp to take his self off, and you pulled the buggy away as fast as you could but it was too late. Within minutes, Jimmy-Paddy began to rock backwards and forwards gasping for air. There was pandemonium on the platform as we shouted for help and for someone to call an ambulance. Jimmy-Paddy couldn't breathe; his face and throat began to show great white lumps as his throat started to close up. We were terrified! Da was so quick. He whisked him out of the buggy, rubbing his back, and tried to blow some air down his throat. You were trying to comfort the rest of us who were scared to death. None of us knew what was happening.

Our train pulled into the station as the ambulance arrived, taking you and Jimmy-Paddy with it to the hospital. Jimmy-Paddy spent his first night in England being treated for anaphylactic shock. The aul tramp must have eaten fish—something Jimmy-Paddy was highly allergic to. Oh, Ma, it was a shit start to a new life. I remember thinking, if this was England, I didn't like it and I wanted to go back home. To make matters worse, we couldn't get the keys to our new house in Durham for three days and we had no money and nowhere to go. So social services made up some beds for us at one of their local shelters for homeless people.

Although the people were kind to us, the beds were lumpy and had aul man's smell on the bedclothes. Nothing looked clean, and when we were given breakfast in the morning, the porridge made me gag. Eating your porridge twice a day had been bad enough, but this porridge was lumpy and thick, and the sausages were big, thick, greasy things that leaked big blobs of fat. If this was English food, I didn't like this either.

Finally we got the keys to our house and a fine looking house it was, we thought. It had three bedrooms and a large garden at the back. We unlocked the front door and were met by the stench. The house was putrid and the aul dirty curtains hung in rags. Everywhere needed a good scrub. It would take all of us weeks to clean it.

The wooden draining board propped up beside the aul sink was covered in dirty aul milk bottles—two hundred and thirty of them. When Da accidently leaned on the sink, all the bottles came crashing down, sounding like a million glasses breaking. You yelled for us to stand still or we'd be cut to ribbons. After the reception you got at the airport from Da and that shithole we had to stay in, your nerves were as jagged as those broken milk bottles, Ma. And, oh God, I knew how you felt. I just wanted to go home—back to where we knew everyone; back to Granny and Granda; back to the dancing when the bus conductor let me keep the sixpence for the bus fare; back to my aul school and my best friend who knew everything about St Olcan's; back to Mr McBaine's English class where I could read books and dream about poetry; back to a time where we could roam the streets and play on the ice in winter; back to when Mrs Granger brought us parcels of knitted jumpers; back to when nobody cared if you were a fenian bastard; back to when nobody got put in Long Kesh for nothing or got shot in their beds; just back and back and back …

We knew we were lucky to escape Northern Ireland. We had made the right move even if we had moved to an 'aul dunderin inn'. It wouldn't take us long to have it looking like a shiny new penny. But I still couldn't shake the feeling of loss, of wanting to go back.

THE BOAT PEOPLE
Isabelle

We'd been in England two years when it was all over the news about people from Vietnam trying to get into England by boat. They were fleeing for their lives from a war in their country too. Maggie Thatcher didn't want these people coming into the country, and I thought she was a cold-hearted cowyard and that if she'd ever had to flee her home for fear of her life, leaving behind everything she owned and the people she loved, she'd have a different song to sing.

I was overcome with pity for the boat people. I told youse that your wee faces may as well be as yellow as theirs because what happened to those poor boat people was the same as what happened to us. Except at least we got to come by plane and not by a rickety boat that sometimes sank and the people got eaten alive by sharks! Those poor souls had risked their lives just to get a bit of peace, too. They had lost everything, leaving their kith and kin behind, trying to start a new life, and who could blame them?

I knew what it felt like to be afraid for your life—thinking you'd be the next to get it, even if ye hadn't done anything to deserve it. I saw the plight of the thousands of boat people fleeing a war-torn land, just the same as my wee family and me. Jesus, Mary and Joseph, why didn't people understand what it was like? But, then again, I thought how could they really know if they hadn't been through it. They hadn't felt the fear, seen the devastation it caused, or felt the heartbreak of families being torn apart. How could anyone understand? They had no idea what it was like to be a refugee. But I did.

Bit by bit the boat people were allowed into England. Those who were Catholic went to the parish priest for help because they had nothing but the clothes they stood up in when they arrived—just like us. The priest contacted the local convent and, at mass that Sunday, he called for volunteers to help the boat people in any way the parishioners could.

'Could anyone make plates of food or donate any aul clothes or bedding? Could anyone decorate a house and get it ready for a family?'

I didn't need to be asked twice. I volunteered myself along with you childer to clean and prepare the council house in our street that had been allocated to a Vietnamese family. Like the house we'd been allocated, the one for the Vietnamese family was putrid. It needed to be scrubbed from top to bottom with bleach.

It took days and days before the water in the buckets stopped turning black from the grime the previous tenants left behind. On and on we cleaned until I was sure the house was clean enough for the family to live in.

Jeez, Berny, we all worked liked navvies, didn't we? And you didn't seem to mind. You all just followed me down there every day till it was done. All the while you wondered what the family would look like and what colour their skin would be. Would it really be yellow like I said? What if they couldn't speak English? How would they get their messages from the shops? Or even go to the doctors? 'What did people eat in Vietnam?' you asked.

'Nora Jones told me they ate cats and dogs and didn't think twice about it.' you said. So you were sort of glad we didn't have a dog or cat just in case.

'Sure people would eat anything including each other if they were hungry enough,' I said, which made you shiver. But I reassured you there'd be enough food for the family, so the street's cats and dogs would be safe. Your da said he wouldn't mind if the Vietnamese ate 'every fucking dog on Earth', then he'd have no more worry about having his arse half eaten off. After the scrubbing, came painting and decorating. Down we all traipsed again to help the Sisters of Mercy—everyone except your da who said his back was still broke from the hiding he got in Rathcoole. He still got me to put the black Belladonna plasters on his back to help the pain and, in truth, I wanted to shove that plaster up his arse for all the trouble he caused. But he would help the cause by looking after Jimmy-Paddy, which kept him from the bookies at least because nobody, not even your da, would be seen dead taking a handicapped child in a buggy into a bookie's shop. That just wouldn't be decent.

Remember the day when the house was nearly finished? We traipsed into the Vietnamese house to discover that the nun in charge had painted the living room ice blue. I stopped and looked for a minute, a shiver running down my spine. 'Jesus, Mary and Joseph! Look at that cold colour on the walls. The place feels like a morgue.'

I asked the nun why had they'd painted the living room such a goddamn awful colour, and the nun dismissed me with a snort. She gruffly stated that the paint had been donated, and that 'Quite frankly beggars couldn't be choosers.' Well that was enough for me to take the head staggers while youse childer stood and watched in disbelief.

'Here! Sister Mary, Mother, what's your face? Do you realise these poor unfortunate refugees have come from a place where they're used to being warm?' The nun just stood there, paintbrush in hand, peering over her bifocal glasses, which were nearly slipping off the end of her sweaty pock-marked nose. The nun flushed red with rage at the audacity of a commoner having the gall to question her charitable efforts. She told me to make myself useful by finishing the rest of the painting.

I was starting to boil.

'Have you no consideration for what these poor people have been through, Sister? These people have been to Hell and back! They've lost everything, including their own kith and kin, and the last thing they'd want is to sit in this freezing country, shivering at the sight of that bloody awful colour.'

That supercilious, pious fecker didn't know what she was doing taking me on that day. I went on.

'They've got little enough choice in what's happening in their lives right now. The least we can do is help them feel warm.' Well the nun said she'd never heard such codswallop and how dare I question her.

'These … these people … should be grateful for anything they get!'

I stood with my arms folded and told the nun I wasn't lifting a paintbrush till the colour of the paint was changed. The nun reared up and told me she'd tell Father Ryan that I was nothing but a trouble-causing bog trotter who had no right to tell a nun what to do. I told her to go right ahead, that I wasn't afraid of either her or fecking Father Ryan!

'We'll see about that,' said the nun as she pushed passed past me with her nose in the air and muttered 'trash' under her breath.

The nun left the Vietnamese house scurrying as fast as her legs could carry her to tell Fr Ryan what I'd said. Before she reached the back door, I lifted the loaded paintbrush and fired it after her, catching it on the back of her pristine navy-blue habit and landing like a big bit of bird shite.

And I called after her, 'G'along ya big tachara and take your fucking ugly paint colour with you.'

We watched as the nun who was now running, as well as glancing behind her, disappeared up the street and out of sight quicker than a coursing hare. I looked round at you childer not saying a word, but then I couldn't stop the smile spreading across my face. Within seconds there were uncontrollable gails of laughter sliding out of all of us, till we couldn't stop the tears, even though I knew it was wrong to fire a paintbrush at a nun.

Now, of course, that's not where it all ended. Father Ryan did come round to our house that night. But when I explained to him how I felt about the poor Vietnamese boat people and how I knew what they'd be feeling, Father Ryan agreed to get me any colour of paint I wanted provided

I told the nun I was sorry for firing the paintbrush at her and wrecking her nice navy-blue habit, as well as saying 'fuck' to a nun. I told him that as long as the paint was the colour of a Vietnamese sunset, I'd agree. And so it was that the living room for the boat people was repainted in burnt orange, the colour of the sunset in Vietnam to help them feel at home. And I told youse childer there are times in life when it's a good thing to eat humble pie as long as it's for a good cause.

THE SILVER JUBILEE
Isabelle

It was 1977 and England was abuzz. Queen Elizabeth II had been on the throne of England for twenty-five years and the whole country wanted to celebrate. Neighbours in our street started talking about a street party with cakes and balloons, bunting, sack races and games for all the childer. Everyone round the doors seemed happier and friendly, stopping to pass the time of day.

Excitement and anticipation filled the air. Even Mr Rajesh, who owned the corner shop in Leyburn Street, put a big poster of Queen Elizabeth resplendent in her crown jewels in his shop's front window, next to the sign for British bacon, tins of mushy peas and pork pies.

Betty and May Wilson, who lived opposite us, put themselves in charge of the street party arrangements, given out jobs to each family. May spoke like the Queen. I heard on the grapevine they'd once been rich and had fallen on hard times when their father lost his entire business—house and all—after a partner had cooked the books and swindled him out of every penny he made. And their mother died of a broken heart because of the disgrace of it all. Betty always wore a pinny even with her pearls, and May always followed Betty about because she only had one good eye. The other eye, being made of glass, didn't sit straight in her head, making it very difficult to know if she really meant what she was saying—she always looked distracted. I knew they were kindly aul souls, salt of the Earth, decent people, English or not.

Now the whole notion of a party for Queen Elizabeth didn't bother me one bit. I was sure that it would have been no easy task trying to run that family business. Sure, didn't they say that half of them were crazy, and that their money made no difference to what genes ran in their blood. Some of them were locked away, out of sight of everyone, in some institution for the rich. This was all due to bad blood. Half of them were related because of intermarrying—cousins and so forth—which wasn't even legal.

Oh, aye, I was glad I wasn't one of them. At least I knew where I came from on that score; there was no inbreeding in my family. What puzzled me was that all the neighbours seemed to be in on the party preparations, not just the Prods but the Catholics too. Even Doris Watson, who served at the wee Christian bookstand at the back of St Mary's, was making table decorations in red, white and blue.

'In under God, would ye look at that,' I exclaimed, as Mr and Mrs Nguyen and their two childer joined in the party. This was the very family who I'd made sure their house was painted the colour of a Vietnamese sunset just so they wouldn't feel cold in the winter. Even the street cats and dogs were still round much to everybody's relief.

This was very strange. Where we'd come from no Catholic or coloured person, no matter where they came from, was welcome at any party that flew the Union Jack, or where the pavements were painted red, white or blue. Those events were for God's own Protestants only, not second-class citizens like us.

I'd kept my thoughts to myself about the jubilee party; I didn't discuss them with anyone outside the house. But one day, to my surprise, Betty and her sister May appeared at our front door with their pearls, pinny and glass eye. They'd come to ask if you kids and I would like to help put the bunting up for the street party.

I started to laugh.

'Now ladies, you know we're Catholic's don't you? And that every stripe on the Union Jack bunting spells nothing but bullets and bombs to us?'

May looked up at me with her glass eye fallen away to one side, which made me take a step back in case it fell out of her head, and she told me they'd be daft if they thought that because most English people didn't give a fiddler's fart about what was going on in Northern Ireland, and to be honest, they didn't care either. So as long as I would bring along a plate to share, well then, we'd all be welcome at the Queen's silver jubilee party.

'Sure, half the Queen's subjects are neither Protestant nor Catholic these days,' declared May.

Well I threw my head back as I laughed. And then May swung her head round laughing too, her glass eye staying exactly where it was so I wasn't sure whether to laugh or not.

'Are ye sure now? I'll only let the childer and me come along if we're welcome?'

'Ehhhhhhhh ... pet ... of course, you and the wee bairns are welcome.'

England had at least given us all a place to exist in relative peace without the worry of bombs or bullets and for that I was very grateful. And if that meant having a red, white and blue street party then that would be okay.

The bunting was strung from lamppost to telegraph pole up and down the street. Long, skinny trestle tables, normally used for hanging wallpaper, were decked with clean, white sheets. The street was awash with Queen Elizabeth's face on every paper plate and cup, and the Union Jack flew high on every flagpole. There was so much food we could hardly believe our eyes. There was enough for everybody; you could even have a whole plate to yourself without having to dish it out round half the street.

Although the air was palpable with excitement and enthusiasm, inside you had felt uneasy, Berny. You weren't sure what to make of it all. Something held you back; it just didn't feel right. You were afraid that any minute someone would tap you on the back and say, 'Get out! This party is not for you. You don't belong here. You're nothing but a lousy fenian bastard.' You kept looking round, not touching any of the food, and trying to catch my eye to gauge what I thought. When I winked at you, you knew that was the go ahead. You picked up the paper plate with Queen Elizabeth's face on it, slowly turning it over in your hands. Her eyes were kind and her face gentle, and you wondered if she was our Queen too.

You touched the Union Jack flag, tracing your fingers over the red, white and blue stripes, and nothing happened. You weren't struck down dead. There was no thunderbolt and lightning. It was just a flag and this was just a street party. Today we weren't different from anybody else in the street. Today we weren't hated because we were Catholics. Nobody was going to burn the Pope on the boney on the glorious twelfth of July. Today we weren't second-class citizens who couldn't even get a decent job. Today it didn't matter if we were Catholic or Protestant.

This party looked like the street parties held in Northern Ireland on the glorious twelfth of July, but it wasn't the same. There were no Orange marching bands with fancy uniforms and shiny maces being thrown up in the air and twirled round by some young buck who thought he was better than us. There were no big drums beating out the victory tunes; no balding middle-aged men in bowler hats and suits with their Orange sashes depicting their lodge membership that no Catholic was allowed a part of; no dancing and singing about how King Billy beat the Catholics in a battle long, long ago; no big boney with a dummy on the top who was meant to be the Pope ready to be burned as the people danced round it; nobody shouting 'fenian bastards', 'fuck the pope', or 'no surrender' at us; and nobody to tell us we couldn't come to the party because we weren't good enough.

All your life you had wondered what it would feel like to be a rich Protestant, Berny, and that day you didn't need to because it didn't matter anyway—we were all the same. And you wondered if Queen Elizabeth would smile too, if she knew our whole street was happy—even us.'

THE BLACKDOG
Isabelle

England was meant to have given us all a new start, peace of mind and a chance to live a normal life, but the troubles seemed to follow us. Bombs were being set off in London and Birmingham, and anyone with an Irish accent was a suspect—and looked at as if we'd planted the bombs. No one in the streets really knew what was happening because only half the story was ever reported on the news. Your da and I were afraid again and we told you childer to keep to yourselves.

'Don't open your mouths; just walk on and tell nobody where you're from.'

The discovery of rotten eggs pelted up against the front of our house didn't help matters one bit.

So once again the front and back doors were laden with bolts to stop anyone coming into the house in the middle of the night. I wasn't coping with life, away from my kith and kin, and everything that was familiar to me. I sank deeper and deeper into depression. The constant struggle to survive with very little money, the loneliness and the isolation, the trouble with your da and the feeling of no way out sent me to the doctors.

I wasn't able to explain to the doctor all of what I'd been through. There wasn't enough time in ten minutes to even begin to tell my story, and what had happened to us all, so I just sobbed and described your da's gambling. In hindsight, I should have looked for another doctor, one who had the time to listen, one who could have got me a good therapist who I could have talked things through with. It wasn't just about your da; we'd been to Hell and back, losing everything and everybody we knew because of what happened in Northern Ireland, and I now realise we should all have had trauma counselling. Jesus, Mary and holy Saint Joseph, it's a wonder we all didn't end up in Purdysburn Asylum, you poor childer and all.

The doctor wrote me a script for Valium, telling me it would help me sleep. So I arrived home and took the tablets. A week later I couldn't function. I couldn't stay awake to even look after wee Jimmy-Paddy. I was out of my mind with worry about what to do. I couldn't survive like this. This was no answer to anything. So I flushed them down the toilet. But a few weeks later the doctor gave me some more Valium and told me I had to take them or I wouldn't be able to cope. And of course doctors, as well as priests, were not usually people who you argued with. They knew what was good for you, so it wasn't long before I couldn't do without the pills.

I felt like I was living a foggy nightmare and it just made my depression seem much worse. And your da was still doing his money in or at the pub at every chance he got. I cried a lot. I cried for my lost life and my love of Jack Kennedy who I should have been with. I cried for the loneliness and the loss of my beloved Ireland and my family. I cried the hardest for my wee childer and the fucking awful life youse had to live, which wasn't what I had dreamed for youse. And I cried that there was nothing I could do about it all but watch youse suffer.

The first time you couldn't wake me up, Berny, you thought I was dead. No matter how foggy I felt, I was always an early riser and had breakfast on the go. So this was strange. My hair was matted to my head, my mouth open and it was then you noticed the empty box of Valium beside the bed. You tried to shake me awake. Your heart was racing as you shook me harder and harder and tried to sit me up.

'Mammy, wake up! Mammy, wake up!'

I was still slumped over in the bed. I was warm so you knew I wasn't really dead, but you couldn't tell if I was breathing right. You ran to the living room, called an ambulance, and you all watched terrified as the ambulance man put a tube down my throat. I was then taken away to the hospital to be pumped out.

A few days later, I was home again. You didn't ask what had happened, but you felt you nearly came close to losing me. Your da said very little. You stayed off school as long as you could until I was back on my feet again. You didn't want to think about what had happened, just that I was okay, because the alternative was too scary. You told me, Berny, that the thought that I might leave you all alone in the world with only your gambling da or that you would end up at Barnardo's, was a worse worry than any fighting or trouble you'd ever seen in Northern Ireland. You were terrified.

The second time you found me unconscious was on the floor of the bathroom. This time you knew what to do and didn't waste any time. You called the ambulance straight away and again I went off to the Memorial to be pumped out.

On this occasion, the doctors realised I was very depressed and their answer for that was shock treatment—electro convulsive therapy. It didn't matter that I would suffer memory loss and be bombed out for days with the most excruciating, blinding headaches, or that shock treatment couldn't fix your da's gambling, drinking ways that kept us in abject poverty, or fix the loneliness within my heart. I got the shock treatment anyway—two courses of ten. And you took more time off school to look after me and the rest of the childer. Your da was made redundant from his job at Cummins and that just made everything worse. Because now he was feeling bad, too, and to ease his pain, he'd gamble and drink even more of his dole money. I pleaded with him to get a job, but he said he wouldn't unless the job he got paid for was more than the dole.

FALLEN ANGEL
Isabelle

I wasn't really improving, even after having the shock treatment. I guess, in the end, even that couldn't cure a broken heart. But I had confided in a hospital social worker about my plight and how desperate I was to live a normal life. I described my unhappiness living with your da and the poverty that had engulfed me all of my married life. The social worker told me she knew of a way that I could get a house of my own and leave him, but it would mean me moving to Leeds and declaring myself homeless for at least six weeks. Although I didn't want to leave youse for a second, I knew this was probably the only way to secure a rented home for us all. Since leaving the house in Antrim, again my name wasn't on the rent book, and I feared that your da could do and say what he liked and there wasn't a damn thing I could do about it. He could literally put me out again. The plan was hatched, you'd stay off school and look after the childer and the house, keep your head low, just do whatever he asked you to do, and I would leave for Leeds. As soon as I could get a place to rent, I'd come and get you all and we'd move to Leeds together, where he would never find us, and we'd live happily ever after. The social worker got me the address of a safe place to stay and then I left, leaving behind only a brief note for your da to say I was leaving him. Da would quiz you at length to see if you knew

264

where I'd gone, Berny, but you said nothing. You told the childer that I needed a break and would be back in a while. Your business holding the house together kept you out of your da's way. Every night you'd tell him you were going for a walk and you'd run to the train station and wait for the Leeds–Durham train. You didn't dare bring the wee ones in case they let it slip they'd seen me.

You were always careful not to look too cheerful when you went back home, so as not to alert your da that something was up. You and I would sit on platform no. 1, trying to keep warm while I filled you in on the details of what I was doing, where I was living and how soon we'd all be together in our own house. You'd let me know about what was happening at home, how all the childer and Jimmy-Paddy were doing, and what your da was up to.

Then an hour later I'd go back to Leeds on the train, with a promise to meet me again the next night after you'd fed the childer, and to make sure your da was looking after Jimmy-Paddy. It wouldn't be too long and we'd be together again. This was the only way to get a house of our own. I hated Leeds, Berny. I found it very difficult to fill my day and being away from you childer drove me deeper into depression. Jesus, I didn't know if I would last the six weeks. You tried to tell me you were okay and that you were taking good care of everyone, and that the house was spotless. But it didn't matter what you said at our nightly secret meetings; I wanted to see all my wee childer. I'd been in Leeds three weeks when I got a severe pain in my back. I went to the doctor who did all the tests of the day and told me to give up the cigarettes. The tests and the X-rays came back okay, but the pain in my back had spread round to the left side of my chest. It was agony. I couldn't sleep and I was frantic now to see you childer. The doctor in Leeds saw me again and, after he'd examined me, simply looked at me and said, 'Mrs Savage, I can't see what's causing the pain in your back, but I suspect that if you don't go back to your children, you'll die of a broken heart'. So after four weeks in Leeds I came home and everybody was delighted I was back, even your da. I think he knew I wouldn't be able to stay away from you childer too long. But the hope of us getting a wee place of our own went out the window; things were right back at square one.

Your da was so glad to see me back, he didn't go to the bookies to do his money in for weeks. But just as we thought life was getting better, he was late home one night and we all knew what that meant. I was distracted by this stage. I'd tried everything to escape only to end up even more depressed and still living with him.

I went to see the doctor one more time and I told him I didn't want Valium, I needed some real help before I did something to your da that I'd regret. You see I still had the fear that I'd snap and run a knife clean through him for all those years of misery. That was why there was never anything sharper than a butter knife in our kitchen drawers and the reason why our potato peelings were half an inch thick. Most other people could put all their peelings in a matchbox, while ours filled the whole sink. And you just had to peel more potatoes till there was enough for everyone's dinner.

This time I recounted to the doctor what I'd been through. How I'd nearly died taking the Valium and how even shock treatment hadn't been able to help me forget about my life with your da. It just made me forget where I'd put my teeth and my wedding ring, and gave me an atrocious headache. Finally, I told the doctor about trying to leave and get a house for us all in Leeds, but how my heart nearly broke and the pain in my back near killed me. The doctor listened, this time carefully, and he knew I was desperate.

'Mrs Savage, do you take a drink?' he asked.

'A drink, Doctor? What do you mean?'

'Do you have a favourite tipple?' he added.

'Oh, I don't drink alcohol, Doctor,' I replied.

'Well, Mrs Savage, I recommend that you find something you like the taste of and have a tipple before bed to relax you. It'll help you sleep. You'll feel a lot better with a good night's sleep. Oh, just one or two, you know, see what helps you sleep.'

266

'Okay, I'll give it a try.'

'Good day, Mrs Savage.'

So I went to the nearest off-licence and asked the proprietor if he could recommend a tipple that would help me sleep, like the doctor had advised, and he recommended rum—rum and coke. He gave me a quarter bottle of Jamaican rum, plopped the money in the till and wished me all the best. I took the tipple and then had another. It didn't taste all that bad with coke, and do you know what? I had my first good night's sleep in years.

I was so pleased. *Why hadn't the doctor recommended this years ago?* And you know, I did feel better with a good night's sleep. I wasn't living a foggy nightmare like what happened with the Valium. I was more able to cope with the stress when your da did his money in, and I began to look forward to my sleep remedy, which I was using as directed by my doctor ... every night.

THE NEIGHBOURS
Isabelle

Durham sits nestled in the north-east of England. Its centre is overlooked by a grand cathedral, with many of its quaint streets still cobbled and crooked—that's where all the wealthy live. You were all quickly settled into schools, and our church was within walking distance. Schools in England were very different to Northern Ireland; the teachers were kinder and nowhere near as strict as the ones we'd left. People were relaxed and no one was interested in whether you were a Catholic or not. For many years, though, when I met someone I'd have to stop myself asking the other person 'that' question: are you a Mick or a Prod? Because that defined everything and whether you could be trusted or not. We lost all contact with family and friends; there were no letters sent back. We thought even the phones may be bugged. There was no choice, so no use complaining about it. That was the way it had to be for safety. The parish priest knew our plight and he often made contact with people who could get us clothes, food and some furniture. You were all very obedient childer, thank God. Causing trouble of any kind was never an option. To add any fuel to a fire of distress that already burned was just unthinkable. You settled into your schools, and support for Jimmy-Paddy was abundant once we negotiated our way round the maze that was disability services.

Your da still did his money in, but he did it less as you childer grew and realised what he was up to. He usually ended up at the pub instead. It wasn't unusual for our Grainne to wait until your da was in a drunken stupor, and then creep into the bedroom to go through his pockets and find a winning bookie's docket, which she would then turn over to me like Robin Hood, much to my cries.

'Jesus, Mary and Joseph, your da'll kill ya if he wakes up.'

When he woke up and searched for the bookie's docket and cash, he thought he was going daft as he couldn't find them. He never knew who the Robin Hood in the family was till the day he died, or if he did, he wasn't game to say it.

I loved my wee garden. It was my refuge. It also meant there was always a place for the childer to play with the goblin ornaments. There was a place for the wee birds to get a drink and something to eat, and a place for Our Lady's statue that you could sit beside to quietly contemplate and say a prayer. There was an apple tree that Gerry planted, a rockery where magical things happened, and a waterfall that I built with my bare hands, which froze over every year. I spent every hour I could out in my garden. It was my pride and joy, and even pulling out the weeds gave me great peace. My daddy always said, 'If you worked in the soil, you'd never go mad.'

A huge hedge separated the neighbours, which was a good job. Your da's health had begun to fail. He smoked heavily, drank way too much and the only exercise he did was to walk to the bookies and back. So, not surprisingly, it wasn't long before he needed major surgery. He was very sick, but it was hard to feel sorry for him after all the hardship he'd caused, and he'd been grumpy for a long time now. He hardly ever told a joke anymore.

The neighbours next door came and went and eventually a young couple with four wee girls, one of them with cystic fibrosis, moved in. The coughs and splutters of that poor wee child were heartbreaking and the doctor was never away from the place. The mother was from the Philippines or somewhere like that by the look of her, with jet-black hair down to her bum and as shiny as a black pair of polished shoes. She was the size of a house, God love her, and every time you saw her, she had either a fag or a big cod's wallop of cake hanging from her bake.

The father was a skinny, long streak of shite, and if he were any older, you'd have said she was one of them mail order brides. The place was a midden. The back garden was more like a rag-and-bone man's yard. It was no wonder with the tribe of 'come all ye' who were in and out of it all day long. Come to think of it, there could well have been drugs going on as well. Initially they were very friendly, but when Saturday and Sunday nights came round, they'd party and fight like cats and dogs until the early hours. No one could get any sleep.

We tried to be tolerant; God only knows we'd done plenty of fighting ourselves. But poor wee Jimmy-Paddy couldn't sleep and his seizures got a lot worse. So I asked them nicely to keep the racket down to no avail.

We were all having Sunday lunch one day when 'him' from next door, drunk as a skunk, near knocks the front door down when Gerry went to answer it. We knew no more till he pulled Gerry out the front door into the garden and was laying into him like a mad man. The scene was chaotic. Your da, who was unable to move from his operation, was shouting for me to come quick. The rest of the childer were trying to see what was happening when all of a sudden I appeared from the back of the house with the hatchet.

'Let go of me child ye drunken fucker!' I yelled. The brawl continued with me yelling again.

'Jesus Christ, I said let go of me child before I cut the fucking skull off ye!'

I knew Gerry wouldn't know how to defend himself or fight back. He was taking a heavy thumping and was lying curled up on the ground. When he didn't let go of Gerry, I leapt into the middle of the fight, hatchet flying all roads. Even Gerry copped a glance accidentally. I was hysterical yelling for the big bastard to let go of me son. Seeing I was only five feet and two inches and poor Gerry couldn't fight his way out of a wet paper bag, you also leapt in to help, Berny, using anything at your disposal including your feet. Gerry was just about freed when the police arrived and took both Gerry and him next door to the police station for questioning—no one got any dinner that night. We were just sitting wondering when Gerry would be back when a policeman knocked on the door and asked to speak to me. 'Mrs Savage, we just wanted to clarify something. Your neighbour is saying that you hit him with a hatchet during that fight outside in your garden? Now that couldn't be true could it?' The policeman looked quite bemused as he glanced at my delicate little frame, knowing the neighbour was six feet and four inches tall.

'Well, actually, yes, I did it. It was me!'

So the policeman promptly took me to the police station to the cries of all you childer. You thought your da was about to die, your brother was almost kicked to death and now your ma was being arrested for using a hatchet on the fucker who started it all. It took a year for the case to come to court and in the meantime Gerry, 'him' and I had to behave ourselves and not bother each other. The nerve, I thought. He had started it all. Then came the stressful bit.

'Ma, tell the judge you're not guilty. Tell him you came out the back, from chopping sticks for the fire, heard the commotion and you didn't even realise the hatchet was in your hand!' you instructed me.

'But I am guilty', I said proudly. 'I did do it and, when I heard that fucker next door beating my poor, soft child, I ran to see which one of the hatchet heads wasn't loose. Oh I meant it all right; I wanted to give him something to remember for picking on our poor Gerry.'

Of course that's not the version the judge heard in court, or he'd have locked me up for sure. After the trial, a police lady stopped me and gave me back the hatchet with a sweet smile. Little did she know the tiger that raged inside my tiny frame. Now we were all bound to keep the peace for a year, but he continued to drink and party with his wife, and the squeals of her when he hit her every week would've put your head away.

I always called the police and they usually calmed things down. One Friday night the raging started again. Your da was very sick, Jimmy Paddy couldn't sleep and I was exhausted. I didn't have the energy to call the police again. The wife screamed and shouted as usual, then things went quiet and the music was turned off.

Thank God for that, I thought, now we can all get some bloody sleep. At about 2 am, we were woken by the blue and red flashing lights of the police cars outside. I slipped the curtain aside to have a duke at what was going on. My legs went to jelly when I saw the police wheel out the black body bag. The only night I didn't call the police and that was the night she was murdered. To my dying day, it's something I'll regret. I might have been able to save her.

Nobody deserves to die like that, and the poor wee childer were left without a mother. You know, he only got a few months because it was done under the influence of alcohol. I fucking well wish I'd hit the bugger harder when I had the chance.

But then I would have been the one in jail, and he would have killed her anyway—the only difference being, you wouldn't have had a ma.

I wouldn't hurt a fly really. You know that. But you know something, Berny, I see her ghost, the girl from next door. She wanders about that back garden looking lost. Her soul's not at rest. I think it was the way she died; I don't think it was her time.

AXY AND BOOTS
Berny

Da was still very sick. He'd had a major bowel operation that left him with a bag on his side. So life was even more hectic and demanding than before. He hadn't been sick in his life, except when the thugs in Rathcoole nearly killed him, so he wasn't used to it. And he made a terrible patient.

He was always calling you to go and see to him, Ma, and on top of wee Jimmy-Paddy's needs and the rest of the family to attend to, you were exhausted and sick of Da's moaning. You found it very difficult to minister to him when he'd caused you so much heartache and given you so many hidings in the past. In fact, you didn't give a tinker's cuss about how much pain he was in. At the time you thought he deserved everything he got. I was petrified, Ma, but not about Da. I was terrified that the day you appeared in court, for hitting the next-door neighbour with a hatchet, you'd be locked up. Every chance I got, when we were alone or out walking, I'd try and coach you about what to say when you went to court. You drove me to distraction.

'Ma, you have to plead not guilty or they'll lock you up.'

'Tell me again why I'm not guilty?'

'Ma, you're not guilty because you didn't mean to hit him with the axe.'

'Aye, but I did mean it. I wanted to take his skull off for starting on our poor Gerry.' Here we go again I thought.

'Ma, you were round the back chopping sticks and you heard the commotion. You didn't realise the axe was in your hand!' I explained.

'But I wasn't. I ran round when I saw him beating Gerry up, and I was purposely looking for the hatchet. I had three of them, two of them with loose heads, so I shook them all to make sure I had the right one.'

I was near to tears with exasperation and fear. *Oh God! She'll never get it before the case was due in court.* I was beside myself with worry at the thought of you going to jail, and us having no ma after all we'd been through; this just can't happen to us. Week after week I coached you, going through the same thing until I was nearly demented.

I couldn't focus or study; all I could think of was you going to jail. I'd spend every hour I could going over the questions I thought the judge might ask you in court. I had to get this right. There was no room for mistakes or we'd be left as good as orphans.

I felt guilty, too, because looking back I wanted you to hit that bastard harder for attacking Gerry when what I should've been doing was trying to get the hatchet off you. It was me who ran to find the hatchet out the back of the house while the police were interviewing you. With a Brillo pad, I scrubbed every bit of blood off it. It was me, too, who'd also joined in, trying to kick the shite out of the bastard for hitting our poor Gerry. You and me got a new nickname at home: Axy and Boots. All the kids laughed when we'd say it to try and make a bit of fun. But inside I was really worried and still couldn't study for the exams that were looming.

Months passed and the day of the court hearing was here. I prepared you again and told you to say you weren't guilty and to tell the judge why in your own words. I sat in the corridor of the magistrates court, shaking with nerves and almost blinded with fear. The door was closed and I wasn't allowed in.

Please, Our Blessed Lady, put the right words in Ma's mouth so she won't go to jail, I prayed over and over.

I watched the barristers, in their long black gowns and white wigs, glide up and down the polished floors outside court room number two, while the hands of the big wall clock ticked away.

You had no solicitor, and I wondered if, for once in your life, you would be able to lie your head off if I wasn't there to remind you how to do it. If you told the truth, it would look really bad. The judge wouldn't understand about Gerry being a big softy and that he could never defend himself. He wouldn't understand that Gerry had been bullied all of his life and you were trying to protect him. He wouldn't understand that your patience was broke with people causing trouble for no reason—that you'd been pushed beyond endurance. He wouldn't understand that what happenned to Gerry was another beating in a life plagued by them. He wouldn't understand that when you have been scared for your life in the past and faced with danger—left with nothing more than the clothes you stood up in—then you will fight like fuck to protect your own. And that you'd had a gut full of it. He wouldn't understand that the day Gerry was trailed out of our house and beaten like a dog for nothing was the straw that broke your back, and you had just snapped. He wouldn't understand that you had to fight because you weren't able to get up and run anymore; you had nowhere else to go.

The clock just kept ticking by, an hour, then another half hour. It felt like the longest day of my life, Ma. Finally the doors were open and out you came with no handcuffs. I ran over to you, hugging you and jumping up and down. You were free and we'd be okay cause our ma wasn't going to jail. As we walked out of the court, a policewoman called out your name, asking you to stop a minute. I immediately thought they'd changed their minds and I was getting ready to run. When all of a sudden the policewoman held aloft the hatchet.

'Mrs Savage, don't forget this or you'll not be chopping any sticks tonight,' she said handing the hatchet back to you. Holy shit, Ma, I still can't believe it to this day. I thought the policewoman had gone crazy for a minute, but of course, she didn't know that you really meant what you did and so we got the hatchet back. Almost a year of worrying and only three weeks to go till my exams. I hadn't been able to lift a book. We were out walking as usual with Jimmy-Paddy and you just happened to ask me about my studies.

'Studies?' I laughed. 'That's a joke, Ma. I haven't been able to look at a book for worrying about you. But that's okay, you're free and it's too late anyway. I can't pass these exams now, not in three weeks.' Well, I knew no more than you stopped dead in your tracks. Jimmy-Paddy clauded his drink because we'd stopped walking and he thought that was the end of his lookout.

'What did you just say?' you asked, your eyes getting wider, your face getting redder.

'I said, Ma, I can't pass the exams. They're only three weeks away!'

You raised your voice and people in the street started to look. I pleaded with you to stop shouting. You turned to me and made me face you like a child.

'Now you listen to me, wee girl. I have loved every hair on your head from the minute you were born, and I never raised any child of mine to be a failure or a victim. Do you hear me? Repeat after me. I will pass the exams.'

When I didn't reply, you got louder.

'Repeat after me! I will pass those exams. Do it now!'

And to shut you up I repeated what you said.

'Louder!' you demanded. So I had to say it till I was shouting at the top of my voice in the middle of the street.

Well ... people stopped and stared at the two of us shouting about exams. One woman walked straight into a lamppost trying to watch the commotion and Jimmy-Paddy trailed his blanket off the wheelchair firing it down the pavement in protest. You told me you didn't want to see my face until after the exams were finished, and that, if it took twenty-four hours a day, I was to study till my brain hurt. And that's what I did. In three weeks, I crammed the contents of a three-year course into my brain and, to my astonishment, I passed. And you smiled and told me it was what you expected. Maybe I wasn't stupid after all.

ALMOST ELECTROCUTED
Isabelle

As Gerry grew up, he didn't make many friends, and those he did make soon became aware of his eccentric ways. He liked to do things in a routine way, and he got very grumpy if anyone got in the way. It didn't matter if he was putting the washing in the machine or baking scones. Gerry had a set way to do it, which he didn't like anyone interfering with. He liked to take Jet the dog for walks, but only to certain places. He went to the movies at the same cinema year after year, and he never liked any commotion in the house. He didn't like anyone fighting or arguing, especially your da and me.

One night when your da was fighting with me, gulldering and carrying on, I knew no more until Gerry had quietly walked into the kitchen, picked up a large glass bottle full of coke, walked into the hallway and smashed it clean over your da's head.

'Now shut the fuck up!' he said and then, as if nothing had happened, he calmly turned away and walked out of the house and down the street, leaving your da sitting dazed on the floor and us all staring in disbelief. Nobody really said much, including your da, who amazingly just went and sat in the living room chair and lit a smoke. Well, it ended the row alright, and from then on everyone was cautious about fighting round Gerry, just in case he really was crazy.

I was distraught about his gatherings and acquisitions, too. Do you remember when we found the shepherd's crook under his bed? That had put the wind up me big style. I'd had Gerry tested by a psychiatrist who told me he couldn't find any mental illness. But if Gerry wasn't crazy, why did he do crazy things? I wasn't taking any chances.

The day I found the shepherd's crook, I decided we'd all sleep in the front room. So I made up a bed on the floor, and I got you to help me push the big chest of drawers up against the bedroom door so, if anything happened during the night, the door couldn't be opened.

Your da slept in the back room. He could take his chances! I don't remember thinking any of this was strange at all, or worrying about yer da and what might befall him if Gerry really was crazy. Funnily enough your da never asked why I was sleeping in the front room on the floor. I didn't tell him about the full-sized shepherd's crook that was under Gerry's bed, which was exactly like the one in the picture of St Patrick that hung in our hallway; the picture of St Patrick chasing all the snakes out of Ireland.

I went back to my own bedroom when the shepherd's crook was gone and I wondered if that meant Gerry wasn't crazy anymore, or if I should still push the chest of drawers up against the bedroom door. But I believed the danger had passed and so, for a short time only, the days and nights passed as if we lived in a normal house.

I remember the day, Berny, when you asked your husband, Gerry, to fix an electric light for you in the bathroom. He had turned off the electricity in the house to do the job. You were heavily pregnant when, out of the corner of your eye, you saw our Gerry walking through the kitchen with the broom held aloft. In seconds you realised he was headed for the electrical circuit and the broom was to reach up and flick the switch back on with your husband's hands inside the light socket.

You dropped the tea plate you were holding screaming, 'No, Gerry!' and rushed out to the hallway just as he was about to flick the switch, which would have killed your husband. You got there just in the nick of time to pull his arm away. You were shaking like a leaf and, when you asked

Gerry why he was turning the electricity back on, he simply said, 'The TV went off.' Any other person would first have asked why the electricity went off in the house. Not our Gerry. It was turned off, so he had to turn it back on. It was a lucky escape for all of us. Jesus, Berny, you could have been left a widow, and your wee childer without a da. You've no idea what it's been like for me all his life—asking for help, looking for help, but each and every time they just told me his IQ was within the normal range and he'd be alright. But he wasn't alright at all. You know, Berny, he never had so much as one true friend his entire life, poor soul.

THE GROG
Berny

I was delighted the first time I saw you start to smile again, Ma. You had more energy and you began to want to go for long walks again with Jimmy-Paddy, Aoife and me. We walked for miles with the wheelchair, Aoife running and skipping ahead of us and me listening to you. We talked and talked about everything—your life, your dreams, your hopes for the future. We talked about Da and how he'd brought you to your knees both emotionally and financially. You also talked about your profound and enduring love for Jack Kennedy and your dreams about what your life would've been like if you'd only married the right man.

Each night after a long walk, we made our way home by way of the off-licence, or 'offy' as we called it, at the corner of Yarm Road and Neasham Road, where you would replenish your stock of the medically-advised tipple of rum and coke. One night the man in the offy saw us enter the shop and, by the time we waited in the queue and you got your money out to pay, he already had your order ready. A quarter-bottle of rum! I was pleased the man was doing something nice so that you didn't have to wait too long, but your face flushed red. You didn't like what the man had done at all.

'Cheeky ballicks, got nothing better to do than stand round

remembering what I'm buying.' And you hurried us all up. I really couldn't figure out why you were so upset.

The next night we walked a different route and called into another offy. You said you didn't want any nosey shite knowing your personal business and that what the doctor had told you to do was certainly no business of any aul ballicks serving in the offy. So every night the walks became different and a lot longer, so that we were visiting a different offy and not going to the same place twice. I didn't mind. I sensed that you were happier when we were outside in the fresh air, and I knew the craic would be grand. Jimmy-Paddy was in his element watching the traffic as we traipsed the roads, the length and breadth of Durham. You always got some sweets at the offy too, so I never minded going along. And I never even thought to question the nightly visits. Even if the penny had dropped with me about the visits, I wouldn't have dared question it because, in those days, it didn't seem to take much for anyone to get their bake bitten off if you said the wrong thing.

Generally you were sleeping well and I was back at school trying to catch up with what I'd missed. It was round this time that a miracle happened in my life. Sister Mary Therese handed me a letter while she smiled and told me to open it. I looked at her unsure of what it could possibly be, and I pulled out an invitation to a dinner—at a fancy hotel. I was to get a school prize. I handed it back to the smiling nun and told her there must be some kind of mistake, and that it couldn't possibly be a school prize for me because, not only had I been absent from school, but I knew I was also stupid. The smiling Sister of Mercy handed the invitation back to me and explained it was a prize for conduct.

'Conduct? What do you mean, Sister?'

'Have a look and read what it says.'

I read the invitation and still didn't understand why it was for me. I was awarded for 'Exemplary Conduct and Unselfish Service'. An award just for being good? I thought it must be a joke. Being good was just what you had to do because causing trouble meant things would only get worse.

And, God almighty, you didn't dare do that if you knew what was good for you.

The only thing more ridiculous than being stupid was making matters worse than they already were. I was so worried, though—a dinner with the Rotary Club in a fine hotel. And I also had to choose a book as my prize. I was distraught. What would I wear? I didn't have anything fancy for a hotel dinner. And what about all the different plates and cutlery? We only had one knife in our house, and that was the blunt butter knife that you peeled the spuds with, which also doubled-up as a screwdriver when you needed one. That was, of course, because with one blunt butter knife, you wouldn't be tempted to run a knife clean through Da. What if I didn't know what knives or forks to use?

We still used plastic bowls and plates at home in case Jimmy-Paddy fired them up against the wall and hit the chipped ornaments, even though by now every ornament was stuck to the mantelpiece with glue. Even Da's dinner plate was unbreakable in case he did the same thing. And what would I wear? The only coat I owned was my school duffle coat.

It was a good job it was winter because maybe everyone else might have duffle coats too. I hoped!

You said you were very pleased that you reared good childer, and asked me what book I was going to choose. I wanted the one with all the poems Mr McBaine had taught us back at St Olcan's. And so it was, *A Choice of Poets,* with a collection of Keats and Wordsworth that I got. The prize night at the fine hotel was very nice indeed. There were only the right amount of knives and forks so nobody saw how stupid I was and I didn't look like a tube. Two other people had duffle coats on too and, by a stroke of luck, we were also required to wear our school uniform.

Your birthday approached and, I must admit, I hadn't really thought about what to get when the day before was suddenly upon me. I couldn't think of what you'd like, but then all at once I thought I'd get you an extra bottle of rum. This way you wouldn't be embarrassed about going to the same offy, and maybe we could go to the park instead.

You opened your homemade gifts from the other childer, thanking them all roads for their little gifts. I'd carefully wrapped mine so that you wouldn't guess straight away what it was. But as you unwrapped my present you stopped laughing. You flushed red like you had done the night the man in the offy had got your order ready. You held the rum up.

'What's this?', you asked. I wasn't sure what to say. I thought you'd be pleased, but you continued.

'A bottle of rum? Is that all you think I'm worth?'

At first I thought maybe I should've got a bigger bottle.

'Is that what you think of me?' you said.

I really didn't know what you were talking about, but I knew you were the angriest I'd seen you and it was aimed straight at me.

'The party's over; get ready for bed. All of you!'

The other childer looked at me as if to say, 'you did this, you made Mammy angry, you spoilt the birthday and you got us sent to bed early'. Why did I have to be so thoughtless and buy you the rum? I felt I'd committed a great crime without knowing quite what it was.

The change in you was becoming more noticeable. I never knew if I was saying or doing the right thing. It was harder to pick it, harder to be good, harder to please you and, funnily enough, even Da watched what he was saying. Your moods became unpredictable and could change like the wind. One minute you'd be happy and laughing till the tears would roll down your cheeks, and the next minute you'd be crying till you thought your heart would break.

One night we'd gone out for our usual dander with Jimmy-Paddy and Aofie skipping ahead. And, as had become the custom, we didn't visit the same offy two nights in a row. We'd walked quite a way this night to get your quarter-bottle of Jamaican rum, but the offy we'd gone to didn't have any sweets for us childer. So we took a detour down Kitchener Street to where we knew there was a corner shop to get the sweets.

The shop was owned by Pakistanis, so we knew it would be open late as those shops were open all the hours God created, seven days a week.

We all piled into the shop—wheelchair and all—and were busy looking at the sweets under the glass counter. After a few minutes, it was obvious the shopkeeper and his wife were having an argument.

His wife, who was up the ladder putting tins of peas away, was berating her husband, who was standing on the tiny cluttered shop floor. She was shaking her fist at him and he was just as loud back. They were talking so fast I'm sure even a Pakistani person would be hard-pressed to keep up. You looked up and noticed the row while waiting patiently to be served. But the row went on and on, with us still all standing there like dummies.

I could see you weren't impressed. You had always said it was the 'height of bad manners' to be talking in your own tongue in front of people who didn't speak it. This was something you never would do, even though you spoke fluent Gaelic. I could see you were beginning to get very annoyed. You took a deep breath and asked, 'Excuse me, are you serving?'

The Pakistani shopkeeper turned round and with a wave of his hand dismissed you.

'Yes, can't you see I'm busy,' he told you with a loud and rude voice. 'Just wait!'

We must have been waiting about fifteen minutes at this point, and you were now furious, your face flushing red as a mad bull. Oh God, here comes trouble, I thought.

When the shopkeeper finished, he strode over, placed both of his hands on the counter and hissed at you.

'Yes! Well what do you want?'

You then turned to me and without warning started speaking to me in Gaelic. What? What was Ma doing? I didn't understand a word of what you were talking about, but I sensed it wasn't good for the shopkeeper.

So you were now keeping him waiting while you spoke in your native tongue. You were giving him a taste of his own medicine and showing him how rude it was to speak another language in front of someone who didn't know what you were talking about. I could feel

284

myself flush with embarrassment. I glanced from you to the shopkeeper and back. You were tapping my foot with yours under the counter so I'd guess what you were up to.

I just nodded to you as if I knew what you were talking about. You kept up the flow of Gaelic including the *Hail Mary*, which I recognised as it was the only prayer in Irish I knew, for about five minutes. Then you turned abruptly to the shopkeeper and smiled. 'Now, I'd like a packet of cornflakes,' you said. They were on the top shelf. Shit, I thought we'd come in for sweets, what were you doing? Then you asked for a packet of tea (again on the top shelf which the shopkeeper had to get the ladder for). Next came a packet of Skips, a bag of spuds and a bottle of HP sauce.

The counter was starting to fill up with all the messages you were ordering. I tried to tug at your sleeve to ask what you were doing, but you motioned me to be quiet and I wasn't game to question you. On and on the list went, until the whole counter was laden with food. I couldn't believe my eyes and my stomach started to churn. We'd only come in for a packet of sweets. You now had the attention of the shopkeeper. This was quite an order, worth a few quid alright—money I knew we didn't have.

When the shopkeeper asked you if there was anything else, you calmly scanned the rest of the shop.

'No, thank you … I think that's all,' you said politely.

He rang up each item; the till receipt getting longer and longer. I felt very nervous. How were we going to pay for all this stuff, never mind get it all home?

Finally, after another five minutes, the shopkeeper finished tallying the total and told you the amount. You looked him straight in the eye. 'Is that right? Well you know what you can do with all that? Shove it up your arse, you ignoramus!'

I didn't even wait for you to say 'run'. My legs were already in action. The brake was off Jimmy-Paddy's wheelchair and I was out that door, knocking over two buckets of yard brush and a stand full of birthday cards on the way out. You were in hot pursuit with Aoife linking your arm, running like we'd just robbed a bank. We ran and ran and ran till I had no breath left in me to push the wheelchair any further.

When you caught up to me, I could hardly speak.

'Ma! What were ye doing?' I rasped. You sat down on the wall beside where we stood, crossing your legs.

'Oh, Jesus Mary and Joseph, may God forgive me! I think I'm going to wet myself.' And you began to laugh. Then we all started laughing till we thought our sides would split. We couldn't stop, the tears streaming down our faces.

'Did ye see the look on that aul ballick's face?' You squealed with laughter.

'That'll fucking teach him to make a buck eejit out of me or anybody else.'

That was one corner shop I was never game to go into again for the rest of the years I lived in England.

I'm not sure when the penny dropped with me, but when you told me five years later you were joining Alcoholics Anonymous, I just looked at you mystified. I really didn't believe you needed to do that. My ma wasn't an alcoholic. Weren't alkies losers who staggered about stocious and couldn't even talk straight? Didn't they hide bottles of grog in airing cupboards and under the stairs? Weren't they found on park benches after dark, slyly sipping their remedies out of brown paper bags? Weren't they dirty, unshaven vagabonds who had nothing to their names? Sure, couldn't you smell alcohol on an alky when they'd had too much? But I wasn't game to say anything in case you ate the bake off me. The one thing I had noticed was that my ma was no longer the same, and it was so hard to pinpoint why.

You told me you were going to your first AA meeting the next night in Bishop Auckland. I wondered if this would be good or bad. What if you didn't want to come on the long walks anymore? What if going to AA meant that you didn't need me to talk to every night? Where would that leave me? Would somebody else be more important in your life? Even though I was desperate for things to get better, I couldn't cope with the change. You were my ma and I still didn't want to share you with anybody, even if it meant you weren't going to drink anymore.

Unbeknown to you, I decided to follow the number one bus all the way to Bishop Auckland on my Honda 90, just to see if that's where you were really going. And to make sure you didn't change your mind and go and find another offy that wouldn't know you. The red double-decker bus stopped in Bishop Auckland Main Street and I watched from across the road as you got off the bus and entered the church hall to go to your first AA meeting.

As I sat across the road, a fine misty rain had started to fall and my heart cried like it was bleeding. I knew instinctively that the winds of change had started to blow and something big had just happened to us, something that could take you away from me for the rest of my life.

I wasn't sure if I felt panic-struck or relieved. It was all mixed up and rolled into a feeling I had never felt before. The game had changed, the lines were no longer clear and I didn't know what the future was going to bring us. What if this meant that all the good things we had shared would stop too? What was going to become of us? Was somebody else going to look after you? What about the craic and the stories? There had only ever been the two of us. We'd never needed anybody else. I was your friend, your confidante—the one who could make you smile. I could fix it, or so I'd believed. It would be years before I understood that, in fact, that was the day you set me free.

The date was the fourth of July 1981. As you were welcomed into the meeting in Bishop Auckland and you introduced yourself.

You simply said, 'Hello, I'm Isabelle, and I'm an alcoholic'.

A SOBER LIFE
Isabelle

Hey, Berny, remember the week after I attended my first AA meeting, I announced I was also giving up the fags and that I was going to see a hypnotist to do it? So the day arrived and the whole tribe of us got ready. Jimmy-Paddy's wheelchair was prepared and we set off to walk to Durham train station and head up to Newcastle city centre.

It was summer and everything in the air smelt good. A sea mist was still hovering when we arrived at the train station, making the platforms look like something from a storybook like *The Lion, the Witch and the Wardrobe*, and we waited for the train to Newcastle. Jimmy-Paddy was ecstatic, pointing to the trains and nodding his head when the whistles blew, and I lit up my cigarette as I usually would with a warning to youse all.

'If ye ever took up smoking, I'll cut the skull of youse.'

It wasn't long before the big InterCity 125 from London entered Newcastle station and, looking round, it was hard to imagine that it was there, in that very station, where the aul tramp had nearly killed Jimmy-Paddy just by a kiss on his cheek because he'd eaten fish. Somehow it seemed such a long time ago and almost like it had happened to someone else.

We arrived at the hypnotist's office, which was four flights of stairs to climb because the lift was broke. We all huddled round Jimmy-Paddy's wheelchair and, like a flock of birds around a plate of seeds, lifted the wheelchair up each stair till we got to the top. I went inside and you all waited in the reception area. No one else was there—only us—and the building was so old even the glass in the window was bevelled as if it hadn't been made straight. This made the outside look crooked and not real.

You childer waited patiently until I came out. You weren't sure how you expected me to look when the hypnotist had finished with me, but I didn't look any different to you, so you weren't convinced the hypnosis had worked. All this way for a joke, you thought. It wasn't until halfway home to Durham on the train that you noticed I hadn't lit a fag and when you asked me about it, I simply said, 'I really don't feel like one.' Although, you still thought it was all a big cod. But I never lit another cigarette for the rest of my life.

I continued to attend the AA meetings and then I also got a sponsor who talked about Bill W and the twelve steps of Alcoholics Anonymous. Your da didn't say much; he just let me talk on. It didn't stop him having his four Carlsberg Specials every morning after his night shifts at the Northern Echo.

By this time you older childer, who were working, would slip me some money of my own. It was money your da couldn't get hold of to run to the bookies. I bought my first new dress and shoes because I had to look half decent going to the AA meetings. There were no more trips to any offy in Durham, and I began to work my way through each of the twelve steps in the recovery program of Alcoholics Anonymous.

There was an open meeting each month that anyone could go to, so you went to have a look at what was going on. You found out about Al-Anon, the group that is for the families of people in AA, and you also went along to that. In October 1981, you met Gerry and fell in love. You were engaged that same Christmas and married in October 1982. I waited for your da outside the Northern Echo just before the wedding, marching him straight to Roger David in Bondgate to buy his suit before he could wager it at the bookies. You were very lucky that he wasn't walking you down the aisle in his work overalls.

Your da had his first heart attack in February 1983 when he was 48 years old. He told me he wanted to go to my next AA meeting when he recovered. His second heart attack took his life six weeks before his first grandchild was born. He was only 49 years old when he died.

For the next twenty years of my life, I became more and more involved with Alcoholics Anonymous, attending meetings whenever I could, and also sponsoring people myself on their journey to sobriety. I lived each day by The Big Book, and worked tirelessly to implement the twelve-step program of recovery and life. I began to share my story at meetings, and I travelled across the UK to attend AA conventions whenever I could.

My confidence grew and grew, and my ability to connect with other alcoholics even took me into the prison system to run AA meetings, as well as psychiatric hospital units—even the same one where I'd been given shock treatment all those years ago. I inspired other souls desperate to quit the grog to reach out and give the twelve-step program of life a go. You've listened to me recite so many readings, prayers and affirmations over the years, but you told me the one you remember the most is 'God grant me the serenity to accept the things I cannot change, the courage to change the things I can and the wisdom to know the difference.'

The strange thing was that your da asked if he could go with me to an AA meeting, but he never saw his first meeting as the heart attack killed him before the nurses could get the crash trolley to him in the coronary care unit. It had taken a lifetime for your da and I to connect with each other, and I finally felt this happened just before he had the heart attack that killed him.

Unbeknown to me he had a life insurance policy with his work, and so for the first time in my life, I had more money than I knew what to do with. I didn't keep it all. I divided some of it up amongst you childer, to make up for what you never got growing up. And I also put some aside for a wee holiday.

THE SOCIAL WORKER
Isabelle

I had my fair share of people coming and going over the years—mainly those who were involved due to Jimmy-Paddy's disability. It's fair to say that most of them didn't know 'B' from a bull's foot when it came to assisting me with his care. There were the bossy ones that always thought they knew better than me in looking after him. There were the suspicious ones who took up valuable time just looking round the house at what I had or didn't have, writing their reports and recommendations without even talking to me about him. And there were the sanctimonious ones who thought they were better than us.

They came and went and over the years and I got so cheesed off that I decided not to let them in the house again. I sent a letter to Disability Services saying that until the day they sent someone with half a brain, don't bother coming and wasting my time and energy. The funny thing is that no one came back to bother me for years until, one day there was a knock at the door and when I answered, it was a young fella, no more than twenty years old, standing there and introducing himself as Jimmy-Paddy's new social worker.

I told him what's what. 'Look son, I don't have social workers coming here, no disrespect to yourself, but most of them were never one bit of use to me when I needed them. It's taken me years, but we found our own way to what we needed and everything is okay, so off you go and see to somebody who needs your help.'

But the young man didn't move. He smiled telling me he just wanted to make sure I was getting all the government allowances I was entitled to. I told him I was and that I really didn't need his help with anything.

The young fella still smiled. He said if it was okay, he'd just like to check to make sure. Now, I was nearly ready to rid the decks with him, which wouldn't have been a pretty picture. But his smile and friendly way, as well as the fact he was so keen to help, softened my stance and I laughed and said, 'Okay, come in and have a cuppa, but I'm telling you now there's no point. What's your name, son?'

'Steve,' was all he said.

'Well, Steve, I never met anyone so persistent in my life. You'll go a long way.'

He checked through the list of entitlements, 'mobility allowance?'

'Yes.'

'Carer's allowance?'

'Yes.'

And on it went.

'Wheelchair? Lift? Bathroom accessories?'

He then asked me if Jimmy-Paddy was incontinent and whether I had a laundry allowance for him.

'Laundry allowance? What's that?'

'Well, Mrs Savage, it's something you're entitled to if you're washing all his clothes and bed linen daily.'

'Ach, that's okay, son. I've washed all his clothes and bedding since the day and hour he was born. It's no hardship to me. It's just what you have to do, and when they're done out, I just buy some more because there's only so many times ye can wash shit off sheets before they start to smell, even if you've boiled them.'

'Oh, well, if it's okay with you, Mrs Savage, would you mind if

I applied for this allowance for you? I'll do all the paperwork so you'll have no extra work.'

'Ach, son, that's really kind.' In my mind's eye, I couldn't imagine what difference a little amount of laundry allowance would make, but to keep the young fella happy, I said okay. Steve finished his paperwork, shook my hand and left, promising he'd be back when he had something to tell me.

Three months passed and I'd almost forgotten about the young social worker who wouldn't take no for an answer, until one day there he was again.

'Ach, hello, Steve. Good to see ye, son. How are ye?'

'Oh, good, Mrs Savage. I've got some great news for you. The laundry allowance I applied for has been approved. You'll start getting it regularly now.'

'Ach, that's great! It was kind of you going to all that trouble.' Steve then asked me to sit down and he handed me an envelope. I looked quizzed.

'What's this Steve?' I said as I dried my hands on my apron. I opened the envelope and inside was a cheque for twenty-nine thousand pounds. I looked up at Steve and said, 'W-h-a-t is this for, Steve?' my hands shaking.

'Oh, I forgot to tell you, Mrs Savage, I asked for the money to be back paid from when Jimmy-Paddy was sixteen.'

Tears sprung forward nearly blinding me. I couldn't talk and control my shakes. This just couldn't be true. This wasn't really happening to me; it must be a dream. But it was true and so I began to laugh and thank Steve, the young social worker, and I also began to plan in my mind the best holiday Jimmy-Paddy would ever have.

Where in the world would a youngster love to go if they had all their dreams come true? I thought … of course, Disneyland in America. Oh Jimmy-Paddy would love that; the big plane and all the cars, buses and rides he could clap his eyes on. Oh, yes, Disneyland! I would need help so I also took two of my girls to help with all the baggage, including his wheelchair and all Jimmy-Paddy's essentials, and off to Disneyland his wheelchair and all Jimmy-Paddy's essentials, and off to Disneyland we went. When good things happened, I always sang the song from *The Sound of Music*.

'Somewhere in my youth or childhood, I must have done something good.' I just couldn't believe how my life was turning round. I neither lit another cigarette nor touched another alcoholic drink in my life again. On the fourth of July 2011, I celebrated thirty years of sobriety—a milestone that is rare even in the circles of Alcoholics Anonymous.

CANADA
Isabelle

Now, my life after your da died was very different. I began to save my money, and because I was such a good manager, it didn't take me long to get a bit behind me. I was heavily involved in AA, travelling and speaking at conventions all over England. I made many friends and was invited to many functions, and I was constantly on call for the people who I sponsored. I started to enjoy little holidays away—first short trips and then later I announced I was taking a tour of Canada. Wow! Canada.

'Why Canada?' you asked. I never really explained fully at the time, but you suspected the reason was to try and find the only man I had ever loved—Jack Kennedy. On my return, I told you of a day trip I took when I was on holiday where I found Jimmy McCoy, Jack Kennedy's best friend. God he'd done well, alright. Those Canadian streets had been paved with gold. He had his very own Irish pub and I just had to go in, opening a door to my past that I'd never dared even to think about until now. I was as nervous as a kitten. I wasn't sure what kind of a reception I was going to get from Jack's best friend, but as much as I was shit-scared to take another step, I willed myself through the front door of that pub.

I had to know one way or the other, once and for all, where he was, whether he was still alive and if he married. The door of the pub swung open easily. Once inside, I was hit with the familiar waft of alcohol and I shivered. The pub was full with lunchtime drinkers and people from city jobs having their lunch. Packed to the rafters, it was, and as I gazed round I thought how much of an exact replica this pub was to the very one at the bottom of Stonemore Road. They must have carted over all the Irish flags, aul kettles, ornaments and Celtic tea cloths and pinned them to the very roof of the bar. The place was bustling, and they were taking money over the bar like a man with no arms right there in the middle of Ontario.

He probably won't even know who I am, I thought. But even at the age of fifty-one, Jimmy McCoy recognised me as soon as he saw me, and screeched my name across the pub.

'In the name of God, it can't be … not in the realms of Heaven and Earth. Is it? I-s-a-b-e-l-l-e?'

He skited across that concrete floor like a lilty and lifted me off my feet, he hugged me that tight. All the regulars were thinking he'd lost his bap.

'Come away in, girl. Wow! Let me have a good look at you. Bye, you look well—not a day over twenty-one. I still can't believe it's you, after all these years. What on Earth are you doing here in Canada? Are ye here on a wee trip?'

We enjoyed the craic for ages, catching up about our families, how many childer we had and I told him your da was dead. He too was shocked because your da was so young. I knew I hadn't much time so I drew up the courage to ask about Jack. 'Do you know, Isabelle McKitterick,' he said, 'you broke my best friend's heart? You know he never married for fifteen years after seeing you pregnant on that bus in Belfast. He never got over you.'

My heart was in my mouth. I was choking back the tears. It was as if Jimmy speaking Jack's name took me right back to that day on the bus. If only Mammy had kept the letters Jack had sent me. If only I hadn't been thrown out of the farm with your da, I'd never have married him. How could I tell his best friend everything that had gone wrong? That it was my mammy that had wrecked both our lives, and that I did wait for him. That he was the only man I had ever loved, and that now it was too late to do anything about it. What was the use now anyway?

'Is he still alive, Jimmy?'

'Ach, aye, he's alive and well and living in America. He's married, Isabelle, and has four grown kids.'

'Is he happy?' I breathed. 'Aye, now he is. It took him long enough. He was so depressed after losing you that I made him stay with me for a while because I was worried he'd jump off a fecking bridge.'

It was at this point the stark, barren, ugly reality of the present cut my heart in two. Jack was married and there was no way on God's Earth I would interfere in his life, not even to tell him the truth about what happened and clear my name. No, that was the end of it all. My dream of finding him was over.

When I arrived home after my holiday in Canada, Berny, you couldn't wait to ask if I'd been able to find out anything about Jack Kennedy. But when I told you what had happened and what I found out, your heart broke for me too. You said it seemed so unfair, that I'd suffered so much at the hands of other people. I'd been to Hell and back with your da, the constant nursing of wee Jimmy-Paddy, the worry of poor Gerry and our escape out of war-torn Northern Ireland. And finally when I had turned the corner, you'd hoped I could also find a bit of happiness for myself. The story about Jack Kennedy seemed pretty final. Logically, there seemed that nothing could be done, but what broke my heart even more was that Jack still didn't know the truth about what really happened. He would never know now. How could he?

You'd wished on many occasions as this story was told to you that Jack and I could have met at least one more time so that I would get the chance to tell him the truth, and strangely you had begun to have a recurring dream that I had. You dreamt we were sitting together, holding hands across a small round table and surrounded by flowers.

'Ach, Berny, you're full of imagination and a born romantic,' I laughed.

'Ma, do you believe in fate, in kismet, the universal power?'

'Universal power, Berny? Well I don't know about that, love, but I believe what's for you won't go past you.'

'Aye, Ma, so do I.'

ALCOHOLICS ANONYMOYOUS—THE TENTH STEP
Berny

Step ten of AA encourages the taking of a personal inventory, which for persons recovering should be a daily process. It is often called one of the maintenance steps and a pressure-relief valve. This may be done in writing at the end of the day. You examine your actions, your reactions and your motives, and you often find you've been doing better than you've been feeling. This allows you to find out where you have gone wrong and admit fault before things get any worse. You promptly admit your faults, not explain them.

You vigorously commence this way of living as you clean up the past. You have entered the world of the spirit. Your next function is to grow in understanding and effectiveness, and continue to watch for selfishness, dishonesty, resentment and fear, and quickly ask God to remove them. You should also discuss them with someone immediately, and make amends quickly if you have harmed anyone. Then you resolutely turn your thoughts to someone you can help—abiding by the code from The Big Book.

'Ah yes, Berny, "Love and tolerance of others", page 84, to be sure.' You know the book so well. Then one day you call me. 'Hello, Berny. Any chance you can come down in the next few days?'

'Is everything alright, Ma?'

'Oh, yes, everything's alright but I need to talk to you one-to-one.'

This was your code for a serious discussion. I did a quick mental scan to check I hadn't inadvertently caused any trouble, and told you I'd see you the next day on my day off work, but my mind was still jittery.

What could Ma want with me that needed such urgent attention? But the late shift at the hospital took my mind off it and into the sluice room, where twenty-seven enemas had been given to the residents, and where in an hour the stink would be strong enough to kill Samson. Then there was no time to dwell on anything except how to clean shit in double-time before the matron thought ye were wasting time, God forbid.

The bus to Durham wound its way through Aycliffe and its new housing estates. Every house looked like a box, most of them flat-roofed, which sort of made the houses look half-baked as if more building work had to be done to make them a whole house. Warm sunlight filtered through the window. I leaned against the side of the seat, resting my head in my hand. I loved the bus, its gentle rumble a bit like being in a big swaying hammock. It wasn't long before I couldn't keep my eyes open and before I could blink, the bus driver was shouting up the bus.

'Terminus final stop. That's it, love, this bus isn't going anywhere else,' he laughed. I was glad that your house was at the end of the bus line. I just had to walk the rest of the way.

You were delighted to see me so I sort of relaxed a bit. Whatever you wanted me for couldn't be that bad. The house was empty except for you and me. Everyone was at work or school, and even Gerry had taken Jet out for a long walk up Yarm Road, past Morrisons supermarket, and out towards the fields and farms beyond.

You made some tea and we sat down.

'So, Ma, what was it you wanted to talk to me about?' You took a long breath and held my hand.

'Berny, I have a story to tell you, a story I'm so ashamed of, a secret I've carried all these years that has broken my heart in two every time I think of it.'

'What, Ma, what could possibly be that bad?' I asked you.

'The burden of guilt and shame has almost crushed me every day I look at you.'

'What? Me? Ma, what are you talking about?' I asked again.

'I need to make amends for what I did, and I need to ask you to forgive me.'

Well you could have pushed me over with a feather; I had no idea what you were talking about. Now I was really confused and worried because you then started to cry. You went on.

'You always were such a good wee child. A tiny wee dot of happiness and I've loved you since the minute I laid eyes on you when you were born. You won't remember what I'm going to tell you. You must have been only three years old. Your da had done his money in again, he'd left me without a brown penny, and I didn't even know where our next meal was going to come from. So I had to go next door to borrow some sugar and tea off Mary Lamb in Rathcoole.

'Gerry was playing in the back garden and I'd put wee Jimmy-Paddy into the big coach pram and strapped him in tight with his reins. You were in the back garden, too, and I told you I was just going next door to see Mrs Lamb and I'd be back soon. I asked you to keep pushing the pram so that he wouldn't cry, but not to take him out of the big pram.'

'I know, Ma, I remember …'

'Oh, Jesus, Mary and Joseph, I thought maybe you'd have been too young to remember.'

'I remember you putting him in the big pram, Ma, but as soon as you left to go and see Mrs Lamb, he started to cry again and I couldn't make him stop. Not even giving him his dummy or patting his head

301

helped.' I spoke quietly as if it was hard to get the words out. I stopped for a second looking at you, and then went on.

'I remember unclipping the baby reins and lifting him out of the big pram, and he stopped crying straight away. I played with him and then I can't remember what happened. I must have left him alone because he was quiet and then … nothing. I can't remember anything after that until I saw you coming round the back garden door with him in your arms.'

It was then and there talking with Ma that it all came back to me. As if a big movie screen dropped down in front of me, the memory of what happened that day rolled before my eyes scene by scene.

You'd come out from Mrs Lamb's house to find him behind the wheel of the ice-cream van that had stopped in the street. You'd screamed in panic and ran to grab him before it took off crushing him. He could have been dead if you'd been a split second later. You rounded the door to the back garden screeching my name.

You grabbed me by the arm, hauling me towards the house with Jimmy-Paddy still in your left arm, all the while screaming. 'Jesus, Mary and Joseph, I just asked you to do one simple thing and you deliberately disobeyed me. The child could've been dead. That's all I would have needed on top of your da and everything else—a dead child. What you have done has scared me half to death.'

I was still looking at you in disbelief—that you were screaming at me. We were then in the house, and you must have put him in the playpen because the next thing I knew I couldn't breathe. The thump on my back must have taken all the air out of my lungs. I couldn't cry either. Nothing would come out. The pain in my back spread all over me; I thought I was choking because I couldn't breathe inward. I felt the next thump across my back and then I must've blacked out. When I could see again, you were crying, shaking me to wake up and I could see our piano stool had only three legs and it was leaning over on the floor. I remember telling you in a whisper that my back was sore and you saying you were sorry.

That night when you got me ready for a bath, you covered your mouth and cried and cried again because the cable pattern of the red Aran jumper you had knitted for me was imprinted on the skin of my tiny back. I was tattooed in cable stitch from top to bottom.

It was a long time before I could take a long breath inward, and even longer for the pain in my back to disappear. The only thought in my three-year-old head was that I was such a bold girl or Mammy wouldn't have hit me. I was never disobedient again. That picture, Berny, of your tiny back imprinted with the jumper's cable stitch has haunted me my whole life. The explosion of anger directed at you as a three-year-old could have killed you, and I have felt so guilty.

'You should never have been left in the garden alone, not even if I went next door. I should've taken Jimmy-Paddy with me and not left you with the responsibility. There is never any need to hit a child. I'd lost control of myself as an adult when I hit you with the leg of the piano stool. I've beaten myself up, mea culpa, ever since and wished I could have worn a crown of thorns to feel the pain you must have felt.

'I'm so sorry, Berny, that your childhood and teenage years have been taken away. You weren't given the chance to be a child; you had to grow up so quick, always having to be so grown-up and so responsible. You never got the chance to be just yourself. I am so sorry for what happened that day. Can you please forgive me for what I've done?'

As I looked at you, Ma, I felt nothing but love and simply smiled with the same unconditional love of the three-year-old within me, and told you there was nothing to forgive. I told you it was probably a good job I didn't get much time to myself or I might have walked round with a limp and a Yankee accent for the rest of my life. Then we both laughed. Your tenth step was complete.

PANDORA'S BOX
Berny

Now, year after year I'd begun to put the pieces of this story together. I was astounded at what Granny had done with Jack's letters to you. In my eyes, the tragedy and hardships that you'd endured were heartbreaking. There were only a few things you ever wanted in life: to be holy, happy and to be a lady. To me, you were all that and a lot more.

As I met and married my husband, the sadness of what happened to you was almost too sad to bear. You deserved better, much better. You were turning seventy and still courageously caring for Jimmy-Paddy—a true woman of substance. And so, sitting in my home on the other side of the world in Australia, I made a decision. I had wished and dreamt it often; it was now time to do it. I wondered if it was possible to clear your name; to let Jack Kennedy know you did wait for him; to tell him the true story. To tell him you never got his letters and, for your whole life, you had only ever loved him. I didn't tell you what I was about to do and some people said I should let sleeping dogs lie. But that wouldn't make things right and you were turning seventy so it was now or never. Maybe it wouldn't be possible, maybe he wouldn't be alive, and maybe he wasn't even in America anymore. It had been over twenty years since your trip to Canada to try and find him. But I had to at least try because it just wasn't right not to. Pandora's Box or not, I just had to do it.

I remembered that when you had taken your trip to Canada almost twenty years before that you'd been to an Irish Pub in Ontario. So it wasn't difficult to find the pub and I spoke to Peter McCoy, whose father Jimmy I'd known was a good friend of both you and Jack when you were young.

I rang the pub explaining who I was and that I was trying to find Jack Kennedy.

'Ach, sure, I have the number right here!' came the response.

I couldn't believe it. I had Jack's telephone number and he was still alive. I checked the time difference and waited, and then dialled the number for New York and left a voice message. I didn't know what would happen. I wasn't sure if I wanted to laugh hysterically or vomit.

I'd been out of the house about forty minutes to pick up some bread, and when I returned my answering machine was flashing with one message. I pressed play and listened to the voice in an American accent on the other end.

'Hi there, this is Jack Kennedy calling from New York. Can you call me back please?'

I let out an audible gasp, as my hand flew up to my mouth. I started to shake and my heart was pounding. I was dizzy with disbelief and shock. *Was it really true? Was it him?* I checked the flashing message again and pressed play for the second time, just to make sure I wasn't dreaming. A million questions spun around my head. Pandora's Box had opened and there was no turning back.

I dialled the New York number again and for the second time in my life I was face-to-face (or almost) with the man you adored. I had to kneel on the bedroom floor in case I fainted, and when the polite male voice answered I thought I would die of fright. I needed to make sure it really was the right person I was speaking to. I began by explaining who I was and that you would be turning seventy on July twentieth. Before I could say another word the voice on the other end of the line interrupted me.

'I know.'

I said, 'Pardon?'

And he replied, 'I know when your mother's birthday is. It's the same day as mine.'

I was so stunned I wasn't sure what to say because that simple statement meant that there was no doubt that I was indeed speaking to the right man. I took a deep breath, to try to focus my thoughts, and went on to explain to Jack that I had two reasons for contacting him.

The first reason was that I had a story to tell him that he didn't know about. The second was a request. I began to tell Jack about what my granny had done all those years ago—about her burning his letters without you knowing.

He was silent the whole time, listening intently, and when I'd finished telling him the story he just said, 'That aul lady never liked me and I never knew why. I was never allowed to call for your mom at the house; I had to wait down the street like some mangy dog, you know. Oh my God, all these years and I never knew the truth.'

'Well,' I said, 'you know now and my request is could you send my ma a birthday card for her seventieth birthday, just for old times' sake, now that you know the truth?'

I went on. 'I know it would mean a great deal to her, and she would be so glad to know her name had been cleared at last.'

His voice seemed tinged with sadness. He then brightened.

'Of course, a birthday card,' he said. I'd be happy to do that. It would be a pleasure.'

So I gave him your address in England.

We chatted for what seemed an eternity, about the dancing years and our mutual dancing teacher Ely Mulligan, and as I was making a move to say goodbye, he suddenly said, 'Wait, please, I have something to tell you too.'

'Yes, what is it?'

'I still have it.'

'Have what?'

'Your mom's engagement ring that I carried with me to Canada fifty years ago; it's still in the same box it was bought in. It was something that I could never bear to part with.'

I was speechless, breathless ... my thoughts still spinning out of control. As I gathered my thoughts I took another deep breath and thought, *well here goes.*

'Well, Jack Kennedy, don't you think it's time that my ma had that ring? I don't suppose you're going to give it to anyone else now?'

He laughed. 'No, it's your mom's ring. It belongs to her.' I knew I was way outside any boundaries that had been drawn here. I didn't know this man, but I thought in for a penny, in for a pound. 'Why don't you send it to her with the birthday card to put old ghosts to bed?'

The line went quiet. I wasn't sure if I'd said too much. Then after the longest pause he said, 'Well, I'll do better than that. I'll give that ring to your mom myself,' he declared.

'What do you mean? You'll go to England from New York?'

'Yes, it's time.'

I don't think I slept for two nights; I was so excited. And then I had to call you in England and tell you what I'd done.

'Ma, I have something to tell you, but I need you to sit down ... No, Ma, it's good news but please sit down and I'll tell you ... Ma, it's about Jack Kennedy. I've found him. He's alive and living in America.'

The line was silent. 'Ma ... Ma? Are ye there?' Then I heard it, low at first, and deep, as fifty years of emotion spilled over the wall of your broken heart.

Slow, moaning sobs of a broken heart, of a lost love and a life of regrets and lost dreams. I silently sobbed too. 'Where is he, Berny?'

'He's in New York, Ma,' and I began to tell you what had just transpired, and that you wouldn't just be seeing me for your seventieth birthday, but also the only man you had ever loved.

You were in total shock. 'He's got the what? My engagement ring? The one he bought for me all those years ago? Jesus, Mary and Joseph.

No ... not after all these years.' You then wept even more because, I realised, you knew for certain that what you'd felt for fifty years had been real, that you hadn't imagined it!

'Oh, Berny, I knew all along that what I'd felt in my heart had been right.'

Now, it's fair to say that once you got over the shock of me telling you that I'd found Jack, you were almost overcome with excitement. There were four months to go until you would see him face to face. You talked about what you'd ask him about his life, what you'd wear and you reminisced about what it had been like when you were both young and so much in love. And that was just week one!

Week two dawned and as usual I called you to see how you were going. What you said next floored me. Your attitude was brusque to say the least; you could hardly keep a civil tongue in your head. 'What's wrong, Ma? I thought you'd be so happy that I'd found him. At last you'll get the chance to talk to him about what happened all those years ago. Isn't that what you wanted?'

You were swift and curt. 'You had no right to do this, Berny. I'm distracted. I'm an aul lady, almost seventy years old. He won't want to see me. He's married so what's the use of him coming here? Nothing can come of it. It's dead, it's over and I wished to God you'd minded your own business and let sleeping dogs lie.'

I was gutted by your reaction; it felt like you had just emotionally slapped me right across the face. I felt so sure from what you had told me over the years that it would have been your dream to see him if you could. I was so totally unprepared for the roller-coaster of emotions that came pouring out of a seventy-year-old's mouth, with a twenty-year-old's heart.

To be honest, I'd been warned that it could all backfire on me, but those people didn't know the whole story, not like me. I was never more certain of anything than this being the right thing to do. But here I was, with you barely speaking to me, unable to sleep with the worry that I'd just caused more trouble for you, and with little or no sympathy from people around me who thought I should have kept my nose out of your past.

To say I took it personally was an understatement. I thought I'd given you the greatest gift anyone could, and here you were throwing it right back in my face. Week three arrived and this time I waited for you to ring me. I couldn't face another tirade of anger for trying to do something good for you. I'd had time to think long and hard during the week.

How could anyone be so ungrateful? What was wrong with you? I thought you'd have given your left arm to see him just one more time. I'd even questioned my own memories of what you'd told me about you both. Was it all just blather and blarney? Had you made it all up for the craic? And me, like a buck eejit, had fallen for it hook, line and sinker?

Now I'd gone and put the cat among the proverbial pigeons, so to speak. You had me as bad as you; I didn't know whether I was coming or going. Or … was it something more … something deeper that you couldn't talk about? Were you afraid to meet him? Afraid of what he might think or say? Afraid he might look at you as an old woman and be disappointed? That you'd be … rejected … the illusion shattered? Had I inadvertently brought your dream of how it was to an end by staring reality in the face? I was beginning to feel like I was walking on emotional quicksand, desperately looking round for something to grab to stop me sinking. I was out of my depth, with no one throwing me a rope and I hadn't a clue what to do about it. The last thing I wanted was to break your heart again.

But there you were the next week on the phone, singing *I Just Called To Say I Love You*, your favourite Stevie Wonder song, and acting all excited, just like the day I broke the news to you. The niggling doubts about seeing Jack again were gone, and you were bright and chirpy and looking forward to seeing him in July. You even made a joke or two about having a tummy tuck and getting a new set of false teeth. I didn't know what to think or what to say at first; I'd been up and down that road several times over the past weeks. I was very cautious about what I said. It was almost as if you didn't remember telling me off.

Week four came and went, and by this time I wasn't surprised when you were down in the doldrums again. What became clear was the outpouring of self-doubt that plagued you once more. I couldn't believe it. Here was the woman I admired most in the world—the strongest, bravest person I knew and you were acting like an ungrateful, moody teenager, as if you didn't have 2ds' worth of sense.

If I'd have carried on like that about a man, you'd have cuffed my ear and told me to get a grip on my knickers. So I decided that this was the tact I was going to take with you. It was either that or cancel my flight back to England in July for your seventieth birthday, and there was no way I was doing that.

So for the next couple of months I kept up the reassurances about Jack when I spoke to you. It was then I realised that when it came to love, your heart really wasn't connected to your head. You were an emotional person first and foremost, and a thinker second. It's what made you spontaneous and passionate, and it's what I loved about you. Sadly, too, it's what had dragged you to emotional Hell. Not that for one second I could tell you that. You'd have eaten the bake off me.

THE BIG DAY
Berny

You were turning seventy, Ma, which was hard to believe as you could have easily passed for a good ten years younger than that. You'd agreed to a party, something very small and intimate. You were never one to wish to be the centre of attention. My sister, Grainne, wanted to make it really special and her idea of a celebration was, 'the bigger the better. Ma deserves the best'. So what was meant to have been a small gathering turned out to be an extravagant garden party complete with an Irish band, lots of balloons and a wonderful feast. And a true and lovely celebration it was.

But what you were more focused on was the visit to England by Jack Kennedy. You two were to meet under the town clock in Durham's market place, and for the week leading up to the meeting, you drove us crazy. One minute you were so choked with excitement and nerves, you couldn't eat or focus on anything. The next you'd state you weren't going to meet him, saying he'd be disappointed you were just an aul woman, and what would Jack's wife think? He wasn't free so what was the point? No, you couldn't go, even to meet him and clear your name.

Then the next minute, 'Alright then I'll go, but just for old times' sake because he's married now and nothing can come of it.' So one minute you were going to meet Jack, the next you wanted to run a mile.

Here we go again, I thought. There it was, yep, the emotional twenty-year-old was out again. It was like a teenager's feelings were pouring out of seventy-year-old's body. We badly needed a good laugh in the house, so to lighten the atmosphere, Grainne had been to the town market and bought a red and black lace bra and knickers set. She came into your house wearing them over the top of her clothes. 'This is what you'll wear tomorrow when you meet Jack, Ma.'

We all laughed till we cried, and you covered your face with mock embarrassment.

'Oh Jesus, Mary and Joseph, and that's a prayer, look at that one, will ye? Take off that paraphernalia. In under Jesus what have I reared?'

This, of course just made my sister dance round in the lacy knickers even more. As we all laughed hysterically, Jimmy-Paddy clauded his magazine and fired his drink of milk across the living room, skiting it all up the wall because, laughter or not, he couldn't stand all the sudden neuration. And I thought, thank God all those ornaments on the mantelpiece are still glued in place.

The big day arrived. Your hair was washed and blow-dried, and your clothes were ironed ready. You almost had to be sedated, you were so nervous and saying your legs wouldn't carry you. But, undaunted, Grainne and I took an arm each and walked you to the steps in front of the town clock on Tubwell Row in Durham, where you were to meet Jack at one o'clock.

You wanted to stand back, well back, so you could see Jack first without him seeing you. And as the town clock struck one o'clock, you said, 'I can't do this. Me legs won't hold me up.'

'C'mon, Ma, you'll be alright. You've waited fifty years for this. Relax.'

'I can't breathe and I think me heart is gonna stop. Have ye got the tablets for under me tongue in case?'

'Ma, you won't need heart tablets,' I said trying to keep her calm.

'The only thing you'll need is them fecking crotchless knickers I bought ye yesterday.' Grainne chirped up.

'Oh Jesus, Mary and holy Saint Joseph, listen to that one, will ye? Don't make me laugh or I'll wet meself.'

The three of us stood watching from the other side of the road, waiting for Jack to appear. Together we scanned the crowd wondering if we would somehow recognise him, and suddenly the crowd thinned.

You just said, 'Jesus, there he is ... look at him... posture as straight as a die, always the dancer.'

I felt your whole body tremble from top to bottom as you gazed upon the man you'd loved your whole life.

Dressed in a smart suit, he belied his seventy-two years. He wore a lemon sports shirt, open at the neck, and stood with his jacket slung over his shoulder. So this was the man who owned your heart and soul. This was the man whose dancing medals I'd found in the secret drawer in Rathcoole. This was the handsome stranger I'd been introduced to in Dublin at the All Ireland Dance Championships. I was speechless. We stood for what seemed like an age allowing you to take it all in, steady your legs and take a deep breath.

'Are you ready, Ma? C'mon, let's go and do this or he'll think you've stood him up again.' I said, the nerves choking me.

We walked arm-in-arm in case you fainted down the steps of Tubwell Row and over the pedestrian crossing towards Jack Kennedy. He saw us immediately and began to smile, slowly shaking his head from left to right. 'Little old woman, Miss McKitterick, I don't think so.' And the gap of fifty years was closed in a heartbeat.

We watched as side by side you strolled off together. We both would have given anything to have been a fly on the wall with you. You had a lot to catch up on. We sat in the Red Lion Pub trying not to choke on our lunch and wondering what was being said between you both knowing this was a miracle for you.

You two spent the afternoon together after fifty years apart. When you came back from your lunch, I suddenly remembered the camera. I quickly whipped it out. 'Hey you two, what about a photo for old times' sake?' He didn't hesitate. Jack slipped his arm round your waist and I captured that precious moment in time.

I had a funny feeling it would be something that would give you great comfort in the years to come. Later that same afternoon Jack introduced us to his wife, and you and Jack's wife clasped each other's hands and hugged. In doing so, you were trying to reassure Jack's wife that she had nothing to fear from an old flame, and Jack's wife in return said, 'It's okay.'

Much later that night, when Jimmy-Paddy had been put to bed and we'd sat down for a cuppa tea, you lit the tea light candles as you always did when evening set in, making the walls of the kitchen dance with flickering shadows. It wasn't quite dark yet, the summer sky still retaining it's pink hue even though the sun had long since set. The first stars had just appeared in the night sky, and it felt as if the world was at peace at long last. I looked at you, waiting to see if you'd start the craic, but it was as if you were savouring your thoughts privately, and going over the events of the day in your own head.

I washed the few dishes that were laid in the sink, wiped round the bench tops and straightened up the cushions on the sofa, until I could stand the suspense no longer.

'Well, Ma, spill the beans.'

'What beans? I will not. Away and mind yer own business, wee girl!' you said as you laughed out loud. 'Wouldn't you like to know?'

You were playing with me now, teasing me, knowing I was bursting with anticipation wanting to know about what happened between you and Jack that afternoon.

'Well,' you said, 'you know what they say, don't you? What's said in the café, stays in the café.'

'Bullshit, Ma. You can't keep it to yerself. I swear I'll not tell a soul.'

Then you started to sing, 'Somewhere in my youth or childhood, I must have done something good. Nothing comes from nothing. Nothing ever could. So somewhere in my youth and childhood, I must have done something good.'

By this time the grin on your face had stretched a mile wide. You only ever sang that song from *The Sound of Music* when something in your life went well. By this time I was jumping out of my skin wanting to hear about every detail, or as much as you were prepared to tell me. And so the craic began.

'We had lunch at the wee garden centre. You know the one just up past the Grange, next to your old school, Berny?'

I must have looked perplexed because you went on to explain. 'You know out past St Augustine's Church?'

'Oh, aye, I know the one, Ma.'

'He let me pick the place and it was an easy walk. We dandered along, getting slower and slower. We didn't want to get there too soon, in case the time went quick.'

'Did he pay for the lunch, Ma?' I asked, my voice raising the expectation that he should treat you.

'Now, hold on there a minute, who's telling this story?' you said laughing away to yourself. I knew you were stringing me along, keeping me in suspense, and you were doing a very good job. Just like you, I had also waited a very long time to find out more about this man.

'Okay, okay, but come on, Ma, what happened next?'

'We found a wee spot, over by the water fountain. The table was made of cast iron and there were wee fancy cushions to sit on. It was quiet; not many people buying plants. I suppose all the summer hanging baskets were about done. It'll soon be time for the chrysanths …'

'Ma, never mind the plants. What happened?'

'Alright, alright, keep yer hair on. I'm getting there. He pulled the chair out for me; I felt like royalty. We must have been talking so much we didn't even realise how much time had gone by. The wee girl who was serving came back three times to ask if we were ready to order anything, and we laughed like a couple of teenagers who'd met for the first time. Jack nodded at me to go first. I felt like such a lady. To be honest, food was the last thing on my mind. I wasn't sure if I could eat a thing, so I just ordered some soup.'

'Soup, Ma, really? Is that all you asked for? Shit, after fifty fecking years, I'd at least have had the lobster.'

'Ach, you know me, Berny. I don't go in for all that fancy stuff.' I smiled to myself thinking that's so typical of you. Even here, even today, you couldn't deliberately take advantage of anybody.

'He asked me if I'd like a drink and I told him I'd have a coke. "A coke," he laughed and said, "I think this calls for something more than coke, don't you, Miss McKitterick?"

'Before I could say a word, he called the wee girl over again, ordered a bottle of Moët & Chandon and said,

"This occasion deserves the best."'

'Shit, Ma! What did you do?' I asked knowing what kind of a position this would have put you in.

'Well, you know, I kind of just smiled and waited for the wee waitress to take off back to the kitchen. I tried to catch Jack's attention, but he started talking ten to the dozen and I started to panic. All I could think of was how was I going to tell him? And would he take off like two men and a wee lad if he finds out who I really am? I took a deep breath, looked him straight in the eye and said, "Jack, I really appreciate the fine wine offer but I don't drink."

"Don't drink? Have you taken the pledge or something, Isabelle? You never were a drinker, even when we were young. I should have remembered that," he said.

'I must have shuffled uncomfortably in the chair because he went on. "What do you mean you don't drink? You don't drink at all?"

'My mind was spinning, Berny. Should I tell him the truth? What will he think of me if I tell him? What if he thinks I'm just a failure and a drunk. What then? This day could be ruined and it'll be all down to me. I thought maybe I should keep shtum and brush it off. He'll be none the wiser. I felt so vunerable and exposed. What if he just got up and took off? Could I handle the rejection? My poor head space was all a jitter. Then a wee voice deep down inside me said, *Fuck that, you've been to Hell and back, girl. If he's going to judge you when you tell him, then he's not worth even having lunch with.'*

Ma, by this time I could feel the tears welling up behind my eyes. I knew how much courage it would have taken for you to tell him and risk his rejection. This chance to spend time with him would probably never happen again. I understood the sheer guts it would have taken for you to lay yourself bare in such a brutally honest way, especially with him. You were risking everything about yourself that you both guarded and cherished. I'd witnessed the battles you'd fought. I'd seen you hit the emotional skids of rock bottom, and I'd seen you get back up off your hands and knees and fight like fury to live again. And I thought if he hurts you, I'll kill him.

I wiped my eyes and blew my nose, giving you time to gather your thoughts.

'Go on, Ma,' I said. 'What happened?'

'Well, I took a deep breath, leaned over the table, touched his hand and said, "Jack, I don't drink at all because I'm a recovering alcoholic."

'Initially I thought he was going to sneer at me. He pulled back slightly and looked at me as if I'd just smacked him across the face. 'Then he let out a deep breath and said, "Jesus Christ, Isabelle, a what? But you ... you never even touched the drink when we were young."

'I told him that I never touched a drink till I was thirty-six years old, and then not again until my fifties. When I did start to drink, it was because my doctor told me to ... to help me sleep. I'd been at my wit's end.

"It's a long story. How long have you got?" I said.

'And he then looked right back at me and said, "As long as it takes. I want to know it all!" I felt my heart leap in my chest, and I breathed a sigh of relief.'

You knew from that minute on you could tell Jack anything and you wouldn't be judged. There's only once place to start with a story like this and that's right back at the beginning and that's exactly what happened.

You got to tell Jack about how you had felt the night you two were supposed to get engaged, when the raven-haired beauty had flung herself at him. You got to tell him about going to the train station the night he was going to Canada and hiding up the back of the platform, wishing he'd turn round and see you there. You told him about your heartbreak when you didn't hear from him, and your jealousy about Jimmy getting a letter still.

You told him about waiting for months and months, running home every day to see if a letter had come from him. You told him how after years of waiting and hearing nothing from him, Da egged you on to go on a date. You told him about how you had never loved Da, and that when you'd both been thrown out of the farm that night after Da had been accused of being a thief, he'd asked you to marry him.

You told him you only married Da to escape the house, and because you believed he wasn't coming back for you. You told him what your introduction to married life had been like with Da, what he'd done with his wedding suit, what a mistake it had been, and about trying to leave him well before any babies were on the way.

You told him that the worst day of your life was meeting him on that bus in Belfast, when you were expecting Gerry. Then finding out that your mammy had burnt all his letters. You told him about your wee childer, including Gerry and wee Jimmy-Paddy, too. You told him what had happened to them, and that your childer were all you'd lived for—that they were what made you get up every day and carry on with life. You told him of your life of abject poverty because of Da's gambling, and the beatings you'd endured.

You also told him about the troubles in Northern Ireland, and our escape out of Rathcoole to get to England. And then about your sad spiral into depression—suicide attempts, shock treatments and eventually the drink.

You told him, too, about your life of recovery in AA, and the important work you were doing in the fellowship. You told him there

318

hadn't been a day go by in your life that you hadn't thought about him, about them both, and the life they should have had together—that there had never been another man on this Earth that you had loved the way you loved him. And that you still did. You told him that you weren't telling him this for sorrow or sympathy, or to interfere with his marriage. You were telling him so he would understand, so that he would know the truth about you waiting for him.

HEART TO HEART
Isabelle

Berny, by the time I'd finished telling him what had happened, he put his hands up to his face and buried his head in them, running his fingers through his hair. For a minute I wasn't sure what he was thinking. When he eventually looked up, and then across the table at me, his face was ashen white and wet with tears. He started to say something and then he caught his breath, not able to speak because his lip trembled so much.

I reached across the table and took hold of his hand. He held mine back, rubbing the back of my hand with his, then he lifted it and gently kissed the back of it. We didn't need to speak. I could tell he was gutted.

Eventually he sighed and looked across at me.

'Jesus, Isabelle,' he said. 'I'm so sorry. If only I'd known, I wouldn't have got right back on that ship again. I'd have taken you to Canada with me, baby or not. What about your wee boy? Have you still got him with you? How do you manage?' The pain in his eyes was fluid.

'Aye, he's still with me, Jack,' I told him, 'and so is Gerry. I swore they'd never be out of my sight. Berny kept me sane in the early days. She was my rock, my wee friend and confidante. That child had my coat ready at the end of her bed many a time, ready for me to jump out the window and run to escape the beatings. She never had a childhood

320

because she was the other little mother in the house. If I hadn't had her to talk to and help me raise the other wee ones, I wouldn't be here to tell the tale.'

'Berny? That's who called me in America, isn't it? Bye Jesus she's got guts,' he said laughing.

'My younger daughter, Grainne, is my right hand now. We've been a team for the past twenty years. I couldn't have done it without her either. My wee girls, their places are assured in Heaven, I can tell you.'

'Why in under God has this happenned to us?' he said and then went on, 'I waited, too, you know … for fifteen years. I couldn't look at another woman. You consumed my days and haunted my nights. I thought I'd die of a broken heart after I'd seen you on the bus that day in Belfast, pregnant with somebody else's baby. The folly of youth, eh? If only I'd sat down beside you and asked you what had happened. I'd have found out there and then. Instead, my stupid head got in the way. My self-conceited arrogance bit me right in the arse. I thought you just hadn't waited. I couldn't believe you'd thrown me away for another fella knowing what we felt for each other and what we'd promised to do. I felt like the biggest eejit in Belfast. Jesus, Isabelle, what a terrible mistake for both of us. If it hadn't been for Jimmy and my job, I'm sure I would have been six foot under, or licking the inside of a bottle myself.'

'How come you're in America, Jack? Why didn't you stay in Ontario with Jimmy? That's where I came to look for you years ago after Harry died.'

'You came to look for me? Ah Jesus, Isabelle, you didn't, did you? Really?' he said taken aback.

'Aye, I did. I was on a wee holiday in Canada and I found Jimmy's pub and went in. He recognised me straight away, and me overy fifty,' I laughed. 'He told me then you were married and that you'd waited for me for fifteen years.'

'Jimmy, the sleeket get! He never told me. Wait till I speak to him next.'

'No, Jack, I didn't tell Jimmy the whole story. I didn't think there was any point and I made him swear on his mother's life not to say a word about me being there looking for you. It was bad enough that it broke my heart about it being too late. That's why I never did anything else. I wouldn't hurt you or your wife for love nor money.'

'Canada wasn't for me, Isabelle. It was cold enough to freeze the balls of a brass monkey in winter. I don't know how Jimmy stands it to be honest. There was more chance of jobs in America, too. And that's where I met Janie. She's a good girl, though everyone thought I was her da at first—me being so much older than her and all that. She's been a good wife and an even better mother. We have four fine boys, you know,' he said with a smile.

'She's always known I had a past. You don't get to the age I was when I met her without one I suppose. I couldn't bear to talk about it, though, and she let it be, didn't try to pry, which I was grateful for. I think she guessed it was about a girl who'd been part of my life. But I buried it deep inside, except on our birthdays. Then and only then did I allow myself to think back, and I've wished you a happy birthday every year of your life. So what now, Isabelle McKitterick?' he said with a relaxed kind of smile.

'What do you mean what now? Jack Kennedy, are you asking me to up and run away with you to Gretna Green?' I laughed. 'Ach, I'm only joking, Jack. That's not what happens in real life, is it? You have your life and your family and I certainly have mine. There's nothing that can happen. It just wouldn't be right. It's enough for me that we had this time together. Enough for me that you now know the truth about what happened. Enough for me that you know I loved you from the day and hour I met you. Is it enough for you, Jack?'

'Aye, Isabelle, it's enough for me. I still love you, my first love.' He paused for ages and then went on.

'And what has been belongs in the past, eh?' he said as he squeezed my hand tenderly.

'Aye, Jack, it surely does.'

Jack reached into his pocket then and pulled out the wee ring he'd bought for me fifty years before, still in its green velvet box. He opened it and winked at me. Can you believe that the cheeky blurt, still flirting? And him over seventy years of age! He lifted my hand and simply said, 'This is yours, Isabelle McKitterick. It always was. Please accept it as a token of my respect and honour, and as a symbol of the love we've shared. And let's close Pandora's box.'

As I gazed lovingly at my beautiful ring, I simply mouthed the words 'thank you' to Jack as he lightly kissed my hand. It was then I heard the hall clock chime three, and it shook me back to reality. God, where had the last few hours gone?

'Now, it's time for bed, Berny Savage. You'd sit there all night and sleep all day; your just like yer da. He was a nighthawk, too. We won't be able to open our eyes in the morning and I have such an early start with wee Jimmy-Paddy.'

'Oh Ma,' you said as you hugged me tight. 'I am so glad I found him and that it wasn't too late. I'm so glad I made that call, even if you did drive me mad for months till you saw him.'

'Ach, Berny, you're a born romantic. Now get to your bed, wee girl, before the eyes fall out of me head.'

As you made your way round the bend of the stairs I shouted after you, 'You know, Berny, it's true what they say about love. It's better to have loved and lost, than never to have loved at all.'

You told me later Berny, that on night before you climbed into your bed, you duked out at the navy velvet night sky, alive with twinkling stars, and mouthed the words 'thank you' to the God of your understanding.

You told me too that it wasn't until you were almost asleep that you shot bolt upright in bed. 'The wish, the dream, the small table surrounded by flowers ... oh my God, how exactly had this all happened? Was it fate, kismet, the power of the universe?' You had imagined my meeting with

Jack exactly as it turned out. That night, I think we both felt that all was right with the world.

'Goodnight, Ma.'

'Goodnight, Berny.'

BLESS ME, FATHER
Berny

Jack promised he'd keep in touch with you ma and he did. For years after that meeting, he sent you roses on your birthday. But as time went on, you grew more and more troubled by this. You weren't sure that sending roses to an old flame was the right thing to do when he was still married, so you asked him to stop and he did.

You wore your ring every day, but as time went by, you began to feel more and more uncomfortable about doing that too. Was it bad karma to wear a ring that had meant so much to you both when Jack was married? There was only one thing you could do. You went to confession.

'Bless me, Father, for I have sinned. It's been a week since my last confession.'

Now no one knows what was said in the confidence of the confessional that misty Saturday evening, but as the candles flickered in St Mary's Church and night time fell, you took off your beloved engagement ring that you once thought you would never see again, kissed it tenderly and dropped it into the church's poor box.

And I wondered about the irony of it all. Wasn't it enough that the Catholic Church had owned your heart and soul? Now they even had the ring.

I made a promise to myself. The next time I interfered would be to write to the parish priest at St Mary's in Durham. Maybe there was a chance I could get that ring back.

EPILOGUE
Berny

I strode across the gravel carpark towards the front door of the lodge—its strong rounded Georgian pillars proudly guarding the memory of the fancy girls' school it had once been. I glanced up at her window, to see if she would be dukin out to see me coming. The keypad numbers clicked easily and the door clunked open.

I slipped in quickly and Miriam as usual shouted with a smile.

'H'way in, pet. She's upstairs in her room. Would you like me to bring a tray of tea?'

'Thanks, Miriam, maybe later,' I said as I carried on towards the huge rounded staircase.

Jane, who was in charge, passed me on the stairs and with a warm and wicked sense of humour chanted, 'Eh, look who's here. Where's the other ugly stepsister?'

'She's meeting us for lunch later,' I said laughing and still keeping with the joke.

'Aye, well, Cinderella's in her room. Give her a hug from me will ya?'

'I will, of course.' God we were lucky. These people were the salt of the Earth. Lynne was sitting in her usual spot, talking away there to Elizabeth who was fast asleep in the other chair. The noisy cheerful clatter in the dining room signalled that morning tea was almost ready. Joe, the big chef, waved his tea tarl in his usual greeting, as he pushed the trolley with all the cups and saucers rattling on it and a batch of homemade scones ready to be handed out.

I glanced down at the precious cargo rolled tight in my hand and wondered what Ma would think. I walked along the corridor, passing Bev who could never find her room, until I saw Ma's photo outside her room. I knocked and then went on in.

'Hey Ma, what about you today?' I exclaimed doing a bit of a jig, which I knew would make her laugh.

'Ach, for God's sake, look who it is. Berny, is that you, love? I thought you'd gone home.'

'No, Ma, I've got another two weeks. We've got lots of time.' It's teatime. Are you having a cuppa?'

'Ach, aye, never say no to a cuppa tea. I haven't had one all day you know.'

'Well there's one on its way. Joe's baked fresh scones and Miriam's bringing a tray up for you,' I said as I glanced over at the two empty tea cups already cold on her bedside table.

'I won't be here long, Berny. England's not for me. As soon as I'm myself again, I'm going back to Belfast, back to me own kith and kin. I'll get a wee flat on The Falls road and I'll be able to visist our Des and Mary. Or maybe I can even live at 26 Stonemore Road if God spares me to live. Now I hope I'm not talking shit, love, because sometimes me head's full of marbles and away with the mixer.'

I just smiled and brought her attention to what I was holding. 'Ma, I've got something for you, something special I want you to see!'

'Oh, what is it?' she said with the excitement of a tiny child.

'Come on, we'll go down into the garden and I'll show you there. It's a lovely day outside.'

'Alright then, lets go. I haven't been over the door step all day, and you know me. I hate to be hemmed in.'

As I snuck one arm through Ma's guiding her to the door, there it was … the photo that I had taken almost twelve years before, still by her bedside, the photo that she still kissed every night before she closed her eyes. There he was, so tall, still handsome in a way only a man could be at seventy-two years old. His back was as straight as a die, a jacket slung over his shoulder, and his other arm was round her waist. Her, with her flaxen blonde hair still the same colour as when she was twenty—all trendy in her neat blue jeans and white lace top.

My God, I thought, as I scanned the photo I now knew so well, did that day really happen? Did she really get to see him just one more time? Did he really keep that ring for fifty years? Did he really wait for fifteen years to find another love when he thought he would never see her again, the only man she had ever loved?

We made our way down the long corridor toward the lift, passing Stan as we went. Ma pulled my arm closer to her as we passed him, and she winked at me in a conspiratorial way. Lowering her voice she whispered to me.

'See that aul lad, Berny? He tried to come into my room last night. I woke up just in the nick of time. I shouted, "Hey, Mac! What the fuck are ye doing in here? Take yerself off, before I kick yer melt in." And I would have, too, you know, because I'm not afraid of him or any other aul lad.'

I didn't doubt for one minute that she would have done it, eighty-two years old or not. She was still as fiesty as ever. I was concerned, though, that the aul lad may have made a simple mistake and wandered into her room accidentally if, in fact, he had at all. I knew he'd been lucky to escape her wrath.

On we walked and turned to face the lift. Just as the lift doors opened, Sarah shuffled out, and reaching for Isabelle's hand greeted her warmly. Ma's eyes lit up and she smiled patting Sarah's arm as we moved on, passing the time of day. As the lift doors closed, she turned to me.

'That's my wee friend, Berny,' she said. Kindly aul soul, even if she is a Prod!'

I had to turn my head away momentarily to stop my smile before she caught me.

The lift opened on the ground floor where a few residents were sitting round. She bent down several times, touching their hands and saying hello with a smile. I was touched to see the carer in her still alive and well, that was until we got past them.

'See them poor souls?' she whispered. 'Most of them are fucking crackers and don't even know what day it is. And do you know something, Berny, I'm getting too old for this work lark, and I haven't been paid a brown penny for all I do here.'

Again, I had to stiffle my laugh or she would've started on me. I wasn't taking that chance. We walked out through the dining room which was now full of residents enjoying the scones Joe had made, and out into the dappled sunlit garden. A light September breeze tossed around the first of the autumn leaves, reminding me instantly of Keats' *Ode to Autumn*.

'Season of mists and mellow fruitfullness, Close bosom-friend of the maturing sun ... Until they think warm days will never cease, for Summer has o'erbrimmed their clammy cells.'

The garden bench was right at the end of the walled garden, its sides supporting an overgrown clematis as a thick, heavy hedge sheilded the back of the garden bench from the winds. When we sat down, I handed the rolled-up papers to her.

'What's this?' she said as she struggled to flick open her smudged glasses hanging round her neck.

'Have a read, Ma, it's for you.' And then again I slipped my arm through hers snuggly as she began to slowly but steadily read aloud.

'I stared again at the hands on my kitchen clock, checking for the umpteenth time what time it would be in England. Eleven hours! Yes, I had it right. It would be just before 7 o'clock in the morning. Ma would have been up and dressed about an hour ago. I wanted to make sure I didn't disturb her morning prayers or meditation from The Big Book. I was nervous; I had a small chance to tell her before she'd be busy with Jimmy-Paddy, getting him off to 'school' ...'

The lump in my throat was so big by this time I couldn't speak. I didn't need to. I thought my heart would burst with pride and pain at the same time watching Ma read the first few lines. Suddenly she stopped reading, turned to me, took off her glasses.

'Oh my God! Berny, this is my story, isn't it?'

I could only nod with joy and wonder as Mammy's past memories lined up in perfect harmony with those of the present ... one more time.

'You know, Berny, he's the only man I ever loved, but I hadn't 2ds' worth of sense when I was a youngster. I didn't know 'B' from a bull's foot, and I didn't know me arse from me elbow where love was concerned. We were soul mates from the day and hour we met. Yer da knew that. I know it tortured him all his life that I couldn't love him back the way he wanted me to. He had my body, but my heart and soul always belonged to Jack.'

'Yeah, I know, Ma.'

'For years it broke my heart to think Jack never knew the truth about what happened all those years ago.'

'Yep, well he knows the truth now, Ma, that's for sure.'

'Did you do this for me, Berny?'

Again I could only nod, and then she started to sing the line that she always sang from *The Sound of Music* when something in her life went well. 'Somewhere in my youth or childhood, I must have done something good. Nothing comes from nothing. Nothing ever could. So somewhere in my youth or childhood, I must have done something good.'

Then she swept her face with her first finger wiping away her tears and, taking a deep breath, straightened herself up and paused in pensiveness for a moment, her thoughts taking her away again. She then shakily took off her tear-stained glasses, letting them drop onto her chest by their thin knotted rope.

'Well, I don't care if it never sees a bookshop, love,' she declared, 'because today you have given me something that money can't buy. Today you've given me hope, and sure isn't that what it's all about, love?'

We sat together snuggled into one another on the old wooden bench at the end of the garden. No words were necessary, and my head lay gently on Ma's shoulder as we held on so tightly to precious moments we knew further time wouldn't allow us to keep, but hoping for just a wee bit longer.

'God, Berny, is that the time, love? That wind's got awful cold. Let's go on in now. I'm feeling a wee bit tired.'

'Aye, Ma, you're right. As soon as the sun goes, the heat is gone. It's almost teatime anyway.'

'Teatime? Oh I better get my skates on, Berny. Yer daddy will be back from the shops any minute, and there's not a thing on the go for his dinner. Jesus, bless us, that's not like me to forget something like that.'

'My da … Ma? Ach, my da's been dead …'

'No, Berny, I said yer daddy. That man has been the only one true love of my life. Some people never get the chance of that kind of happiness. I'm so lucky, you know.'

'Aye, Ma, umm, well let's get in before you freeze.'

I'd never, ever heard her talk like this. The confusion was definitely getting much worse.

'Ach, look, Berny, there he is. Just look at him standing there with me in that photo, his back as straight as a die. That's the Irish dancer in him, that beautiful posture. I love every hair on his head. We were quite the couple you know, back in them days. People turned wherever we went. Do you know that wild horses couldn't keep us apart when we were young? What a life we have had; it's been wonderful. He never so much as looked at another woman again when he met me.

'Hey Berny, did I ever tell you the tale about the wee girl in my class at school who became a nun? Jesus, Mary and Joseph, now that's a story and a half. We're both women of the world, aren't we? You'll be blushing to the roots of yer scalp when I tell you this one.'

'Aye, we are, Ma, go on …'

As I left the nursing home that night I looked up to the night sky and again whispered 'thanks' to the God of my understanding. It didn't matter that Ma couldn't remember what she'd eaten for breakfast, where she was or what day of the week or year it was. It didn't matter what she thought she was doing there or where she'd left her slippers. In her mind, she was living the dream.

Ma's world was perfect—just as it was meant to be. She was with him in her thoughts, remembering everything she needed to. She was back in Belfast holding hands with Jack Kennedy. It was his photo beside her bed she would kiss goodnight. It would be him she'd be thinking of as she closed her eyes because nothing takes that kind of love away.

P.S. If anyone is wondering if I ever chased after gold in the arsehole of nowhere, well of course I did. The minute I stepped into Sovernign Hill at Ballarat, I swear I could hear Mary McKitterick's ghost snigger when she saw me up to my ankles in that river, swilling that pan like a man with no arms, and the look on my face when I spotted the glint of gold … well, I'm afraid it's in my blood.

THE END

GLOSSARY

alisalamin: a crawler; sucking up to someone; being all over them in a smarmy way

aul: old

away like two men an a wee lad: two and a half men

away with the mixer: confused

big ballicks: big, nasty male person

boney: bonfire

buck eejit: big fool

bye: short for 'by God'

childer: children

come all ye's: a whole tribe or bunch of people

cowyard: female name-calling, in reference to the farmyard animal, 'cow'

craic: gossip

dead on: just right

dirty mare: female name-calling, in reference to the farmyard animal, 'horse'

do the neatful: finish the job

duke: look

eejit: fool

feck: polite way of saying 'fuck' without actually swearing

gullder: shout

hallion: hooligan

laste: Old English for a shoe last—a model of the human foot for shaping shoes

Nanna Mokan: disheveled-looking woman

neatful: needs explaining

neuration: used colloquially to mean a commotion; creating a disturbance

no goat's toe: very grand

oxter: armpit

peelers: police

pigerina: female name-calling, in reference to the farmyard animal, 'pig'

pished: pissed or wet oneself

poor crater: (or poor wee thing) a phrase of endearment

Prod: a Protestant

Purdysburn: a mental hospital

shtum: quiet

sizza: sister

skeg: look or observe

sleeket get: sly person

stocious: drunk

stounced: bounded

tachara: female name-calling meaning big, nasty person

taking the head staggars: going mad, but can mean 'angry' or 'crazy' too

tarl: towel

thumpadonian: dogmatic

2ds' worth of sense: tuppence worth of sense (meaning not much sense as tuppence wasn't a lot of money)

walkers: nits

wee: small; little; young

ACKNOWLEDGMENTS

To my girlfriends Jean, Martha, Effie and Leanne, thank you for listening to my story and sharing those of your own life journeys, and your endless encouragement to write the story.

A special thank you to Jean for typing the early chapters—your support was infectious and invaluable.

To Colin, thank you for your encouragement and constant question 'Where's my book?' every time I saw you.

To Iain and Geoff who read the early manuscript, thank you for your colourful and honest feedback.

To Colum, thank you for all the titbits and tales you were able to help with.

Thank you to my wonderful family, especially my daughter Claire who patiently and tirelessly updated my skills with a PC and Word, and who was honest enough to tell me 'Mum, you need to go back to the beginning and do it all again'. Ahhh!

To my son Richie, thank you for always believing this was possible.

To my husband Paul, thank you for the endless cups of tea in the study, and your support as the story began to take shape.

To Pam Collins who assisted with early advice and the manuscript appraisal—thank you.

To Angela Tannous who has been my dynamic right hand in the editing process, I am eternally grateful for all your help and collaboration with the team at New Holland.

To the team at New Holland:

To Diane Ward, Publisher, thank you for reading the manuscript submission, taking a chance on me, and passing it on to the team. Thank you from the bottom of my heart—it is a dream come true.

To Susie Stevens, Project Editor, my deepest thanks for the amazing job you have done in turning my ordinary words into something magical.

To the graphics and printing team, the cover has brought the book to life. Thank you everyone—I am happy and fortunate.